FISHING
STORIES

BOOKS BY NICK LYONS

The Seasonable Angler
Jones Very: Selected Poems (editor)
Fisherman's Bounty (editor)
The Sony Vision
Locked Jaws
Fishing Widows
Two Fish Tales
Bright Rivers
Confessions of a Fly-Fishing Addict
Trout River (text for photographs by Larry Madison)
Spring Creek
A Flyfisher's World
My Secret Fish-Book Life
Sphinx Mountain and Brown Trout
Full Creel
In Praise of Wild Trout (editor)
Hemingway's Many-Hearted Fox River
The Quotable Fisherman (editor)
Classic Fishing Stories (editor)
Hemingway on Fishing (editor)
Traver on Fishing (editor)
Best Fishing Stories (editor)
Fishing Stories

FISHING STORIES

A Lifetime of Adventures and Misadventures on
Rivers, Lakes, and Seas

Nick Lyons

Illustrations by
Mari Lyons

Skyhorse Publishing

Contents

Introduction

Fishing Stories is a roundup of stuff I've written over almost half a century. The first two stories I wrote one summer in the mid-1960s—"First Trout, First Lie" and "Mecca"—are here and I guess I like them about as well as any of the several hundred I wrote thereafter. They were what snared me away from the academic essays and articles I had been writing since my days as a graduate student, and I've long been especially grateful to them for giving me a much earthier voice, one much closer to something my own, and a path that gave me a life far from the academy. The span of this collection after those stories follows irregularly the arc of my life—full of stolen days astream, great adventure and travel, triumphs and disasters, and days that were chiefly just great fun. At the end, there's even a piece about the Indian summer of a fisherman.

Most of these stories and recollections have appeared somewhere before in a magazine, anthology, or book—and occasionally in different form. In some cases I've tried to correct rotten phrasing or sentences that leave wrong impressions. But mostly they appear as written, some more than forty years ago. In a few cases, I've included work not published in a trade book of my own before, like "Hemingway's Many-Hearted Fox River," which I wrote on assignment for *National Geographic* magazine, then revised for a limited edition published by Jane Timken. I've always liked that article for giving me a chance to speak about an author (and a story of his) who had meant a great deal to me when I first began to write. The trip was memorable and revealing.

Because they were written at different times the stories vary greatly—but this is less for their occasional changes in style and point of view than because of the circumstances of my life at the time they were written. When I wrote the long opening section of *Bright Rivers*, part of which I've included here, the contrast between my fishing life and the challenges of living in New York City, with a large family, could not have been greater. There is a manic, feverish quality to parts of the book, and sharp contrasts, and I rarely wrote like that again.

I think I always love to read and then to write what I call "shaggy fish tales," somewhat true perhaps but hovering at the edges of truth, where truth bleeds comfortably into fun and even fantasy of an innocent sort. These I wrote with an unalloyed pleasure that I've always hoped gave readers some of the same. Some of these stories are close to straight reminiscence, hewing rather close to what actually happened—warts and pratfalls included, which I didn't need to tinker with. A few come purely from my imagination, like "The Metamorphosis," of course. And at times some of my deep-rooted questions are at the heart of a story—some plea for conserving the clean environment without which no fishing is possible, some quarrels with matters that have crept into the world of fishing, like competition, commercialism, or other qualities I could not help getting my two cents in about. In most cases you'll know which is true, which isn't, and always you'll know where I've come down on social and environmental matters. I've tried to keep the fun of fishing in what I wrote and to avoid exaggerating the size or number of the fish I caught flagrantly, to avoid bragging, and hopefully to keep at the heart of the stories some of the joy fishing has given me.

I competed with full force when I played basketball, which I once loved, but I've found little sense in competing with my neighbor or a fish, or watching it, or writing about it. I guess I feel fishing is a lot more intimate than all that, more personal—at least that's the only way I can do it. Maybe I don't brag about big fish caught because I have been too slender in that department. Nor will you find much about how to do it here, something others do with great skill and which I admire, though I have three thumbs. As a book publisher I met dozens of experts with great skills to share, and many became friends; but I am not an expert.

What I love are the stories—real or imagined; I love the delicious feel of them that lets us live in them and believe them. I love the structure that draws us into them and holds us, and the surprise and suspense and delight that they imp from the fishing itself. I love the stories that tell us as much about the fisherman as the fish or the fishing. I treasure the link we feel toward anyone who pursues gamefish with rod and line. What great fun it all is! How wrong-headed it can be to freight it down with all that is ponderous, pretentious, commercial, competitive, ultimately unworthy and silly.

I see there are a lot of family stories here, though in retrospect I'd have loved to spend much more time on the water with my four children. Well, I have four grandchildren and more time now than I once had, and perhaps I won't be so anxious for these children of my children to fish that I scare them away.

I've fished for more than seventy-five years and these stories are drawn from practically my earliest days prowling a Catskill creek until my Indian summer. Some are light, some serious. Some are clownish, dramatic, sad, quietly triumphant. I've tried over the years to register the fullness of my fishing life, the excitement and breadth and variety of the pursuit. I've had great pleasure writing these stories and hope you take pleasure reading them.

—Nick Lyons
Woodstock, New York
May 2014

M.

First Trout, First Lie

My first angling experiences were in the lake that bordered the property my grandfather owned when the Laurel House in Haines Falls, New York, was his. At first no one gave me instructions or encouragement, I had no fishing buddies, and most adults in my world only attempted to dissuade me: they could only be considered the enemy.

It was a small, heavily padded lake, little larger than a pond, and it contained only perch, shiners, punkinseeds, and pickerel. No bass. No trout. Invariably I fished with a long cane pole, cork bobber, string or length of gut, and snelled hook. Worms were my standby, though after a huge pickerel swiped at a small shiner I was diddling with, I used shiners for bait also, and caught a good number of reputable pickerel. One went a full four pounds and nearly caused my Aunt Blanche to leap into the lake when, after a momentous tug, it flopped near her feet; she was wearing open sandals. She screeched and I leaped toward her—to protect my fish.

I also caught pickerel as they lay still in the quiet water below the dam and spillway. It was not beneath me to use devious methods; I was in those days cunning and resourceful and would lean far over the concrete dam to snare the pickerel with piano-wire loops. It took keen discipline to lower the wire at the end of a broomstick or willow sapling, down into the water behind the sticklike fish, slip it abruptly (or with impeccable slowness) forward to the gills, and yank.

After the water spilled over at the dam it formed several pools in which I sometimes caught small perch, and then it meandered through swamp and woods until it met a clear spring creek; together they formed a rather sizeable stream, which washed over the famous Kaaterskill Falls behind the Laurel House and down into the awesome cleft.

Often I would hunt for crayfish, frogs, and newts, in one or another of the sections of the creek—and use them for such delightful purposes as frightening the deliciously frightenable little girls, some of whom were blood (if not spiritual) relations.

One summer a comedian who later achieved some reputation as a double-talker elicited my aid in supplying him with small frogs and crayfish; it was the custom to have the cups turned down at the table settings in the huge dining room, and he would place my little creatures under the cups of those who would react most noticeably. They did. Chiefly, though, I released what I caught in a day or so, taking my best pleasure in the catching itself, in cupping my hand down quickly on a small stream frog, grasping a bull frog firmly around its plump midsection, or trapping the elusive backdancers as they scuttered from under upturned rocks in the creek bed.

Barefoot in the creek, I often saw small brightly colored fish no more than four inches long, darting here and there. Their spots—bright red and gold and purple—and their soft bodies intrigued me, but they were too difficult to catch and too small to be worth my time.

That is, until I saw the big one under the log in the long pool beneath a neglected wooden bridge far back in the woods. From his shape and coloration, the fish seemed to be of the same species, and was easily sixteen or seventeen inches long. It was my eighth summer, and that fish completely changed my life.

In August of that summer, one of the guests at the hotel was a trout fisherman named Dr. Hertz. He was a bald, burly, jovial man, well over six-foot-three, with knee-cap difficulties that kept him from traveling very far by foot without severe pains. He was quite obviously an enthusiast: he had a whole car-trunk-full of fly-fishing gear and was, of course, immediately referred to me, the resident expert on matters piscatorial.

But he was an adult, so we at once had an incident between us: he refused, absolutely refused, to believe I had taken a four-pound pickerel from "that duck pond," and when he did acknowledge the catch, his attitude was condescending, unconvinced.

I bristled. Wasn't my word unimpeachable? Had I ever lied about what I caught? What reason would I have to lie?

Yet there was no evidence, since the cooks had dispatched the monster—and could not speak English. Nor could I find anyone at the hotel to verify the catch authoritatively. Aunt Blanche, when I recalled that catching to her in Dr. Hertz's presence, only groaned "Ughhh!"—and thus lost my respect forever.

Bass there might be in that padded pond, the knowledgeable man assured me: pickerel, never. So we wasted a full week while I first supplied him with innumerable crayfish and he then fished them for bass. Naturally, he didn't even catch a punkinseed.

But it was the stream—in which there were obviously no fish at all—that most intrigued him, and he frequently hobbled down to a convenient spot behind the hotel and scanned the water for long moments. "No reason why there shouldn't be trout in it, boy," he'd say. "Water's like flowing crystal and there's good stream life. See. See those flies coming off the water."

I had to admit that, Yes I did see little bugs coming off the water, but they probably bit like the devil and were too tiny to use for bait anyway. How could you get them on the hook? About the presence of trout—whatever they might be—I was not convinced.

And I told him so.

[3]

But old Dr. Hertz got out his long bamboo rod, his delicate equipment, and tried tiny feathered flies that floated and tiny flies that sank in the deep convenient pools where the creek gathered before rushing over the falls and down into the cleft.

Naturally, he caught nothing.

He never even got a nibble—or a look, or a flash. I was not surprised. If there *were* trout in the creek, or anywhere for that matter, worms were the only logical bait. And I told him so. Worms and shiners were the only baits that would take *any* fish, I firmly announced, and shiners had their limitations.

But I did genuinely enjoy going with him, standing by his left side as he cast his long yellow line gracefully back and forth until he dropped a fly noiselessly upon the deep clear pools and then twitched it back and forth or let it rest motionless, perched high and proud. If you could actually catch fish, any fish, this way, I could see its advantages. And the man unquestionably had his skill—though I had not seen him catch a fish, even a sunny, in more than a week.

And that mattered.

As for me, I regularly rose a good deal earlier than even the cooks and slipped down to the lake for a little fishing by the shore. I had never been able to persuade the boat-boy, who did not fish, to leave a boat unchained for me; unquestionably, though he was only fourteen, he had already capitulated to the adults and their narrow, unimaginative morality. One morning in the middle of Dr. Hertz's second, and last, week, I grew bored with the few sunfish and shiners and midget perch available from the dock and followed the creek down through the woods until I came to the little wooden bridge.

I lay on it, stretching myself out full length, feeling the rough weathered boards scrape against my belly and thighs, and peered down into the clear water.

A few tiny dace flittered here and there. I spied a small bullfrog squatting in the mud and rushes on the far left bank—and decided it was not worth my time to take him. Several pebbles slipped through the boards and plunked loudly into the pool. A kingfisher twitted in some nearby oak branches, and another swept low along the stream's alley and seemed to catch some unseen insect in flight. A small punkinseed zig-zagged across my sight. Several tiny whirling bugs spun and danced around the surface of the water. The shadows wavered, auburn and dark, along the sandy bottom of the creek; I watched my own shimmering shadow among them.

And then I saw him.

Or rather, saw just his nose. For the fish was resting, absolutely still, beneath the log-bottom brace of the bridge, with only a trifle more than his rounded snout showing. It was not a punkinseed or a pickerel; shiners would not remain so quiet; it was scarcely a large perch.

And then I saw all of him, for he emerged all at once from beneath the log, moved with long swift gestures—not the streak of the pickerel or the zig-zag of the sunfish—and rose to the surface right below my head, no more than two feet below me, breaking the water in a neat little dimple, turning so I could see him, massy, brilliantly colored, sleek and long. And then he returned to beneath the log.

It all happened in a moment: but I knew.

Something dramatic, miraculous, had occurred, and I still feel a quickening of my heart when I conjure up the scene. There was a strong nobility about his movements, a swift surety, a sense of purpose—even of intelligence. Here was a quarry worthy or all a young boy's skill and ingenuity. Here, clearly, was the fish Dr. Hertz pursued with all his elaborate equipment. And I knew that, no matter what, I had to take that trout.

I debated for several hours whether to tell Dr. Hertz about the fish and finally decided that, since I had discovered him, he should be mine. All that day he lay beneath a log in my mind, while I tried to find some way out of certain unpleasant chores, certain social obligations like entertaining a visiting nephew my age—who simply hated the water. In desperation, I took him to my huge compost pile under the back porch and frightened the living devil out of him with some huge night crawlers—for which I was sent to my room. At dinner I learned that Dr. Hertz had gone off shopping and then to a movie with his wife; good thing, I suppose, for I would surely have spilled it all that evening.

That night I prepared my simple equipment, chose a dozen of my best worms from the compost pile, and tried to sleep.

I could not.

Over and over the massive trout rose in my mind, turned, and returned to beneath the log. I must have stayed awake so long that, out of tiredness, I got up late the next morning—about six.

I slipped quickly out of the deathly still hotel, too preoccupied to nod even to my friend the night clerk, and half ran through the woods to the wooden bridge.

He was still there! He was still in the same spot beneath the log!

First I went directly upstream of the bridge and floated a worm down to him six or seven times.

Not a budge. Not a look. Was it possible?

I had expected to take him, without fail, on the first drift—which would have been the case were he a perch or a huge punkinseed—and then march proudly back to the Laurel House in time to display my prize to Dr. Hertz at breakfast.

I paused and surveyed the situation. Surely trout must eat worms, I speculated. And the morning is always the best time to fish. Something must be wrong with the way the bait is coming to him. That was it.

I drifted the worm down again and noted with satisfaction that it dangled a full four or five inches above his head. Not daring to get closer, I tried casting across stream and allowing the worm to swing around in front of him; but this still did not drop the bait sufficiently. Then I tried letting it drift past him, so that I could suddenly lower the bamboo pole and provide slack line and thus force the worm to drop near him. This almost worked, but, standing on my tip toes, I could see that it was still too high.

Sinkers? Perhaps that was the answer.

I rummaged around in my pockets, and then turned them out onto a flat rock: penknife, dirty handkerchief, two dried worms, extra snelled hooks wrapped in cellophane, two wine-bottle corks, eleven cents, a couple of keys, two rubber bands, dirt, a crayfish's paw—but no sinkers, not even a washer or a nut or a screw. I hadn't used split shot in a full month, not since I had discovered that a freely drifting worm would do much better in the lake and would get quite deep enough in its own sweet time if you had patience.

Which I was long on.

I scoured the shore for a tiny pebble or flat rock and came up with several promising bits of slate; but I could not, with my trembling fingers, adequately fashion them to stay tied to the line. And by now I was sorely hungry, so I decided to get some split shot in town and come back later. That old trout would still be there. He had not budged in all the time I'd fished over him.

I tried for that trout each of the remaining days that week. I fished for him early in the morning and during the afternoon and immediately after supper. I fished for him right up until dark, and twice frightened my mother by returning to the hotel about nine-thirty. I did not tell her about the trout, either.

Would she understand?

And the old monster? He was always there, always beneath the log except for one or two of those sure yet leisurely sweeps to the surface of the crystal stream, haunting, tantalizing.

I brooded about whether to tell Dr. Hertz after all and let him have a go at my trout with his fancy paraphernalia. But it had become a private challenge of wits between that trout and me. He was not like the huge pickerel that haunted the channels between the pads in the lake. Those I would have been glad to share. This was my fish: he was not in the public domain. And anyway, I reasoned, old Dr. Hertz could not possibly walk through the tangled, pathless woods with his bum legs.

On Sunday, the day Dr. Hertz was to leave, I rose especially early—before light had broken—packed every last bit of equipment I owned into a canvas bag, and trekked quickly through the wet woods to the familiar wooden bridge. As I had done each morning that week, I first crept out along the bridge, hearing only the sprinkling of several pebbles that fell between the boards down into the creek, and the twitting of the stream birds, and the bass horn of the bullfrog. Water had stopped coming over the dam at the lake the day before, and I noticed that the stream level had dropped a full six inches. A few dace dimpled the surface, and a few small sunfish meandered here and there.

The trout was still beneath the log.

I tried for him in all the usual ways—upstream, downstream, and from high above him on the bridge. I had by now, with the help of the split shot, managed to get my worm within a millimeter of his nose, regularly; in fact, I several times that morning actually bumped his rounded snout with my worm. The old trout did not seem to mind. He would sort of nudge it away, or ignore it, or shift his position deftly. Clearly he considered me no threat. It was humbling, humiliating.

I worked exceptionally hard for about three hours, missed breakfast, and kept fishing on into late morning on a growling stomach. I even tried floating grasshoppers down to the fish, and then a newt, even a little sunfish I caught upstream, several dace I trapped, and finally a crayfish.

Nothing would budge that confounded monster.

At last I went back to my little canvas pack and began to gather my scattered equipment. I was beaten. And I was starved. I'd tell Dr. Hertz about the fish and if he felt up to it he could try for him.

Despondently, I shoved my gear back into the pack.

And then it happened!

I pricked my finger sorely with a huge carlisle hook, snelled, which I used for the largest pickerel. I sat down on a rock and looked at it for a moment, pressing the blood out to avoid infection, washing my finger in the spring-cold stream, and then wrapping it with a bit of shirt I tore off—which I'd get hell for. But who cared.

The carlisle hook! Perhaps, I thought. Perhaps.

I had more than once thought of snaring that trout with piano wire lowered from the bridge, but too little of his nose was exposed. It simply would not have worked.

Carefully I tied the snelled hook directly onto the end of my ten-foot bamboo pole, leaving about two inches of firm gut trailing from the end. I pulled it to make sure it was firmly attached, found that it wasn't, then wrapped a few more feet of gut around the end of the pole to secure it.

Then, taking the pole in my right hand, I lay on my belly and began to crawl with painful slowness along the bottom logs of the bridge so that I would eventually pass directly above the trout. It took a full ten minutes. Then, finally, there I was, no more than a foot from the nose of my quarry, directly over him.

I scrutinized him closely for a long moment, lowering my head until my nose twitched the surface of the low water but a few inches from his nose.

He did not move.

I did not move.

I watched the gills dilate slowly; I followed the length of him as far back beneath the log as I could; I could have counted his speckles. And I trembled.

Then I began to lower the end of the rod slowly, slowly, slowly into the water, slightly upstream, moving the long bare carlisle hook closer and closer to his nose.

The trout opened and closed its mouth just a trifle every few seconds.

Now the hook was fractions of an inch from its mouth. Should I jerk hard? Try for the under lip? No, it might slip away—and there would be only one chance.

Instead, I meticulously slipped the bare hook directly toward the slight slit that was his mouth, guiding it down, into, and behind the curve of his lip.

He did not budge. I did not breathe.

And then I jerked abruptly up!

The fish lurched. I yanked. The bamboo rod splintered but held. The trout flipped up out of his element and into mine and flopped against the buttresses of the bridge. I pounced on him with both hands, and it was all over. It had taken no more than a few seconds.

Back at the hotel I headed immediately for Dr. Hertz's room, the seventeen-inch trout casually hanging from a forked stick in my right hand. To my immense disappointment, he had gone.

I wrote to him that very afternoon, lying in my teeth.

Dear Doctor Hertz:

> I caught a great big trout on a worm this morning and brought it to your room but you had gone home already. I have put into this letter a diagram of the fish that I drew. I caught him on a worm.

I *could* have caught him on a worm, eventually, and anyway I wanted to rub it in that he'd nearly wasted two weeks of my time and would never catch anything on those feathers. It would be a valuable lesson for him.

Several days later I received the letter below, which I found some months ago in one of my three closets crammed with fly boxes, waders, fly-tying tools and materials, delicate fly-rods, and the rest of that equipment needed for an art no less exhaustible than "Mathematics."

Dear Nicky:

I am glad you caught a big trout. But after fishing that creek for a whole two weeks I am convinced that there just weren't any trout in it. Are you sure it wasn't a perch? Your amusing picture looked like it. I wish you'd sent me a photograph instead, so I could be sure. Perhaps next year we can fish a *real* trout stream together.

Your friend,
Thos. Hertz, M.D.

Real? Was that unnamed creek not the realest I have ever fished? And "*your friend.*" How could he say that?

But let him doubt: I had, by hook and by crook, caught my first trout.

mari lyons

A Fisherman's Childhood in Brooklyn

Bedford Avenue in Brooklyn was sterile ground for a budding sportsman. We had the Dodgers and our own intense half-court basketball games at Wingate Field; we had stickball in the street, with the manhole in front of Ira's house as homeplate, bike rides to Bensonhurst and Bushwick, stoop ball, tough touch football on the fenced-in cement field near P.S. 193; but there was not water closer than Steeplechase Pier at Coney Island—and the fishing there could only be rated as poor.

I had started to fish at my grandfather's hotel, the Laurel House, in an obscure corner of the Catskills, before memory. Then, fatherless, I continued to fish in a sump called Ice Pond during all those grim years from four to eight at a frightening boarding school in Peekskill, where my growing passion for fishing surely buoyed my spirits and possibly saved my life. When my mother and my stepfather brought me to Brooklyn, I was ten, and the first thing I noticed was all the cement. The place was lousy with gray. There was no fishing, not anywhere.

Summer camp, on Lake Ellis in the foothills of the Berkshires, helped. I caught bullhead there, perch and several varieties of panfish, and my first bass. On a picnic to Bull's Bridge on the Housatonic, I saw a magnificent trout rise to an unseen insect, and though I did not fish for trout for some years, that image never left me; the fish, nearly two feet long, starting as a shadow, turning into the shape of a fish—sleek and spotted—that slipped downstream with the current and then angled up so gently that its white mouth barely opened and there was only a slight bending down of the surface and then that neat spreading circle sliding down stream. At Steeplechase Pier, on cold November or February days, we used two-ounce sinkers, frozen spearing, and thick glass rods to catch skate, mackerel, fluke, flounder, hacklehead, occasional snappers, and whiting. They were not pretty fish, this grab bag of the seas, and the fun of it was all contained in that little tug forty-five feet below and then the sight of a wriggling thing as we hoisted it upward, reeling like mad.

Every afternoon during my early teens I worked for a gardener who tended lawns and backyards in the neighborhood. He was a high school math teacher and I usually got to his house first, around three o'clock, readied the tools, and then sat atop the bags of mulch and pungent fertilizer in the carryall he attached to his car, waiting for him to arrive. With the little money I earned I bought my first spinning reel, various lines, hooks, and lures, my first fly rod (made of white glass), and bait for my saltwater sojourns, and I subscribed to four outdoor magazines. In the mid-to-late 1940s, I could not wait each month to get the magazines, my windows on the great outside world of angling. Lee Wulff, Joe Brooks, Ted Trueblood, A. J. McClane, H. G. Tapply, and Ed Zern became household names to me, though no one in my house fished or hunted and my stepfather thought it pretty stupid; I fished with those men from the Keys to Newfoundland, from the Beaverkill to the Deschutes. With Lee Wulff I jumped off a bridge over the Battenkill to see whether you'd die if you went underwater in waders, and I got just a little better (what with my three thumbs) at tackle tinkering by reading Tap Tapply—and I fell madly in love with Ted Trueblood's West.

Eventually I found books. Ray Bergman's *Trout* was first—as it has been for many thousands of other trout fishermen. I was looking for some logic to it all—the history I now became aware of, the never-ending stream of tackle, the conflicting techniques, the practical lore of a thousand kinds without which one cannot really be a complete angler. *Trout* included a measure of everything one went to "the Word" for. Bergman's patient, steady, thoughtful voice made good sense out of the mysteries of the craft and the greater mysteries of why a trout—under various circumstances— behaves as it does. His early experiences, decades earlier, paralleled those I was having—with their inescapable movement from "crude" to "more refined," from unknowing to knowing. His instinctive dislike of hordes of people and of those "who are not in accord with the true spirit of nature" defined my own growing uneasiness with such people. I might, by circumstance, live in the heart of a gray city but my ancestors must have been Tapplys or Bergmans—with at least one Leatherstocking in the batch.

Even before I tied my first fly onto a leader, Bergman gave me eyes to see what was in rivers—and he gave form and focus to my eventual love of fly fishing. He introduced me to wet flies, streamers, nymphs, and dries, and how they should be used; he described water I'd seen and was only just beginning to understand from my worming and spinning; he led me, also, to think as much about what respect I owed my fellow fishermen and my quarry as what a trout sees and how to play it more deftly once hooked.

All this was in stony Brooklyn, far from rivers of any stripe— though by now I had in fact discovered that with some vigorous travel I could find flowing water only several hours away. From the age of thirteen on, and without ever missing an Opening

Day or half a dozen trips each April and May, Mort and then Bernie and Don and I would take wearying treks north. We were all drawn to moving water—and we all still are, nearly fifty years later. The fishing was not very good, based on what I've experienced since; mostly stocked fish with a few holdovers, all caught rather unceremoniously in a passage of water between two city reservoirs, on worms first, then spinning lures. But we loved it. And we learned great lessons on those hard-fishing waters. Those days stolen from the gray city streets meant worlds to me then—and we had nights and Opening Day mornings that were as full of excitement as anything I've known since. A 15-inch holdover brown—with a bright orange belly and a bit of a kype—was a prize not soon forgotten.

To fish those Westchester and Dutchess County rivers we needed bait, and the best, always, had been worms. Working for a gardener, I was in a position of great privilege; in an afternoon of hard spade work I could always slip ten or twenty choice garden worms into the Prince Albert tobacco can I kept in my back pocket; neither my boss or my clients cared. But better, I knew the lawns that had automatic sprinklers or owners who were conscientious users of the hose—and I had scouted out the lawns filled with little mud mounds with a hole in the center of each, the telltale mark of nightcrawlers. With flashlight and coffee can I could, whether it had rained or not, always count on collecting three or four dozen nightcrawlers on any spring night. Once the light had flashed across their shining backs, I'd turn it away, bend and grab quickly for the spot where the long worm entered the earth, then tease it out, like Arthur the great sword from the stone. When Mort and I worked in tandem, we'd keep an eye out for suspicious homeowners or the police and whisper loudly when we had some success—whispers sometimes punctuated with "A double!," which meant we'd gotten two at one thrust, joined at the neck, in their act.

Those days and the worlds of the sport I read in book and magazine led me to dream of fishing in states far-flung. I felt linked by my passion for fishing to every other fisherman in every other part of this diverse country—from the catfisherman in Missouri to steelheaders in Oregon to a bream fisherman on a bayou in Louisiana. I even ordered from some of the two dozen mail-order catalogs I got each spring lures and hooks that could be used only in such places. Ted Trueblood and A. J. McClane were my eyes and ears, and my soul, long before I knew anything about them other than what appeared in their articles; they gave me skills and techniques and made me a westerner and southerner long before I ever fished such waters. They gave me ethic, too—one that has only grown stronger, more a part of me, over the many years.

Slowly, then, our worlds broadened. To summer camp and Sheepshead Bay and the Croton watershed rivers we added the great Catskill rivers, the huge St. Lawrence (for smallmouth bass and pike, with Mort's father), then (in college) rivers in Pennsylvania, Connecticut, and Vermont. At first we took trains or buses; later we hitchhiked, barnstorming through the East, pursuing faint rumors and glimmers of promising water, gleaned from stocking reports that Bernie got from the New York State Conservation Department or from magazine articles or from hearsay. The great Sportsman's Show—filled with hundreds of irresistible displays of lures, rods, reels, and lodges—came to Madison Square Garden every winter and we never missed it. It too gave us new dreams. We collected every travel brochure in the place and learned that the great landlocked salmon and outsized trout from the Maine and Canada exhibits were taken to a place called, ungraciously, Reservoir 3, in Westchester County—which proved, for us, only a very good lake in which to catch big crappies.

Then, in 1955, the summer I got out of the army, I bought a black 1946 Ford convertible with twin silver exhaust pipes. It was my first car and it gave me the West. I loaded it with fishing tackle and headed across America for the first time. It was a miraculous trip, filled with revelations; after the cities and eastern mountain ranges, the day-long flatness of the prairie and my first sight of the snow-tipped Rockies, looming in the distance for hours before I reached them. I went north, then south, crisscrossing the Continental Divide; to the Madison, the Henry's Fork, the Big Hole, then down to the great Gunnison in Colorado. I went up again to Silver Creek and the Big Lost River in Idaho, and found some unnamed spring creeks whose trout were mammoth—and, for me, uncatchable. I had never seen such water—so much of it and so wild, fecund. Eventually I wandered through Oregon, camped in the shadow of Mount Shasta, and then, on the way back, got vapor lock in the desert and had to be towed thirty miles. I had seen more water than I could fish in ten lifetimes, more fish of greater size than I'd seen in my entire childhood. If I stayed an extra day or two in a dry desert town waiting for my car to be fixed, it did nothing to blur the miracle of cold water.

Back in the Rockies I remembered a lake an army friend had said held "big ones." It did. I caught eight or ten truly huge trout, packed them carefully in ice, and raced back to Brooklyn. Don still remembers the day I arrived on East 24th Street in my 1946 Ford convertible and stopped in the middle of the street, where he was playing stickball, to show him my fish. He had never seen such trout. No one had. We talked for hours in my backyard, the tiny patch of gray summer grass surrounded by cement appearing even smaller—by a lot—than I remembered it. I had stopped working for the gardener when he paid me one dollar to cut my own grass and charged my parents ten dollars for the job; I had long skinned the yard of any nightcrawlers, and it was untended and dry now.

I told Don and Mort everything I had seen. They looked at the trout, my bona fides, and nodded. I swore I'd go back;

I swore I could learn how to fish for those elusive spring creek trout in Idaho. There was a vast world beyond Brooklyn. We'd seen nothing.

I knew I would always be a visitor to such places and I knew too that I would treat them with perhaps even more respect than those who lived there did—for the sad rivers of my childhood were auguries of what could happen to rivers anywhere. I was shocked, years later, to see some local fishermen beach a rubber raft above Varney Bridge on the Madison and display a full limit of huge trout, laid out like frozen meat slabs in an ice chest; the limit was ten or fifteen in those days. It was during the stonefly hatch and they had caught their fish on live stoneflies. There were four of them in that little boat, jammed in like city subway riders, cackling. They boasted that they had time before dark to float from McAtee down again and take another limit each.

But by then I knew that rivers belong to those who love them, and that these men were no friends of this river.

That afternoon in the backyard in Brooklyn I knew I would go west again, and south and north, too. Suddenly there was a whole country full of rivers and lakes to fish—or fish again.

And so I have.

And so I will.

Confessions of an Early Wormer

When I was fifteen and we lived in Brooklyn and all the other guys were off hunting girls, I would often sneak out of my house on a muggy late-March evening, wearing sneakers and carrying a flashlight and coffee can. On the corner of the Bedford Avenue and Avenue J, I would meet my friend Mort, and the two of us, with great bounding strides, would head without a word for the huge abandoned house several blocks away, its windows dark, a "For Sale" sign stuck prominently into the front lawn. And among the high clumps of untended grass, only barely green, our hearts would quicken and we would begin to hunt worms.

More snake than worm, these night crawlers were long, floppy, gooey things, often stretched out to six or seven inches on their spawning crawl. We would shine the light so that only its edge illuminated the shiny back of a worm, then plunge quickly to catch one where it left the earth, pinning it lightly, firmly, then easing it up out of its hole. Later we learned to put red paper over the faces of our flashlights, and we could shine the dimmer light directly on these night crawlers without their moving. We often caught the old hermaphrodites at it, quite passionately joined together at the necks, and now and again Mort or I would say, in a loud whisper, "Double," and we'd display two with as much pride as a wing-shooter after his feat.

We were always quick and intent about our business. We had to be. More than twenty minutes on any lawn usually meant the cops. We had "safe" lawns, where we could linger, and some well-tended lawns whose owners thought we were madmen, burglars, or worse. Carefully trimmed and watered lawns were usually the most fecund, and one old lady, whose immaculate lawn was irresistible, often sat shotgun so we "beastly boys" wouldn't pinch *her* worms.

It was a strange, mystical rite—this catching of night crawlers on moist spring nights—and we somehow took almost as much pleasure in it as we did in fishing. Rarely did we return with fewer than several dozen good worms. We even experimented with scores of different materials in which to store the bait—from cut newspaper to grass—and finally settled on sphagnum moss, which we bought in vast quantities from a dealer in Arkansas. We packed the moss and worms in shoeboxes, and I, who had an understanding mother, kept them in the vegetable section of my refrigerator.

They were our foremost baits for trout, these snakelike night crawlers, and for several years we caught all our early-season trout on them. Though by May, when the water was low and clear and we switched to small garden worms—a firmer, more compact creature—all our April fishing was done with these preposterous monsters. And we caught fish. Big two- and even three-pound holdover brown trout, from hard-fished public waters, fell to our ungainly rigs.

We gave them up not for flies but for spinning lures, and spent the last few years of our teens becoming lethal with this new tool that enabled you to flip a 1/16-ounce spinner forty feet, to the base of a fallen tree, and retrieve it with subtle fluttering.

Spinning taught me much that I've put to good use when streamer fishing—but probably condemned me to a floppy casting wrist for life; only years of careful fly casting have burned away the haste, the impatience, the nervous movement spinning taught me so well. None of my previous fishing prepared me for the challenge of the dry fly, and only recently have I begun to appreciate how much I learned about wet-fly and nymph fishing from my early worming.

At first we fished worms on long, unwieldy telescopic fly rods. We did not so much cast as heave or lob the rig out—a big night crawler hooked lightly in its orange band with a #8 Eagle Claw hook, then ten inches of leader, then as much split shot as we needed to get the thing where we wanted it. We used four of the biggest shot in the Big Bend Pool, merely one in the deep Swamp Pool, none in several slow glides where we'd fish in straight upstream and follow its progress down with the tip of the rod. On Opening Day, we used the most primitive methods and fished the deepest, slowest pools, smack in the middle, dead still, right on the bottom. On warmer days, we'd fish the head of a pool, drifting a worm from the riffle down into the center or sides—still as deep as possible. And even with "bugs" hatching all around us and trout rising with bacchanalian slurps, we fished— and caught fish—with worms We'd use the smallest worms then, the lightest leaders; we'd fish shallow runs or riffles, or wherever we saw fish rising. We fished upstream and watched the worm come back toward us, a few inches beneath the surface—and often enough we'd see one of the better trout cease all that peanut grabbing and head for a good, decent munch of worm.

How did all this early worming affect me when I became a fly fisherman?

I suppose at first it merely humiliated me to have done it. I mentioned it not at all, could find no connection between it and the dry-fly fishing I now did—except that I had always caught a lot of fish on worms.

But then I realized that there was a certain "pool" of stream lore I had developed before I caught any fish, even on worms—a knowledge of where, at a particular time of the year and day, fish would be; a sense of what will frighten them; an inkling of what they would eat and under what circumstances they would take it. I had begun to learn this kind of lore while worming. Before long, I learned that trout were rarely taken in open, exposed water; they wanted protection from the heavy flow, and from predators, and they wanted a spot where vulnerable fish would come to them. Pockets behind rocks, with their broken water and eddies, were ideal; here the trout had protection and had ready access to food caught and stunned and perhaps eddying in the broken water.

After the holocaust of Opening Day, our most regular success came from fishing these spots, what Al Troth calls the supermarkets of the river, with immense care. We learned that we could not drop a worm smack in the middle of such a pocket because the turbulence would scoot it right out and into the main flow; we had to get the worm slightly upstream first, then give enough slack so the bait would sink to the proper depth, then manipulate the rod in such cunning ways that the bait would remain in the pockets. Bends in the river created under-cut banks and greater water depth, and we also took fish by working a worm slowly, naturally, into their depths.

Naturally.

That, I think, is the key word. Mort used to say, when a dumb hatchery fish took a quickly retrieved worm: "Mistook that one for a worm swimming upstream." And we'd continue the conceit with references to "hatches" of upstream-swimming worms and other unnatural absurdities. No. The tough fish, the good-sized fish, were only caught when you fished the worm naturally. And since a worm does not usually swim upstream, or hang suspended from a leader on the bottom of a river, *natural* meant dead drift: with the worm cast upstream, gaining a bit of depth as it moved down, without encumbrance, tumbling as close to the bottom as possible.

We learned to hold the rod forward and then bring it downstream as the worm came toward and past us. We learned to see the telltale twitch of line or leader, the wink of white under water when a trout's mouth opened. We learned to manipulate the bait to the depth at which the fish were; we learned to judge currents and eddies in the process. We learned holding water and feeding lanes and how to use our eyes and hands, and we learned the absolute need for quick, light strikes.

Though we didn't know it, we were beginning to learn how to fish the nymph.

Now and again, when I hear someone tell me how they learned to fly fish when they were five or ten or twelve, I get a touch of envy, a sense of regret, a feeling that all of my green years, when my feelings and passions were freshest, might have been better spent. As I look back, I was from the beginning fated to be a fly fisherman: everything I love about fishing pointed me in that direction. Now and again, when I think back on my early years, I regret I did not find fly fishing sooner.

But lately, especially in late March, when Mort and I first went forth with flashlight and coffee can, I remember the lowly worm: the moist night on which we hunted them, the engaging *peck-peck-peck* when a fish took one, the whole ritual of worm fishing. But beyond all that, beyond that world to which I cannot return, I am grateful to the worm. It was a damned good teacher.

The Lure of Opening Day

"Who so that first to mille comth, first grynt."
—GEOFFREY CHAUCER, PROLOGUE TO "THE WIFE OF BATH'S TALE"

The whole madness of Opening Day fever is quite beyond me: it deserves the complexities of a Jung or a Kafka, for it is archetypal and rampant with ambiguity. And still you would not have it.

It is simply the beginning of a new season, after months of winter dreams?

That it is the *one* day—like a special parade, with clowns and trumpets—that is bound by short time, unpredictable weather, habit, ritual?

That it is some massive endurance test?

Or the fact that the usually overfished streams are as virgin as they'll ever be?

That there are big fish astream—for you have caught your largest on this day?

Masochism—pure and simple?

A submergence syndrome?

That you are the first of the year—or hope to be? And will "first grynt?"

I don't know. I simply cannot explain it. When I am wise and strong enough (or bludgeoned enough), I know I shall resist even thinking of it.

I know for sure only that March is the cruelest month—for trout fisherman. And that the weakest succumb, while even the strongest must consciously avoid the pernicious lure of Opening Day.

On approximately March fourth, give or take a day—I get up from my desk year after year and industriously slip into the reference room, where I spend hours busily studying the *Encyclopaedia Britannica*, Volume I, under "Angling": looking at pictures of fat brook trout being taken from the Nipigon River, impossible Atlantic salmon bent heavy in a ghillie's net, reading about Halford and Skues and the immaculate Gordon and some fool in Macedonia who perhaps started it all.

Then on lunch hours I'll head like a rainbow trout, upstream, to the Angler's Cove or the Roost or the ninth floor at Abercrombie's—sidle up to groups rehashing trips to the Miramichi, the Dennys, the Madison, the Au Sable, the Beaverkill, and "this lovely little river filled with nothing less than two-pounders, and everyone of 'em dupes for a number twenty-six Rube Winger."

It is hell.

I listen intently, unobtrusively, as each trout is caught, make allowances for the inescapable fancy, and then spend the rest of the day at my desk scheming for this year's trips and doodling new fly patterns on manuscripts I am supposed to be editing. Or some days I'll head downstream, and study the long counter of luscious flies under glass at the elegant William Mills's, hunting for new patterns to tie during the last March flurry of vise activity. It is a vice—all of it: the dreaming, the reading (Aston to Zern), the talking, the scant hours (in proportion to all else) of fishing itself. How many days in March I try to get a decent afternoon's work done, only to be plagued, bruited, and beaten by images of browns rising steadily to Light Cahills on the Amawalk, manic Green Drake hatches on the big Beaverkill, with dozens of fat fish sharking down the ample duns in slow water. I fish a dozen remembered streams, two dozen from my reading, a dozen times each, every riffle and eddy and run and rip and pool of them, every March in my mind. I become quite convinced that I am going mad. Downright berserk. Fantasy becomes reality. I will be reading at my desk and my body will suddenly stiffen, lurch back from the strike; I will see, actually see, four, five, six trout rolling and flouncing under the alder branch near my dictionary, glutting on leafrollers—or a long dark shadow under a far ledge of books, emerging, dimpling the surface, returning to its feeding post.

My desk does not help. I have it filled with every conceivable aid to such fantasies. *Matching the Hatch,* Art Flick's *Streamside Guide, The Dry Fly and Fast Water* reside safely behind brown paper covers—always available. There are six or seven catalogs of fly-fishing equipment—from Orvis and Norm Thompson and Dan Bailey and Herter's and Mills; travel folders from Maine, Idaho, Quebec, Colorado—all with unmentionable photos of gigantic trout and salmon on them; I have four Sulfur Duns that Jim Mulligan dropped off on a visit—that I *could* bring home; and there is even a small box of #16 Mustad dry-fly hooks and some yellow-green wool, from which I can tie up a few heretical leafrollers periodically, hooking the barb into a soft part of the end of the desk, and working rapidly, furtively, so no one will catch me and think me quite so troutsick mad as I am.

But no. It is no good. I will not make it this year. I cannot wait until mid-May, when even then there will be difficulty abandoning Mari and my children (still under trouting size) for even a day's outing.

And yet for many years there was this dilemma: after years of deadly worming and spinning, I became for a time a rabid purist, shunning even streamers and wet flies. How could I fish Opening Day with dries? It was ludicrous. It was nearly fatal.

But it was not always so.

I can remember vividly my first Opening Day, and I can remember, individually, each of the ten that succeeded it, once at the expense of the College Entrance examinations, once when I went AWOL from Fort Dix, and once ... well ... when I was in love.

A worm dangled from a nine-foot steel telescopic rod took my second trout. He was only a stocked brown of about nine inches, and I took him after three hours of fishing below the Brewster bridge of the East Branch of the Croton; I was just thirteen and it was the height of the summer.

On Opening Days you can always see pictures of the spot in the New York papers. Draped men, like manikins, pose near the falls upstream; and Joe X of 54-32 Seventy-third Avenue is standing proudly with his four mummy buddies, displaying his fat sixteen-inch holdover brown, the prize of the day; a buddy had ten—are they smelt? You do not die of loneliness on the East Branch of the Croton these days.

Probably it was always like that. But memory is maverick: the crowds are not what I remember about the East Branch—not, certainly, what I remember about my first day.

In the five years since I caught my first trout, I had fished often for large-mouth bass, pickerel, perch, sunfish, catfish, crappies, and even shiners—always with live bait, usually with worms, always in lakes and ponds. Once, when my mother tried to interest me in horseback riding, I paused at a creek along the trail, dismounted, and spent an hour fishing with a pocket rig I always carried.

It could not have been the nine-inch hollow-and gray-bellied brown that intrigued me all that winter. Perhaps it was the moving water of the stream, the heightened complexity of this kind of fishing. Perhaps it was the great mystery of moving water. What does Hesse's Siddhartha see in the river? "He saw that the water continually flowed and flowed and yet it was always there; it was always the same and yet every moment it was new." He saw, I suppose, men, and ages, and civilizations, and natural processes.

Whatever the cause, the stream hooked me, too. All that winter I planned for my first Opening Day. There were periodic trips to the tackle stores on Nassau Street, near my stepfather's office; interminable lists of necessary equipment; constant and thorough study of all the outdoor magazines, which I would pounce on the day they reached the stands.

My parents were out of town the weekend the season was to open, and my old grandmother was staying with me. My plan was to make the 5:45 milk train out of Grand Central and arrive in Brewster, alone, about eight. My trip had been approved.

I arose, scarcely having slept, at two-thirty by the alarm and went directly to the cellar, where all my gear had been carefully laid out. For a full ten days.

I had my steel fly rod neatly tied in its canvas case, 150 worms (so that I would not be caught short), seventy-five #10 Eagle Claw hooks (for the same reason), two jackknives (in case I lost one), an extra spool of level fly line, two sweaters (to go with the sweat shirt, sweater, and woolen shirt I already wore under my Mackinaw), a rain cape, four cans of Heinz pork and beans, a whole box of kitchen matches in a rubber bag (one of the sporting magazines had recommended this), a small frying pan, a large frying pan, a spoon, three forks, three extra pairs of woolen socks, two pairs of underwear, three extra T-shirts, an article from one of the magazines on "Early Season Angling" (which I had plucked from my burgeoning files), two tin cups, a bottle of Coca-Cola, a pair of corduroy trousers, a stringer, about a pound and a half of split shot, seven hand-tied leaders, my bait-casting reel, my fly reel, and nine slices of rye bread. Since I had brought them down to the cellar several days earlier, the rye bread was stale.

All of this went (as I knew it would, since I had packed four times, for practice) into my upper pack. To it I attached a slightly smaller, lower pack, into which I had already put my hip boots, two cans of Sterno, two pairs of shoes, and a gigantic thermos of hot chocolate (by then cold). Once the two packs were fastened tightly, I tied my rod across the top (so that my hands would be free), flopped my felt hat down hard on my head, and began to mount my cross.

Unfortunately, my arms would not bend sufficiently beneath the Mackinaw, the sweater, the woolen shirt, and the sweat shirt—I had not planned on this—and I could not get my left arm through the arm-strap.

My old grandmother had risen to see me off with a good hot breakfast, and hearing me moan and struggle, came down to be of help.

She was of enormous help.

She got behind me, right down on the floor, on my instructions, in the dimly lit basement at three in the morning, and pushed me up. I pushed down.

After a few moments I could feel the canvas strap.

"Just a little further, Grandma," I said. "Uhhhh. A ... litt ... ul ... more."

She pushed and pushed, groaning now nearly as loudly as I was, and then I said, "NOW!" quite loudly and the good old lady leaped and pushed up with all her might and I pushed down and my fingers were inside the strap and in another moment the momentous double pack was on my back.

I looked thankfully at my grandmother standing (with her huge breasts half out of her nightgown) beneath the hanging light bulb. She looked bushed. After a short round of congratulations, I told her to go up the narrow stairs first. Wisely she advised otherwise, and I began the ascent. But after two steps I remembered that I hadn't taken my creel, which happened to contain three apples, two bananas, my toothbrush, a half pound of raisins, and two newly made salami sandwiches.

Since it would be a trifle difficult to turn around, and I was too much out of breath to talk, I simply motioned to her to hand me the creel from the table. She did so, and I laboriously strapped it around my body, running the straps, with Grandma's help, under the pack.

Then I took a step. And then another. I could not take the third. My steel fly rod, flanged out at the sides, had gotten wedged into the narrow stairwell. In fact, since I had moved upstairs with some determination, it was jammed tightly between the two-by-four banister and the bottom of the ceiling.

It was a terrifying moment. I *could* be there all day. For weeks.

And then I'd miss Opening Day.

Which I'd planned all that winter.

I pulled. Grandma pushed. We got nowhere. But then, in her wisdom, she found the solution: remove the rod. She soon did so, and I promptly sailed up the stairs at one a minute. ...

A few moments later I was at the door. "I'll ... have ... to hurry," I panted. "It's three thirty-five . . . already."

She nodded and patted me on the hump. As I trudged out into the icy night I heard her say, "Such a pack! Such a little man!"

The walk to the subway was only seventeen blocks, and I made it despite that lower pack smacking painfully at each step against my rump. I dared not get out of my packs in the subway, so I stood all the way to Grand Central, in nearly empty cars, glared at by two bums, one high-school couple returning from a dress dance, and several early workers who appeared to have seen worse.

The five forty-five milk train left on time, and I was on it. I unhitched my packs (which I did not—could not—replace all that long day, and thus carried by hand) and tried to sleep. But I could not: I never sleep before I fish.

The train arrived at eight, and I went directly to the flooding East Branch and rigged up. It was cold as a witch's nose, and the line kept freezing at the guides. I'd suck out the ice, cast twice and fine ice caked at the guides again. After a few moments at a pool, I'd pick up all my gear, cradling it in my arms, and push on for another likely spot.

Four hours later I had still not gotten my first nibble.

Then a sleety sort of rain began, which slowly penetrated through all my many layers of clothing right to the marrow-bone.

But by four o'clock my luck had begun to change. For one good thing, I had managed to lose my lower pack and thus, after a few frantic moments of searching, realized that I was much less weighted down. For another, it had stopped raining and the temperature had risen to slightly above freezing. And finally, I had reached a little feeder creek and had begun to catch fish steadily. One, then another, and then two more in quick succession.

They weren't trout, but a plump greenish fish that I could not identify. They certainly weren't yellow perch or the grayish largemouth bass I had caught. But they were about twelve to fourteen inches long and gave quite an account of themselves after they took my night crawler and the red and white bobber bounced under water. They stripped line from my fly reel, jumped two or three times, and would not be brought to net without an impressive struggle.

Could they be green perch?

Whatever they were, I was quite pleased with myself and had strung four of them onto my stringer and just lofted out another night crawler when a genial man with green trousers and short green jacket approached.

"How're you doin', son?" he asked.

"Very well," I said, without turning around. I didn't want to miss that bobber going under.

"Trout?"

"Nope. Not sure what they are. Are there green perch in this stream?"

"Green perch?"

Just then the bobber went under abruptly and I struck back and was into another fine fish. I played him with particular care for my audience and in a few moments brought him, belly up, to the net.

The gentleman in back of me had stepped close. "Better release him right in the water, son; won't hurt him that way."

"I guess I'll keep this one, too," I said, raising the fish high in the net. It was a beautiful fish—all shining green and fat and still flopping in the black meshes of the net. I was thrilled. Especially since I'd had an audience.

"Better return him now," the man said, a bit more firmly. "Bass season doesn't start until July first."

"Bass?"

"Yep. You've got a nice smallmouth there. They come up this creek every spring to spawn. Did'ya say you'd caught some more?"

I knew the bass season didn't start until July. Anybody with half a brain knew that. So when the man in green said it was a bass I disengaged the hook quickly and slipped the fish carefully back into the water.

"I'm a warden, son," the man said. "Did you say you'd caught s'more of these bass?"

"Yes," I said, beginning to shake. It was still very cold and the sun had begun to drop. "Four."

"Kill them?" he asked sternly.

"They're on my stringer," I said, and proceeded to walk the few yards upstream to where the four fish, threaded through the gills, were fanning the cold water slowly.

"Certainly hope those fish aren't dead," said the warden.

I did not take the stringer out of the icy water but, with all the grace and sensitivity I could possibly muster, and with shaking hands, began to slip the fish off and into the current. The first floated out and immediately began to swim off slowly; so did the other two—each a bit more slowly. The fourth had been on the stringer for about fifteen minutes. I had my doubts. Carefully I slipped the cord through his gills and pushed him out, too.

He floated downstream, belly up, for a few moments.

"Hmmm," murmured the warden. "Don't think this one will make it."

Together we walked downstream, following the fish intently. Every now and then it would turn ever so slowly, fan its tail, and flop back belly up again.

There was no hope.

Down the current it floated, feeble, mangled by an outright poacher, near goner. When it reached the end of the feeder creek and was about to enter the main water, it swirled listlessly in a small eddy, tangled in the reeds, and was absolutely still for a long moment. Absolutely still.

But then it made a momentous effort, taking its will from my will perhaps, and its green back was up and it was wriggling and its green back stayed up and I nearly jumped ten feet with joy.

"Guess he'll make it," said the warden.

"Guess so," I said, matter-of-factly.

"Don't take any more of those green perch now, will you?" he said, poker-faced, as he turned and walked back up the hill. "And get a good identification book!"

I breathed heavily, smiled sheepishly, and realized that my feet were almost frozen solid. So I began to fold in my rod, gather together my various remaining goods—almost all unused—and prepare to leave. I cradled my pack in my arms and trudged up the hill to the railway station, glad I'd taken some fish, glad the fish had lived.

It was ten o'clock that night when I returned. Somehow I stumbled up the stairs and, with a brave whistle, kissed my grandmother on the cheek. She did not look like she would survive the shock of me. Then, without a word. I collapsed.

Though I had 104-degree fever the next day and missed a full week of school, my first Opening Day had scarcely been a failure. I had seen a few trout caught and marked where and how they had been caught. In particular, I had seen a new kind of rod and reel, the spinning outfit, which could do everything I had wanted to do with my fly rod but could not. I had seen it take trout on a small spinner fifty feet across stream from beneath an upturned tree stump—a fine fourteen-inch brown that slashed across and downstream furiously. With the trees coming directly to the water's edge, I had simply not known how to fish that fishy section with a fly rod. I had been confined, so far as I could tell, to the pools and the runs along my own bank.

That spring I worked afternoons for a gardener and soon earned enough to purchase a spinning rod of my own. I bought the longest, thinnest glass rod I could find, a Mitchel reel, and several hundred yards of braided line (monofilament had not yet appeared). I practiced with it constantly and soon, without instruction, learned to keep the rubber practice plug low and soft and accurate. I practiced underhand, side-arm, and overhand—and did not bother to fiddle with fancy bow-and-arrow or trick casts.

That summer I found my first two angling companions, Clyde and Mort, at camp, and all that fall and winter we plotted my second Opening Day with all the strategies of master generals.

This time it was not a disaster.

For us.

It *was* for the trout.

Clyde rapped on my bedroom window promptly at four o'clock, I picked up my new efficient single pack quickly, and we met Mort at Grand Central in time for the milk train.

All the way to Brewster we talked and planned, and when we arrived we marched to the stream like the four gunmen coming into town after Gary Cooper in *High Noon*. Only it was eight o'clock and freezing, and we got what we had come for.

Our spinning weapons worked with uncanny skill. By ten, Mort and I had two good trout each; Clyde had four. We picked up another seven among us before we left that afternoon and came back proud and triumphant.

Rarely after that year did we return with less than limits—often interspersed with fifteen- and sixteen-inch holdover browns. Clyde had discovered a large turn in the stream that opened into a huge deep pool with a shallow glide at its tail; midway through it a fallen tree cut the flow and provided highly productive eddies in front and below. We dubbed it the "Big Bend" (and also named a dozen other favorite spots), and it was there that we began each Opening Day for the next half-dozen years, lined up in a row. Once, when the season started at six in the morning, we told Clyde we'd miss this year and drove to Brewster without him. At five thirty, in order to beat the now mounting crowds that had found our East Branch, we headed downstream to the Big Bend.

The mists were still on the water and we felt all the old excitement sweep away the confusions of college. It was still dark and cold and no one had arrived yet as we stepped swiftly through the stark trees toward the Big Bend. As it came into view, we both felt charged with anticipation; we looked at each other and smiled.

But there was someone there before us! Up to his chest, half-hidden in the mists—and fast to a good trout! And there was someone nearby, leaping up and down.

It was Clyde—jumping the gun. And on the bank was his girlfriend—a very beautiful girlfriend. He heard our approach and half turned, without taking his eye from the struggling fish.

Since we'd outrightly lied to him about not making it this year, we expected a bitter moment, but Clyde simply shouted, "Don't stand there! Bring the net. Quick!"

Later, when a warden saw him in the water, fast to his third pre-season trout—while we were standing glumly and honestly by—he simply lay his rod down on the bank held up his hand, and let the trout roam about until six on a slack line.

Some years later, when the fever was particularly severe, when I could not wait until late April, I determined to strike out boldly. I would fish Opening Day again, rid myself of the dread fever and bring home a full limit of hatchery trout. Someone else would if I didn't. I would fish with my son Paul's spinning rod. With worms. I was that desperate.

So I called Mort, and then there we were, zipping along Route 22 at eleven thirty on March 31st in Mort's huge Chrysler wagon; the season started at midnight again. The night was nipping cold, though clear; all the old feeling was there. But now I was trimly efficient—with minimal gear, maximum comfort. It would be a killing.

It was colder than we'd thought, below freezing, but we rigged quickly, divided the noble worms, and headed directly downstream through the stark black trees. The moon was slightly more than a pale-yellow sliver, but our flashlights led us swiftly toward the scene of so many Opening Day slaughters.

The Big Bend was indeed high. The water went some ten yards higher upon the land than I had remembered it, and a close look with my flashlight showed the churning water to be thickly brownish, filled with leaves and other debris—snow water. But all the old feeling was there. I stepped out boldly up to my waist, then a bit further. The cold shot through my Totes and a small streak of icy wetness began to seep through above my knees and down into my boots. I worked myself slowly to the spot where I remembered the old fallen tree had been, the one that jutted out and cut the flow.

Ten hours later, frozen, exhausted, fishless, after one of the most unpleasant days (and nights) of my life, I felt the car stopping, opened both eyes rapidly, widely, and shouted—irrationally and unaccountably shrilly—"Thank God! We've made it!"

Mort helped collect up all my tackle and clothes. They were in a tangled mass. I put his furniture blanket over my head and began to walk away. He hauled it back and the two of us nearly collapsed on the pavement.

"This is hell," said Mort.

As I reached back spasmodically to grasp a night crawler working its moist way down my spine, I saw my wife and children standing on the stoop. For some reason they were unable to say a word. Even my four remarkably vocal children were stark silent. I stuck my tongue out at them, and two scurried behind my wife.

The Generous Bluegill

They were the first fish I—and most of us—caught: bright flopping jewels of blue, crimson, green, and coral. I caught them on bent pins first, then snelled hooks and eyed hooks, on breadballs, crickets, grubs, caterpillars, bits of pork rind, corn kernels, and worms. Mostly I caught them on garden worms.

I spit on the breadballs and pork rind for luck, and I used bobbers made of quills, balsa wood, and wine corks threaded right onto the line with a large needle.

I started to catch bluegills before memory began, so as far as I know I've always been catching them.

After a while I caught them on flies. Bluegills were the first fish I caught on flies and with the first flies I used—deliciously gaudy wet flies, the brighter the better: McGinty, Parmachene Belle, and Silver Doctor. Drab flies, like those I later used with such success for trout, never worked as well. Anything with rubber legs, though, was a killer.

I first fished flies for bluegills on a Berkshire foothills lake called Ellis, wading the shorelines in sneakers on July and August evenings after I'd finished waiting on tables. I used one of those clumsy white-glass fly rods and a level line, and first put the line through the keeper ring. I could barely slap the line down twenty feet out when

I started; until I rethreaded the line, outside of the keeper ring, the casts were considerably briefer. But the bluegills didn't much care. If they were there, you could see them trail after the fly as I retrieved it with short slow pulls, a few inches below the surface; you could see them come after it, their little mouths pursed and ready, and then they'd snap at it and pretty much hook themselves.

Since all the action was visible in the shallow water, from the moment the fly hit the water until the fish was hooked, bluegills gave me a short course in how fish strike and why. The regular, steady retrieve, for instance, rarely brought the number of strikes that irregular twitches brought—slow, then fast, quick and erratic. I could see how deep the fly rode in the thin water and the fish's response at various depths, to kinds of retrieve, particular colors, and so much else—knowledge of fish behavior that, over time, became instinct and helped me catch a thousand fish with bigger reputations but no more heart.

No, they were not what trout fishermen call "selective"; but they had their preferences. They did not mind when a beginner's bad casts fell like balls of hail on the flat evening lake. They did not ask for seventy-foot casts. They were the most generous of instructors and I couldn't catch enough of them—and I seemed to learn more with each fish that trailed my fly.

Bluegills are of course the ideal fish on which to start fly fishing. Since they take the fly so readily, you can have the pleasure of catching *something* immediately, and they always fight with circling pluck and ardor. They are tolerant of our mistakes and are willing to give us a day's sport as soon as we get the line out of the keeper ring.

Though colorful wet flies and chenille-bodied flies with rubber legs were how I started, I soon found that small cork popping bugs were much more fun; I still prefer them, whenever they've got the slimmest chance to work. That first summer, as I taught myself to cast thirty, even forty feet, to reach some parallel stretch of shoreline I could not wade, I found that I had a distinct preference for the floating bug. I'd choose the very smallest I could find in a local hardware store—about twenty cents apiece, from a card that held a few dozen of them—and choose, too, the ones with little cupped heads, which would make a bit of disturbance when I tugged them. I'd fish them near the lily pads, let them sit for a moment or two, pop and ploop them gently, and if there were bluegill around they'd crash up for the bug, with a happy pinching and clefting of the surface. Oddly, they always stopped at dusk—which was when I caught my first few bass on flies; and all I had learned fishing for bluegills immediately stood me in good stead with their larger cousins.

How I wish I had started my three sons on bluegills instead of trout! We took long trips in their early teens to great rivers to which I'd lost my heart, and usually they caught nothing but a huge dose of boredom. There has got to be *some* encouragement for a beginning teenager with little other fishing experience; a day of listening to a lunatic father talk about bugs with Latin names and about fish that *might* start rising in another hour or two or four, and slapping down casts a couple of dozen feet for those trout when they do finally rise, will not get a youngster interested. We did best on Great Pond, near Amherst, Maine, where we bunked in an old cabin for a week many years ago. Here there was excitement: the water near the island was lousy with bluegills and we all got a good dose of them, several of which, on the way in, found their way into a pickerel's mouth—which added to the fun.

After I lost my heart to trout and became involved in the minute and exacting business of learning to extract a few now and then, sometimes under very challenging circumstances, I forgot about bluegills for some years. They were fine, I thought, when there was nothing else to do, but I wouldn't travel very far for them.

I guess it was Thom Green, an oil geologist from Tulsa, who got me to travel for them—and when he did I traveled a full two thousand miles. That was fifteen years ago. We were fishing

Henry's Lake in Idaho for very large rainbow and hybrid rainbow-cutthroat trout and Thom was one of the most tenacious—and skillful—fly casters on the lake, up at 4:30, in at 10:30 a.m., out again in the evening and on the lake until dark. And he got some of the largest trout, on a special leech he tied and could cast spectacularly. With a shooting-head line he regularly cast a full hundred feet; here was a big-fish fisherman if I'd ever seen one. One night, seeing his pleasure, I asked him if he enjoyed this lake more than any other fishing he did and he replied without hesitation: "No, I like bluegill most. I really like those bluegill when they're up on the beds and you can take them on little popping bugs. Gosh, that's a barrel of fun."

I said I'd always liked them too and a few days later we'd arranged to meet in Utah the next spring to explore a lake that, allegedly, had two- and even three-pound bluegills. Utah is two thousand miles from where I live ... but those are *very* big bluegills.

We were a few weeks early but the fish were every bit as large as the reports Thom had been given. This was a rich alkaline lake and a delicate combination of abundant food supply and severe winter kills had created—at least for a while—a large number of gargantuan bluegills. Thom saw at once that they were not yet on the beds, so he tied up some of those chenille-bodied flies on long-shank hooks, with drooping rubber legs, and we took a slew of fish up to two and a half pounds in the deepest water, and had a marvelous time, worth every mile of the trip.

Most bluegills are much smaller, of course, and the best sport is usually close to home. That's one of their greatest virtues: they remind us that the heart of fishing, the great fun we have at it, is not high-tech, far-flung, expensive sport. It's as close as the nearest farm pond. It's the meeting of an angler or two, with the least possible gear, and a game fish in another element. There's always a bit of mystery and with bluegills there's always a whole measure of fun—and there's a certain unpressured, noncompetitive, happy, Huck Finn-like, earthy quality to it all that I've longed for more than once when I've done "Big Time" fishing.

Give me small-time bluegills half a dozen times every year, to keep the human measure to my angling; give me a long light fly rod and a single plastic box of bugs and wet flies, and I'll have as much fun as I can have anywhere on the water.

I like a stiff #4 rod these days—light but strong enough to throw a bug into the wind. I like a variety of small bugs, usually with dyed feathers for the tail and a couple of strands of rubber coming from the sides. I use a simple double-taper line and a seven- or eight-foot leader, tapered to no lighter than 4X; I think that lighter tippets flop in the wind, won't straighten out a bug, and break off too quickly on obstructions. You tire a fish less using the heaviest possible leader, which of course enables you to bring fish in quicker, and bluegills are not leader shy.

Along with bluegills, you often catch perch, pickerel, rock bass, crappie, and other panfish. All can be lots of fun, too, on a fly rod, and all can be caught with pretty much the same techniques that work for bluegills, though I always retrieve flies with the greatest possible speed when I'm specifically after pickerel.

I like to wade wet for bluegills in the late spring, fishing to the beds with a little popper. I generally do so alone, so I can travel at my own pace, though this is genial, friendly fishing not nearly so intense as fishing—say— a tough spring creek and it's often pleasant to talk over the water to a good friend, sharing a fish that may be a full inch or two larger than the average you've both been catching, comparing notes on which bugs work best. But I often fish for them from an old wooden rowboat or a canoe, tooling down the shoreline slowly and casting in to those targets of lighter sand that are the bluegill beds, each, often, with an auburn shape in it that is the fish.

After that trip to Utah I've never traveled very far for bluegills, though they've several times saved a slow day of bass fishing that

I'd come a great distance to try. I know five, six little ponds, some that you can cast across, some a mile or so around, some with larger bluegills, some with bluegills that must go seven or eight to the pound. I'll fish any one of them any chance I get—often in the later afternoon, when the heat of a late spring day just begins to break and the sun is beginning to angle off the water. My casting is much better now than it was when I first fished for them, and often I'll practice a double-haul or see if I can reach a log some seventy feet away, and then turn the cast into some good fishing by working the bug back with little twitches and pops. But mostly, bluegill fishing requires no more than thirty feet or so, and I simply make my casts as gentle as possible and work each fly in with care.

I'll amble down to a certain half-acre pond I know about six o'clock on an August evening, and feel the same sense of expectation I feel when I fish one of those great name rivers for big trout. The water is flat and there's just a bit of swirling mist on it, as the temperature changes. A couple of mallards climb off the water as I approach, shattering the stillness; a few robins exchange one branch for another. I'm wearing sneakers and khaki pants, a long-sleeved khaki shirt to keep the bugs off my arms (and the chill that will come up in a couple of hours); I've got a single box of flies and bugs, an old rod, dark glasses that I'll shed when the sun goes down, and a baseball cap. If I want to keep a few fish—and they're of course sweet and delicious when fried, though bony—I may take the old wicker creel I no longer wear near trout streams; I always liked the weight of it on my shoulders and lining it with wet grasses for the fish I caught. Mostly I travel very light.

The pond is shaped like a watermelon, with a swimming dock that floats on barrels at one end. I can just about cast fully across it at its narrowest point. The cattails and marsh grasses are high this time of the year so I'll only have two or three spots I can cast from, but from those I can reach every corner of this pond.

It is an intimate place and I love it, and as I work out a couple of dozen feet of line for my first short casts I remember dozens of fish I've taken over the years from this very spot.

I've chosen to make my stand with a tiny cork bug painted yellow, with soft red feathers for a tail and a couple of pairs of rubber legs—like cat's whiskers—near the head. It casts well and its concave head lets me pop it loudly when I'm of a mind to see such a pleasant disturbance on the flat surface of the pond, or think it will attract some attention; I like to watch the little thing chug and swirl on the surface of this little pond, its rubber legs vibrating back and forth, and I've seen fish come from even the deepest parts to the top for it.

This is a good night. I get a fat old pumpkinseed with a bright orange belly, big enough to take two hands to hold, on my fourth cast. It may be the largest fish I've ever taken in this pond, except for a three-pound bass I once got at dusk. Then there are four or five bright bluegills, considerably smaller, but quite satisfying. The fish are coming to the popper readily tonight.

A frog jumps in near the dock. I see a deer up the hill, near a stand of aspen. I shift to another side of the pond and then when I catch nothing, to the dock. On top of the dock, a couple of feet into the pond and above the water, I can fish most of the far bank and I start to do so systematically, as if I were fishing a salmon pool. About eight o'clock there's a sudden pocking of the water near the reeds and I hook the biggest bluegill of the evening—not nearly the size of the ones I caught in Utah, nor even as large as the pumpkinseed. but twice the size of those I've been catching, a trophy.

I smooth back its dorsal with my hand so I can grasp it without the points sticking me and look at it as the light begins to fail—the fish of my youth and of my late middle years: an eager emblem—small but of stout and generous heart—of all the simple good sport we all too often forget when we fish these days.

Then I head home. Or was I there already?

Family Interludes

He that views the ancient ecclesiastical canons shall
find hunting to be forbidden to churchmen, as being
a toilsome, perplexing recreation; and shall find angling
allowed to clergymen, as being a harmless recreation,
a recreation that invites them to contemplation and quietness.

—IZAAK WALTON

Though the relationship of an avid fisherman to his family may be said to have no season, or to be always "in season," it reaches the peak of its intensity—or aggravation—in the very height of the trouter's year.

There are, I am sure, innumerable arcane and esoteric reasons for this.

But the safe pragmatic reason is simply this: the trout-fisher is at his moment of greatest self- and trout-absorption—and least resistance; and his family, flourishing under the beneficence of his year-long support and devotion, and the ideal weather, is at maximum strength.

Days are long; children are indefatigable; wives acquire an alarming propensity for shopping and house-hunting and "just walking together, like a *real* family, in the park." In the early days I did not have an ally among them, and my secret fishing life suffered much at the hands of my family.

There were the little things: two missing barred-rock necks that turned up under Anthony-the-thief's pillow; a notorious departure from the Schoharie in the midst of a massive Hendrickson hatch, after I had waited three hours for it to appear (my wife called them "Morgans" and pleaded that we leave "this bug-infested place"); innumerable engagements that took precedence; irony; caustic wit to the effect that "grown men" did not act in the ridiculous way I acted about trout. I must be painfully truthful about it, for it all reached a crisis, a momentous crisis, in an incident still painful to recall.

My fishing friends say I am too generous with women and little children. Perhaps. For I suppose Mari, Paul, Charles, Jennifer, and Anthony owe their survival of that Father's Day trip to my extraordinary equanimity. I am not at all sure how I survived.

The spring, troutless and city-bound that year, had been long, but Father's Day weekend was longer.

We left in a flurry, all six of us, on Friday, but despite my best efforts, my speed and my scheming, it was still too late even to make the latest moments of the evening rise on the closest streams. So I settled into a family habit of mind, decided to bide my good time, and set about enjoying a harmless day of visiting friends and swimming on Saturday. After that we could easily fulfill the most prominent of our trip's simple purposes: as I had engineered my wife into saying, "A few solid hours of fly fishing for Dad—poor Dad, who never gets out on the streams anymore because he loves us so much."

Not that I believed her, or had much confidence that at this particular season of my married life I would actually get to drop a few flies—but her gesture seemed sincere and I took it at face value. "A turning point," I thought with quiet satisfaction. Thus, hopefully, I had stashed my little Thomas and my vest carefully in the corner of our rented station wagon. I had heard of such turning points.

The temperature was ninety-eight degrees when we left our friends at three o'clock that Saturday: too hot to fish, no doubt, so I allowed Mari to persuade me that Vermont would be cooler, that we would have time to fish that evening and all day Sunday. "A nice drive will keep us cool," she insisted.

It was little less than 150 degrees in the car once we hit the crowded highway: I cannot remember being able to drive faster than thirty-five. But up Routes 5 and then 91 to Brattleboro we went, pausing to examine, while we sped, a half dozen or more promising waterways. It had been part of my plan (cunningly conceived, I must admit) to inject my oldest son, Paul, with the trout fever, and the serum had taken with a vengeance. Before I could see a stream, he'd spot one and call out, "Can we stop here, Dad? It looks like a terrific place for tremendous trout."

He did this several dozen times.

The serum nearly cracked me.

By the time we reached Vermont, all four children were howling wildly, stepping on each other's toes and pride and souls. Dinner took two hours, motel-hunting another hour, and precisely at dusk we were established in cool Vermont, exhausted. Had I been on the Schoharie, at Hendrickson time, I would not have been able to lift my arm to cast.

"Tomorrow we'll get some big ones," I said to Paul as we turned off the lights and settled, all six of us, into the quiet and cool of the air-conditioned room.

"Do you promise, Dad?"

"I promise," I said

"Can I get some gig ones, too?" asked Anthony, my four-year-old, in the dark room.

"Maybe"

"Me too?" asked Charles with his foghorn voice. "If Paul does, I want to get some big ones, too."

"Let's sleep now, children."

It was quiet for five full minutes and, motionless, pooped, I was nearly into a pleasant dream about the Green Drake hatch on the Beaverkill when Jennifer whispered loudly, "You'll let me catch some big ones too, won't you Daddy?"

"Shussssssh!" said my wife. And then, sardonically, "Trout!"

Well, Sunday it was raining long thick droplets of rain: a day-long pernicious rain if I'd ever seen one.

"Didn't you say fishing was best in the rain, Dad?" asked Paul.

"You *wouldn't* take the boy out in a rain like this, would you, Nick?" asked Mari.

"Not when it's heavy, Paul," I said quietly.

"And you *wouldn't* expect the rest of us to sit in a muggy car while you were out catching pneumonia, would you?"

"We will not fish in this weather," I assured my wife, sullenly.

"You promised, Dad!"

"It will not rain all day," I told Paul. "And maybe it's not raining in New York State."

So we drove and we sang a hundred songs and we munched some of our genuine Vermont maple sugar—which did not quite justify Saturday's trip to cool Vermont, and which made Jennifer dreadfully nauseous—and we made our way slowly through the blinding Fathers' Day rain that was sure to kill any decent fly-fishing for a full three days, along the winding, twisting Molly Stark Trail, and the children stopped singing, and then fought and bellowed, and Mari became irritated and blamed me, and then Paul blamed me for not finding him a "dry trout stream."

We crossed into New York, where it was pouring nails, at about twelve-thirty, had a long lunch, and then started gloomily, for a Father's Day—or any day—down Route 22. The Hoosic River, I noted, was impossibly brown, and the rain still showed no signs of growing less frantic. The Green River, a sprightly spring-fed creek, was clearer, but the rain continued and Mari would have none of sitting in a muggy car while I got pneumonia.

"If you could find us a nice clean beach, where we could get some sun and have something to do for an hour or so ... But you really can't expect me ..."

"Scarcely," I said

"You promised," said Paul

A disaster either way. Straight home: the only solution.

There is absolutely no question in my mind that I should indeed have gone home. Right then. Tragedy was imminent. Had I simply read the signs of the times, I could have avoided disaster.

Yes, blithely I was heading home, peace in my soul, capitulation painless, when, as we approached Brewster, the sun broke out suddenly—brightly, fetchingly. I could not resist a quick look at the Sodom section of the East Branch of the Croton River.

"We won't do any fishing," I promised. "I just want a fast look at an old friend. I used to fish this stream when I was a kid, every Opening Day. Came up the first time when I was ..."

"Thirteen. I know. You mention it every time we pass this silly creeek."

"Do I really? Do I mention it *every* time we pass?"

"Yes, you do. 'I used to fish the Left Branch of the Croydon every Opening Day when I was a kid.' Every time."

"East Branch. Croton," I muttered. "A short look. Three minutes. Perhaps less."

"I sincerely hope less."

Miraculously, the water below and above the bridge was admirably clear, not crystal but a translucent auburn, perhaps because it traveled to this point over a long cobblestone sluice after shooting down from the top of the reservoir. Interesting, I thought; very interesting.

I scurried back to the car with the happy news.

"Well, if you think you can catch a few trout for supper," Mari said, "you can drop Anthony and me off at a coffee shop for half an hour and take the rest of your children fishing in the Left Branch of the Croydon, or whatever it is."

"*All* of them?"

"I want to go with Daddy," shouted Jennifer.

"If Paul goes, I have to go too, Dad," said Charles petulantly.

"At least make it forty-five minutes," I said

"With Anthony? In a coffee shop?"

"All right, children: a half hour to catch two fat trout for supper."

"Nick, you haven't brought home a trout in two years. You talk about fishing day and night; read about it constantly; tie those confounded bugs by the evening; go on and on and on— and never bring home any fish."

Since the clock was running, I did not choose to explain that despite the tragedy of being married I still *caught* trout now and then, though I rarely kept them anymore. One such argument, with my mother-in-law, who thought I kept a mistress on the banks of the "Croydon," led me to stomp out of the room with the profound truism: "Do golfers eat golf balls?"

"Two fat trout for dinner, children—in one half hour."

I dropped my wife off at ten of five, spent seven minutes acquiring some night crawlers, another four setting up Paul's spinning rod, and was on the stream by one minute after five exactly.

"Lovely," I said "The water's beautiful, Paul. We're going to get four or five."

"Really, Dad?"

"Can't miss. Look: that fellow right under the bridge has one—see him splashing?"

The children crowded together along the bank, watching the brisk battle of a thrashing and leaping eleven-inch brown. I took the time to sneak in six or seven casts, but did not even get a tap.

Then Paul wanted the rod and I gave it to him, telling him how to cast across and slightly upstream, how to hold the rod tip down in anticipation of the strike, how to keep delicate control of the moving bait. He managed his casts well, and I watched eagerly as the night crawler floated downstream and out of sight. Before his fourth cast, Charles wanted his turn too. No, I had promised Paul he'd catch a trout first, I told him gently.

"I want *my* turn, Daddy," said Jennifer.

"We only have one rod."

"Not fair. It's not fair, Dad," said Charles gruffly.

"Can't you keep these infants quiet so I can fish?" demanded Paul.

"Don't get nasty," I advised.

"They're bothering me, Dad."

"After Paul gets a fish," I promised Jennifer and Charles wisely, "you two get a turn each."

"Only one," said Jennifer

"Two trout," said Paul.

But he got no strikes in the next fourteen or fifteen casts, and I noticed that it was now 5:18. I was glad I'd left my Thomas in the car. Another ten minutes of this madness—no more.

To get the younger children out of Paul's way, I decided to go up on the bridge itself for the last few minutes, though I noted with alarm how fast the cars sped by. I flattened the children against the edge, warned them sharply not to climb up the low wall, and leaned far over to peer down into the fairly clear auburn water.

A few flies were coming off the water—small darkish flies—but I paid them no heed.

Then I saw it: a long dark shadow, nose upstream, slightly to the left of a large submerged boulder. Now and then it would rise slowly to the right or left and, almost imperceptibly, break the surface of the flat stream. The fish was well over a foot long.

I tried to point it out to Jennifer and Charles, lifting one in each arm so both could see at exactly the same time, but when they scrambled further onto the low wall I spooked and put them back on the pavement, whereupon they raced back and forth across the bridge several times while cars shot by menacingly.

I told Paul about the fish and he promptly climbed up the bank and onto the bridge. He plunked his worm loudly down into the water and it bobbed to the surface and waved there, without the slightest threat of ever being disturbed by a trout.

But the long trout kept rising, once or twice every minute— was it really 5:23 already?—and when I tossed it several bits of a worm, it swirled and snapped at them, though it did not finally take any.

Then a few of the small darkish flies rose to my level, and I leaned out incautiously and grabbed several of them.

Dark blue; tiny. Most curious.

What were they? Iron Blue Duns. Not more than three or four a minute, but a steady hatch. *Acentrella*—about #18. Weren't they a late-April mayfly, though? No matter. *Acentrella*—nothing else.

Not much of a dinner, but the long trout was unmistakably settling for them. Had I tied a few last winter? Yes, one each, a #18 and a #16.

The trout rose again—and then again, this time with a definite sucking-down of the water, a turning of its sleek yellow body that showed it to be of considerable size and weight.

Five twenty-eight.

I could stand it no longer. Grabbing Jennifer and Charles by the collars, I rushed back to the car, plucked out my aluminum rod case and vest, and then tugged the children—silent, frightened— down the muddy bank, past a flourishing garden of shiny poison ivy, and toward the downstream section below the bridge.

Swiftly I unhoused and jointed my delicate Thomas, a simple, lovely idea in bamboo. I managed to mount the fly reel and slip the line through the first two guides, but then began to fumble. The line slipped back through to the reel. Then I worked the line through four guides and discovered that it was twisted around the rod after the second. Then it was through all of them, but the spidery 6X tippet would not shake loose and got tangled in itself, and I had to select another. Then I couldn't find my Iron Blue Dun in #18. Should I try the #16? Or an Adams in #18? Or a small Leadwing Coachman?

Finally I found the Blue in with the Adamses, its hackles a bit bent, and I poked the film of head lacquer out after only six or seven tries and then knotted the fly to the leader on my fourth attempt.

Five thirty-five. She should be furious already—even on Father's Day.

"Quiet. You children have got to be absolutely quiet. Not a sound"—they had said nothing—"good children. You're not going to spoil Daddy's sixteen-incher, are you?"

"How big is a sixteen-incher, Daddy?"

"Big, Jennifer. Very big. Quiet. Quiet. Quiet, now."

"PAUL! DADDY'S GOING TO CATCH A SIXTEEN-INCHER!" Jennifer howled in her high-pitched shrilly voice.

"Can I help you, Dad?" asked Charles.

Paul, on the bridge, had leaned far over to see the action. Clouds were forming rapidly in the sky.

"*Paul! Get back!*" I called, nearly flopping over on the muddy bank. "But WATCH OUT FOR THE CARS! Not too far back!"

Damn, no waders. No matter. The moment was here.

I stepped in boldly—in my Father's Day shoes, in my neatly creased trousers, in my Father's Day sport jacket—tumbled to one arm on a mossy rock, climbed over the riffles slowly, bent my hand to steady myself on another rock (soaking the new sports jacket up to the elbow and along the hemline), and meticulously surveyed the long flat pool.

A few soft small drops of rain began to fall.

"Paul! Paul! Look what Daddy's doing!"

"Dad, can I go wading, too?" shouted Charles.

"Can we, Daddy?"

"Will all my very good children kindly be ab-so-lute-ly quiet for ten minutes. I love you all. I really do. But *please, please* be quiet."

"Daddy, Daddy," called Jennifer. "Charles is in the water. Charles is in the water. Charles is …"

"*I am not! I am not!*"

"Charles! Get out and stay out! Now!"

Another foot. Not too close. Whoops! Almost slipped that time. Don't rain. Don't rain, yet! "Paul! Will you *please* get off that railing?"

"My line's tangled, Dad. And I can't see a thing."

"Then come down. But carefully! Watch out for the cars. And the poison ivy."

"Will you fix my line, Dad?"

"In a minute. In just one minute."

"Five *thirty-eight!*"

"Charles is in the water. Charles is …"

"I am not!"

"Charles, if you don't stay out of the water I'll break your little arm!"

I could not see the fish beside the boulder, but thought that amid the steady raindrops and bubbles on the surface I detected the characteristic dimple of a trout's rise. "Now," I murmured audibly. I looped out several yards of line, checked behind me for trees or shrubs or sons or daughter.

The old feeling. That glorious old feeling. After twelve full months, it was all still there.

One more false cast.

"Now."

The line sped out, long and straight; the leader unfolded; the fly turned the last fold and dropped, quietly, five inches below the base of the bridge. Perfect.

I retrieved line slowly, watching for drag, squinting into the steadily increasing rain, along the rim of the dark water, to see that tiny dark-blue fly. In another moment it would be over the spot.

There was a heavy splash below me. Then another and another.

"Charles is throwing stones, Daddy. Charles is …"

"CHARLES!"

Whammo!

The tiny Iron Blue Dun disappeared in a solid sucking-down of the water. I raised the rod swiftly, felt the line tighten along its length and hold. Not too hard. Not too hard, Nick. I did not want to snap the 6X leader.

I had him. A good brown. A really good brown. I felt his weight against the quick arcing of my little Thomas. Sixteen inches for sure. Not an inch less. The trout turned, swirled at the surface, and bolted upstream.

"Daddy caught one!" shouted Jennifer.

There were momentous splashes downstream.

"CHARLES!"

Out of the corner of my wet eye I could see Paul, in his short pants, hopping through the great garden of poison ivy. "Got a fish, Dad?" he called.

"Got a big one, kids," I said proudly, holding the Thomas high, reeling in the line before the first guide to fight him from the reel. "Your ol' dad's got a good one this time—*whoaaa!*"

Just then Paul slipped on the muddy slope and slid rawly— through more poison ivy—to the brink of the stream.

The rain was steady and thick now, and I felt it trickle down past my jacket collar and along my spine.

The trout had run far up under the bridge and I was playing him safely from the reel. Several time he heaped high into the air, shaking, splattering silver in all directions, twisting like a snake.

"I'll help you, Dad," shouted Charles, splashing vigorously toward me.

"Didn't I tell you——-?"

But before I finished, the huge trout began to shoot downstream rapidly, directly toward me. I retrieved line frantically. He was no more than four yards from me and I could see the 6X leader trailing from the corner of his partly opened mouth; the jaw was already beginning to hook.

Charles was quite close to me now, behind me, and I half turned to shoo him back to shore. His hair was plastered flat on his head from the rain, and he had a long, thick stick in his hands and was holding it out, in the direction of the trout.

"I'll get him, Dad, I'll get him," he said. His tone was sincere and helpful.

"*No!*" I shouted, and turned to wrest it away from him.

The gesture was too sudden. The leather-soled shoes were no match for the mossy rocks. With gusts of heavy rain pelting my face, I felt my left foot slipping, tried to catch myself and my tangled line, felt my right foot slipping too, and holding my delicate, my beloved Thomas high overhead, went down, disastrously, flat on my rump, up to my chest, and kept going, the Thomas slamming wildly against a rock ...

I consider it a holy miracle of the first water that I survived that day.

And I consider it a fine miracle of physics that my Thomas survived. With only minor scratches.

And I consider it sure evidence of my extraordinary equanimity and good cheer that my family survived. Yet there may well have been a touch of clairvoyance in my ensuing patience: for pragmatically, how could I have known than that Paul would become a favorite fishing partner, Charles a skilled and careful net man, and that on a memorable June evening I would baptize Mari in the holy waters of the Beaverkill?

Yes, Paul had caught the fever. And the very next year, fishing the little Sawkill near Woodstock, in mid-April, he caught his first trout.

We had taken only one outfit, his spinning rod, and I proceeded to give him some instruction, casting six or seven times up under the bridge. They had not yet stocked the stream but I knew there were always a number of solid holdover browns that survived in the deep ledge-pools.

Since the water was fairly low, I decided it would be best if we went upstream and Paul cast down, so that there would be less chance of the lure snagging on the bottom. He went up on the rocks by himself and cast twice, across and downstream, with no results. The casts were well executed and he retrieved the little C.P. Swing with neat, short jerks.

On the third cast the rod suddenly arced sharply. I thought it was a rock but Paul insisted it was moving.

I didn't believe him until the trout leaped. It was a splendid brown, well over a foot, and all of us—Paul, Charles, Jennifer, and Anthony—began to shout at once.

The fish raced across that little pool wildly. But he was well hooked, the drag gave line when needed, and soon Paul had him up close.

Charles, who was now a properly equipped net man, slipped the net under the large fish with genuine talent. And we had him.

I grasped the trout around the head and flexed back its neck abruptly. Jennifer flinched and Paul asked me why I had to be so cruel. I told him that this was the quickest way and that it kept the trout from secreting bile. "If you're going to keep them," I began, but then realized that it does not occur to a young boy to release what he has caught. Especially not a first trout! That could come later.

It was a splendid event. Charles carried the fish, hung by the jaw from a forked stick, up the hill. Even Mari was impressed.

We took the trout directly to Frank Mele's house, and he treated that first prize with all the ceremony it deserved. First he got out his ruler and measured it out at fourteen and a half inches. Then, with his razor-sharp pocket knife, he showed Paul and Charles how to dress it carefully, showed them how to slit from the vent forward, remove the innards, thumb out the blood clot, and cut out the gills. They were fascinated.

"Now," said Frank, "we'll have to trace it. Just like they do in the fancy sporting clubs."

He got out a strip of butcher paper and Paul laid his fish upon it and traced its outlines with my pen. Below it, Frank advised, Paul should put the vital information.

Years later, the memento of that first trout still hangs proudly in Paul's room. The brown butcher paper is rolling up on the ends but a few silver scales are still stuck to the body area, and beneath the silhouette reads:

brown Troute, 14 1/2 inches
caught by Paul B. Lyons

Sawkille, Woodstock
4/16/67

It seemed at the time the beginning of something.

Mecca

Mecca (mĕk' å), *n.* 1..... a holy city;
hence, any place sought, especially
by great numbers of persons, as a
supremely desirable goal.

One spring there was no spring. March lingered into mid-
April; late April was a wintry February; and by the end of May
you might have been convinced that, since not even the Quill
Gordon had arrived, someone was taking a special vengeance on
fly fishers. On all except me.

Emergence dates would be postponed; few trout would be
taken in the fly-only stretches I had begun to haunt; June (unless
someone was vengeful toward fly fishers) would be perfect. While
small clusters of distressed anglers grumbled in the tackle shops, I
gloated. June was the only time I would be free, and June would
be ideal. Even Brannigan was morose. I was serenely gleeful.

All winter I had corresponded from the city with Mike, a fanatic
like myself but one who had taken the plunge and now lived chiefly—
and blissfully—for fishing. What other way is there? Brannigan
constantly wrote me of his friend Hawkes, a knowledgeable old
Catskill trouting genius whom I had never met. But Hawkes was

more than knowledgeable, more than a rumor: he was a myth. In an increasing number of understated and sometimes unconscious ways, the old trout fisher—in off seasons, a cellist—began to emerge from Mike's letters as a figure of outrageous proportions. He had, so far as I could tell, a special formula for dyeing leaders to within a chromophore of the color of eight different streams at a dozen different times of the year. He no longer kept emergence tables, but could tell (by extrasensory perception?) not only which fly would be hatching on a particular day, but at what time of the day, even to the hour, the fly would emerge. And in what numbers! Of course I believed none of it. Who would? It was all the fiction of that wild Irishman. Brannigan was obviously a madman, more afflicted even than I, who had lost two jobs because of his trout neurosis, and almost a wife: he was given to exaggeration, fantasy, mirage, and fly-tying. I had only almost lost my wife.

But I was curious. Who wouldn't be? And I had asked four or five times, covertly, whether or not Hawkes would fish with us when I got away for a week in June.

"Rarely fishes anymore," wrote Brannigan. "Most streams have become rather easy for him; most hatches too pedestrian. Except for the Green Drake. Says there's still something to be learned there."

The Green Drake, yes—the most exciting and mysterious of them all. *Ephemera guttulata Pictet*, yes, which brought the lunkers, the old soaks, out of the deep pools, which emerged in massive and manic hatches, sometimes for only a few days, perhaps a week. Sometimes the circus occurred on the Beaverkill. Perhaps this year, with Hawkes, that was an ambition worth the four months of brooding and scheming. To return to the Beaverkill, which I had not fished in ten years, with the old myth himself, yes—it would be Mecca, a vision to hold me throughout another long dry city winter.

But there was no adequate imitation of *Ephemera guttulata*—that was common knowledge. White Wulffs took a few fish; dyed light-green hackle flies took some; the attempts at exact imitation took very few; and, in the spinner stage, there was the adequate waxy-white and funereal Coffin Fly.

So I experimented that spring, to while away the wait, and finally, in mid-May, accomplished what to my mind was a major innovation, a contribution to the angling fraternity of staggering proportions. I called it the Pigeon Drake, for the pigeon quill body I had used after a long quill had fluttered down to me, quite mystically, at the very moment I was thinking about this fly one dreary lunch hour. That quill was a portent, and I promptly sent my two older sons out to collect me a several dozen in the park at a penny a quill. They brought in ninety-seven, but I used only thirty in my experiments, and ultimately made only four or five usable flies.

The result is hard to describe. It was not a small fly, nor a particularly neat fly. The tip of the quill, through which I had inserted exactly three stems of stripped badger hackle for the tail, had to be strapped firmly to the shank of the #12 hook. Peering up through specially purchased contact lenses from the bottom of a filled bathtub at numerous flies floating there (the door had to be locked to keep out my skeptical wife and distracting children), I observed that the white impala wings of the Wulff flies, sparsely tied, closely resembled the translucent wings of the Green Drake (and many other flies, which perhaps explains part of its extraordinary success). I dyed pure white hackle in green tea. The pigeon quill body, however, is what made the fly: it was natural, translucent, and would cock slightly upward if properly strapped to the shank. Frankly, it was the work of genius, and I could not wait to fish it with Mike and Hawkes on the Beaverkill—Mecca.

But if rained the first three days of my week's vacation, and all I could do was take Brannigan's abuse to the effect that a man who had not been out on the streams *once* by June ninth was a fallen man, fallen indeed, a man given over to mercantilism and paternalism and other such crimes and moral diseases as were destroying the world, or at least a noble sport. "These are dangerous years for you, Nick" he advised me. "Worse will lead to worse."

The fourth day was Brannigan's one day of work, his one day of homage to mercantilism and paternalism, and since Hawkes was not to be heard from (apparently he had disappeared), I went out glumly to a small mountain stream nearby and surprised myself by having a delightful day catching seven- and eight-inch brookies and browns on tiny #18 and #20 Cahills and Adamses, dry. It was fun watching the spirited streaks of trout shoot out of their cover and gulp the little flies: it was real sport handling them on 6X tippets. But it was not Mecca.

That night I could bear it no longer. Indirections lead to indirections, and I, a mercantilist, had no business being subtle. "Mike," I said, "it's the tenth of June. There have been no reports that the Green Drake hatch has started and it's due momentarily. Don't you have *any* idea where Hawkes is? Can't you simply hunt him up and ask him if he'll go to the Beaverkill with us tomorrow?"

Brannigan roared. "Sure. I know where Hawkes is. But you just don't ask him like that. It takes some engineering, and some luck. He's got to ask you."

"Dammit. What is he, Mike, a saint?"

Mike smiled and sipped at his fourth beer.

"Did you make the damn guy up?"

"All right. All right. I suppose I can find him. But I can't promise a thing."

Two days later, the night before I had to leave, after two days of mediocre fishing in the Esopus, Brannigan said simply, "Hawkes is going tomorrow; said we could come if we want to."

I tried to answer calmly. Though I still didn't believe a word about Hawkes, not a word of it, a myth is a myth, and it comes with ineluctable power, a power elusive and haunting.

The next morning at eight o'clock Brannigan was at his garage arranging his tackle, selecting from his six fly rods the best for the day.

"Hawkes thinks there might be a Green Drake hatch this evening," the bright white-haired Irishman said, "but that there might not."

Already a hedge; the tricks of the prophets, the ambiguities of the mediums. He didn't exist. Not the Hawkes I'd dreamed about.

Then, as I got out my gear and piled it beside Brannigan's, Hawkes arrived in his 1946 Dodge. His gaunt, lined face was that of a saint, or a gunman. His eyes were deep set, limned with shadowy black globes; his fingers were long and thin and obviously arthritic. He walked stiffly toward us.

"Brannigan, old Branny, so this is our young friend," he said, extending his bony hand. "Has he made all the adequate preparations? If he is to be admitted into our little club, he must agree to will his ashes to us, that we may sprinkle them upon the waters of the Beaverkill"

Brannigan tried to suppress a smile. I tried, gently, to remove my hand from Hawkes's firm but friendly grasp.

"The Beaverkill," he continued, looking warmly at me, smiling, "home of Gordon and Darbee and Dettee: Mecca. Tell me, Nick, do you face the Beaverkill every morning and evening at sunset? Do you pray to the gods?

"Of course he does, Hawkes," said Mike. "Now let's get started. This will be his only real day of trout fishing for the year."

"Very curious," said Hawkes, shaking his head. "One day of trout fishing. I'm sure our young friend has the burdens of the world upon him, then. Nevertheless, one day of real fishing can be enough. Especially at Mecca. It can be made to serve the whole of the year."

I smiled, an embarrassed, naive smile that spread and spread all day, until my cheeks hurt, on that long unforgettable drive to Mecca.

The drive to the Beaverkill should have taken no more than an hour. It was nine o'clock, and I had all hopes of catching the late-morning rise. But it took about an hour for us merely to pack

Hawkes's old Dodge, an immaculate, impeccably ordered vehicle, with each object in its proper place: rods, waders, vest, extra fly boxes, net, and Jack Daniel's whisky. There was a holder for his pipe above the dashboard, disposal bags, and four cans of beer neatly packed into the ample glove compartment. Hawkes placed each of our items of equipment carefully into the car, with such measured movements that he might have been giving them permanent homes. As he picked up each piece of tackle he would contemplate it for a moment and then comment on its appropriateness to the sport. "Branny, you know that felt is best for the Beaverkill—and yet you bring hobnails. Curious. Is there a special reason for that, Branny? Do you know something you're not telling? Have reports reached you of great mountains of silt and mud being washed into it? You surely would not be using them simply to impress the pedestrian likes of Nick and me, to taunt us with the fruit of some large sale of flies to a posh New York City tackle shop?"

And then, when the felt waders were brought out from Brannigan's garage, after another five minutes of slow, meticulous scrutiny, "I suppose you know that the glue you've used won't last the day. But the Irish are knowledgeable men, and if you've failed to use the preparation I gave you last winter, I'm sure you have your reasons."

At eleven we set out. Too late for the morning rise, but still early enough for a long day on the river. We wouldn't even have to stop for lunch, I thought, hopefully: pick up a sandwich or two for the vest, and hit the stream as soon as possible. I had a raging fever to be on the stream.

The old Dodge scrunched slowly out of Brannigan's pebbled driveway, made the semicircle onto the tarred road, and started, with incredible slowness, west—to Mecca.

Hawkes opened and closed his long arthritic fingers slowly around the wheel. "This is a day not to be rushed," he said. "It is going to be an experience, an event. It must be savored."

"Come off it, Hawkes," said Brannigan.

Hawkes stopped the car abruptly. Smack in the middle of the highway. Without taking his eyes away from the windshield in front of him, he said with dead seriousness: "If this is to be a day of cynicism, of doubt, of feverish behavior by an unruly Irishman, I would be glad to turn around, return said Irishman to his own car, and make my peace elsewhere. I have my doubts that the Green Drakes will appear anyway; the temperature dropped to fifty-two degrees night before last—which, I take it, the less sensitive scholars of the streams *did not notice*—the barometer is falling, if slowly, and the moon was not to be seen last night. My fingers are tight, I have a telltale itch along my right thigh, and this *could* become a highly dubious proposition all the way around."

"Okay, okay, Hawkes. I apologize. Please—let's go."

"You're tense, man. Sink into the day. Don't force it. The electricity of such feverish thinking is transmuted imperceptibly but ineluctably to Mr. Brown Trout. The result you can well guess."

My smile spread, my cheeks ached. Three miles down the road Hawkes stopped at a gas station, got out, and asked the attendant about the composition of gasoline. Hawkes got a drop on his fingers, smelled it, touched it gently to his lips, smiled, and wiped his fingers carefully on some paper toweling. "It is quite possible after all, gentlemen, that the Green Drake *will* make his appearance this afternoon. Very curious."

We started out again, and this time Hawkes was silent, thoughtful, meditative for five minutes. Several times he stopped the car at small mountain creeks, got out of the car, scrutinized the water, threw boysenberries into the eddies, and began to hum quietly. "Boys," he said nodding, "it's really going to be a day. This is going to be an event"

Three more miles down the road, feeling immeasurably dry, he had to get a small bracer at a roadside tavern. We each ended having three tall beers apiece. Another mile, feeling too wet, he had to relieve himself, and did so in a conspicuously high arc. Half a mile farther and he stopped abruptly, whistled a long clear whistle, and watched a blonde farm girl carrying a child walk slowly across a field of knee-high corn shoots. "It is a day of poetry, of cosmic stillness," he informed us. "She is the Madonna agrarianistically developed."

When I noted, unobtrusively, that it was now two thirty, he advised: "There are lessons to be learned on a day like this. Let it not be rushed; let it be savored. It is a day composed on the celestial lyre. An event. We need only stop at the Blue Goose tavern, my dear Nick, and we will get to Mecca in good time. Branny, where is that oasis?"

Mike did not remember, but several inquiries proved that it was seven miles out of our way, up an unpaved road. No matter. It was impossible to fish the Beaverkill during the Green Drake hatch without first stopping at the Blue Goose. It was ritual. Part of the sacraments. The Blue Goose was a holy place, a temple pilgrimages were made to.

It looked like a cruddy over-aged bar to me. We stayed an hour, but only two miracles occurred: the floor rose three inches on my fourth beer, and I was able to walk out. We took a six-pack with us and were on our way, due west, over the last little mountains, pilgrims, pioneers, seekers of the holy Mecca.

We arrived in Roscoe at five thirty, still in time for a long evening's fishing, but Hawkes thought we should look up Bishop Harry Darbee before heading for the stream, to seek his blessings as well as his advice. This could not be done directly. It was first necessary to head for the Antrim Lodge, to the cool dark cellar for a few stronger snorts than we'd had. Hawkes invoked us each to empty two double shots of Jack Daniel's, when done, he launched into a series of incisive questions of the good bartender. But when that dispenser of firewater said that the water had been high and that a few men had been in that very afternoon with limits they'd taken on spinning rods, Hawkes became violent and Brannigan had to grab his arm, even hold his mouth, as he shouted, "Coffee grinders! Hoodlums! Saracens!"

Darbee was not to be found, but Walt Dette was home, and Hawkes conned him out of a dozen hackles from a natural blue dun, after an hour of talk about the breeding of this rare bird.

At seven o'clock we hit the stream. Not ten miles downriver, where Dette had told us to go, but a spot directly below Junction Pool. One look at the water, after that interminable drive, and I had insisted. Hawkes shrugged. It did not make much difference, he said.

Once parked, Mike and I suited and set up hurriedly. Hawkes sat back and puffed at his pipe. "Long as you two have the Saint Vitus's dance, you might as well indulge it. Go on. Git, you two. Takes an old man like me a while to get into the proper frame of mind for this holy stream. It is not to be rushed."

We wasted no time. Brannigan headed downstream, I up— and we were flailing away wildly at waters for a full twenty minutes before Hawkes, on stiff legs, puffing contentedly on his pipe, ambled to the spot on the stream nearest the car. Fish were beginning to rise steadily just at that moment, and the large pale-green duns began to rise in swarms from the water. I switched from a Cahill to a #12 Pale Watery Dun, and then to a White Miller, a White Wulff, and then to an imitation Drake. All in rapid succession. Nothing. Something was missing. My mind was beer-fogged, my casting was sloppy, I was wobbly, and something important was trying to press itself out of my unconscious. Below me, Brannigan, fishing nymphs dead drift, took nothing.

Hawkes waded out a few feet, stood stark still like a crane, fixed his glasses, took the temperature of the water, tested it with his hand, peered long into the swirling duns, the many dimples of fish, and selected a fly from his single aluminum case. It took him a full minute to affix it, but when he had he looked at the water again, clipped off the fly, and started the process again. He pulled the leader tight, clipped off the end bit, ran the leader through his mouth six or seven times, and peeled off line.

I was staggered when his first cast brought a strike only moments after the fly had alighted. Deftly he played an eleven-inch brown, drew it close until it turned belly up, and then neatly netted it.

The scene was unbelievable. The sun was several feet above the tree line now, and seemed to hang, luminous and diffused, ready to drop at any moment. The hatch was fantastic, the large pale-green drakes thick as locusts, heavy-winged and fat. Leisurely two- and even three-pound trout stalked them, inches beneath the surface. It was like a slow-motion film. They would cruise, like sharks, their dorsals extended above the water line, and heavily suck down the fallen drakes. Everything took place on the surface—methodically, devastatingly. There must have been fifty trout cruising in that long flat pool—no doubt, many were denizens of the large lake like pool several hundred yards downstream. They were in no hurry. For them it was an event, an annual feast some of them had probably partaken of for two or three years. My hands and limbs were shaking.

Hawkes's next cast brought another strike, but it was short and he retrieved the line quietly, without a ruffle of the surface.

I made a full twelve casts before he cast again, and this time the rise to his fly—which I could not see—was not short. While playing what was obviously a two-pound trout or better, he called softly for me to come to his position. I scampered through the water like a water buffalo, convinced that he had both the right spot and the right fly, and scurried to his side just as he netted a fine eighteen-inch brown, broke its neck, and creeled it.

I was frantic. There could not be more than another thirty-five minutes of visibility. Wildly I tried four or five different flies, my back cast slapping the water behind me noisily. Hawkes did not frown. He did not take his eyes from the water. I had never seen such intense concentration.

Then I remembered—*how could I have forgotten?*—and my entire body shook with excitement as I did: the Pigeon Drake.

I was so unhinged that it took five tries before I got the leader through the eye of this miraculous fly, and when I jerked the knot tight the line broke. I tried again and this time managed. The Pigeon Drake hung convincingly from my line.

Carefully I false-cast out fifteen, then twenty feet of line. I felt calm and confident now, as icy and knowledgeable and canny as Hawkes. Then I released the last few feet of line, shot them through the guides, and happily, expectantly, watched the fly drop to the water.

It landed like a shot pigeon. But immediately one of those slow-motion monsters glided portentously toward it. I watched, heart beating wildly, while the dorsal neared. The spotted back of the fine brown and each and every aspect of his awesome body were clear to me as he moved, inches below the surface. Then he stopped, the fly not four inches from his nose. The trout was motionless, but not tense. "Take it. Take it, you old soak," I whispered. I twitted the fly. "Take it," I murmured again. Once more I twitched the fly, and this time the movement did it. When the reverberations in the water ceased, the fly began to sink, like the City in the Sea, majestically down. Unmistakably, the trout turned its nose up. It did, I'll swear to it. And then, with noble calm it glided toward a nearby natural, and took it. It had been a sneer—the sophisticated sneer of a wiseacre trout if I'd ever seen one. And it finished me. Dejectedly I retrieved my line, clipped off the fly, dropped it into the water (where it promptly sank like a stone), reeled in my line, and dismantled my rod.

In the remaining half hour of visibility Hawkes calmly took three more fish, the largest a full twenty inches, minutes before darkness set in.

The drive home, after Hawkes had finished three almost raw hamburgers and two cups of black coffee, took exactly sixty-two minutes. Hawkes did not particularly race along the road.

All the way back I had visions of those swarms of greenish duns rising from the flat pool, fluttering clumsily, falling back, drifting downstream, and being leisurely sharked down by slow-motion monsters. Brannigan had caught nothing; I had caught nothing; three anglers we met had taken one small trout among them; innumerable trout-fishers throughout the East take nothing during the massive Green Drake hatches; but Hawkes had taken six in about an hour, using no more than several dozen casts. Alas, I can only further the myth about Hawkes: I certainly cannot disprove it.

He evaded all our questions for the first forty-five minutes of that quick drive home with a skill to dwarf Falstaff's.

"Yes, it did seem like the Green Drake, *Ephemera guttulata Pictet,* was the major hatch."

"You're not saying they weren't taking those duns, are you?" asked Mike pointedly. "I saw them take a dozen myself."

"Exactly what were you using?" I asked.

"How, how, how! An extraordinary question. Not at all an easy question to answer, my dear Nick. There are a dozen subtle factors involved that ..."

"Come off it, Hawkes," said Brannigan.

"... that the unenlightened Irishmen who slash the streams—and whom it has been my misfortune to fall in with during my decline—would scarcely understand. Brannigan, Branny old boy, did you see the innocence, the absolute simplicity of that farm girl holding her child this afternoon? The Madonna—no less."

"Will you simply tell us what fly you were using?" Mike persisted.

"A question impossible to answer—beyond my power to answer. Ah, but did you see the colors of the sun settling below the tree line, the ochers, the magentas, the great song of the heavens? You must scatter my ashes there, Branny. It is so written."

We were silent while he dropped us off at Brannigan's house, carefully unloading all our tackle—this time without comment. He asked if we'd like a fish apiece (though not the two trophies).

We both said no.

Then he got back into his car stiffly, turned over the motor, looked at us both with those ancient and shadowy eyes, smiled, and said: "It was an event, gentlemen—was it not? We have been to Mecca. And it will last longer than these six trout, which I shall dispatch shortly—the least part of our trip."

"You won't tell us what you took them on?" I asked.

"You've missed the point. Nick," he said taking my hand in his bony fingers, "until next year ..."

With that he drove off around Brannigan's graveled circle and up the road. We could see the old Dodge pause on the highway. Hawkes leaned far out of the car, looked up at the moon, and said something that we could not hear.

"Perhaps it *will* last longer," said Mike, putting his arm around my shoulder and smiling broadly there in the moonlight. I started preparing for the long trip back to the city, for the long year.

"Perhaps," I said.

And it has.

The Legacy

I had never known Ed Halliday, of course—neither personally nor by reputation. For a while after that night I tried to find someone who had: someone who had fished with the man, someone who could tell me how he approached a pool, what rivers he loved, how softly he could lay down a dry fly, what size stripers he took from which lonely beaches, whether he preferred flat water or the riffles, whether he fished often, in the early mornings, weekdays, autumns, or when and where and how.

But I was not very successful and to tell the truth I didn't try very hard. After that evening I had my own image of the man and whatever he actually was has by now been transformed in my imagination. I have never even seen a photograph of him. Once I was tempted to ask Tom for one, but I never did. Not even after he finally saw his father. After all, his legacy was not mine.

My former student Tom Halliday had called late one night to ask my advice. His father had died a few months earlier and there was, he said, a certain amount of fishing equipment in the estate. Would I come over and give him an educated opinion?

"Doesn't anyone in the family fish?" I asked. I was rather too busy that wet December to go tramping the bleak cold city looking at some poor dead bloke's cod rods. I hadn't mentioned fishing for three months and my marriage was flourishing. I knew Tom had never cast a line, for I now and then made allusions to trouting in my classes: there are metaphors in it for most of what goes on in the world. He had never risen, except once, to ask a sharp and probing question about the "morality" of trout fishing. I had rather worked my way out of the trout-killing business, and he said it was worse to play with them and then throw them back; he could understand a man fishing for food.

Tom had never mentioned his father to me, though the number of times he came to me for certain advice might have suggested that he had no father to ask—or that, as for so many young people today, the bridge had been blown up. I knew he was searching for values, for a guide; he was not by nature a rebel and his solitary nature kept him from joining the fashionable student mobs. We shared certain solitary habits of mind.

No. None of the family fished; neither of his two sisters, certainly not his mother, none of his uncles. And they didn't want to bring in a dealer until they had some idea how much the lot was worth. The man had fished a great deal, Tom told me, and his sisters thought the equipment might have substantial value.

"Are any of the rods in metal cases?" I asked. "Tubes?"

Tom did not remember. He only knew there was now a mass of it in several closets where his sisters lived and that he had been given a quick look a few weeks after the funeral.

"Didn't you see it in the house? I asked. "When your father was alive?"

"I didn't live with my father. My parents were divorced. I was only allowed to see him three, maybe four times."

I agreed to take a quick look and, to the best of my limited ability with such matters, let him know if I thought the tackle had much value. The next evening I met him in the lobby of a dowdy apartment building on the upper West Side.

The apartment was in shambles. Beer cans were littered everywhere; clothes and newspapers were carelessly heaped in the corners; I thought I detected the odor of marijuana. The television was blasting from the other end of the living room and the lights were dimmed. A seductive but sleazy girl in her mid-twenties was scrunched down into the shoulder of the couch and, as we came in, a bearded young man moved over to the opposite arm lazily, frowned, and then stared back at the set.

Tom said the girl was Clarise, his older sister; he'd never seen this particular friend of hers. He brought me directly into a large cluttered room and told me to wait a moment while he fetched his younger sister, Julie. I pivoted slowly in the dim room, trying to find some logic to this bewildering mess.

I could not.

A few moments later a whole spate of fishing rods, clustered and extended like lances, came thrusting into the room. There were eight or nine of them together, with one long stick projecting ahead of the others. Even before I saw who was carrying them, I saw the long rod catch against a cardboard crate and bend suddenly in a sharp arc. I leaped for it, shouted wildly, and managed to shove the crate back. I was too late.

"Damn," I muttered. "Clean split."

The girl—quite short, scraggly, and obviously very hip—was unruffled. "Did something drop?" she asked.

"No," I said after a short pause.'

"What was that sound? Like didn't you hear something, Tommy?"

"You broke one of the rods," I said. I still couldn't see, among the mess of sticks, which had been snapped. Most of them were thick saltwater affairs.

"I couldn't have!" she announced.

I turned the light on, went over to the pile of rods she'd summarily dropped on the daybed, and showed her the split tip section. I shut my eyes. It was a fine light-ocher bamboo.

The girl looked at it closely, running her fingers across the severed strands. Then she proclaimed, in a miraculous tone like admitting something she rarely admitted: "Like you're right!"

Tom had come over, and he, too, wanted to see the rod.

I disengaged it carefully from the others and held it out, the splintered tip hanging limply where it had broken. It was a fly rod—about eight feet, I judged— and a fine one. I grasped the cork handle instinctively, thumb ahead. Fine fly rods come alive in your hand: this one leaped, then died. I could feel it in my stomach.

Then my eyes darted to the butt.

The signature read:

Dickerson   *7604*   *Ed Halliday*

"No. No. No."

"Is it a good one?" asked Tom.

"One of the best," I muttered. "Custom-made, too. Is there another tip for this?"

The girl said she'd look and skipped out of the room.

Tom could see that I was upset and asked if the rod could be fixed. I told him it couldn't, not anymore, but that a company in the West could probably match the broken section from their stock, or build another. It would be expensive, and the rod would probably never be quite the same.

"I don't like to see fine things destroyed," Tom said soberly. "I don't know a Dickerson from a Weyerhaeuser, but if you say it's one of the best …"

"It should have been in a metal case. I can't imagine why it was set up like that," I said, bending the splintered tip gently so that the pieces came together—imperfectly.

"Julie!" called Tom. "Have you found a case for this rod? Or another … another …?"

"Tip," I said quietly. "Tip section."

"Another tip?"

She came into the room with a heaping armful of tackle, cases, and boxes, dumped them onto the daybed, and went back for more. "No cases yet. But I think I saw some near the radiator."

I shuddered visibly and Tom asked me if I wanted a drink.

"Two."

"Let's go into the kitchen."

Several quick shots of Jack Daniel's didn't help. And I was anxious and troubled about returning to the room. When we got back the pile had grown substantially. Julie was bringing in, she said, the last of it. She did. She dropped a couple of fly boxes, a handful of empty reel cases, and a net upon the rest, sighed, and said: "I never realized Ed had so much junk. Clarise brought some over the day we closed up his place, and I took some over in a duffel bag on Harvey's bike, and the uncles carried some. I never saw it all together like this before. There's a regular mountain of it, this junk, isn't there, Tommy?"

Though the equipment was in wild disarray, and most of it buried, it was simple enough to see that it had substantial value. There were seven or eight Wheatley fly boxes, six or seven aluminum rod tubes in canvas or leather carrying cases, a fisherman's carryall, a fine pair of Hodgman waders, a lovely English wicker creel, seven or eight expensive saltwater reels to go with the heavy rods I'd seen. And more.

Much more.

It was also simple enough to see that though the equipment was heaped and disordered now, the man himself had been meticulous. One quick look into the opened top of a Wheatley fly box disclosed that. Here and there were corners of his fishing life untouched by his pelican daughters.

I held out my arms, smiled, and said, with as little irony as possible: "How can I help?"

Tom explained that the provisions of their father's will had simply said that all his worldly possessions were to become, jointly, the property of Julie, Clarise, and himself. His mother, Rena, had gotten some cash and, when it was secured, had gone off on one of her frequent trips—this time, one of the girls thought, to South America. But they weren't sure.

They had decided to sell all this fishing "junk" and divide the proceeds equally—if indeed it had any value; but Tom could have his choice of several items if he had any use for them; the girls certainly didn't. They had heard hostile talk about fishing from their mother for as long as they could remember. "I suppose what we'd like is some evaluation of it all," said Tom, "and perhaps some help for me in choosing one outfit. I didn't want any of it at first, but there's something fascinating about it, isn't there?" I doubt that I'll ever use any of it, but I guess that since these things obviously meant something to him, I should keep some of it."

"All right," I said, "let's unravel the debris."

I began by extracting the saltwater equipment. The big rods were good fiberglass; I suggested their commonness and minimal resale value. Some of the big-game reels looked expensive and I mentioned several places that dealt in such used equipment; I told the confused legatees to try them all, and to take the best offer.

In a half hour we had gone through all of the heavy gear—surf-casting rods and spinning reels, boat rods and reels, carryalls full of hooks and lures and wire leaders. It all probably had cost in excess of a thousand dollars, but I told them to be satisfied with several hundred. Through private sales they might get more; but they would have to advertise, and without someone knowledgeable on hand, it would be a cumbersome business.

The freshwater tackle was another matter.

Nothing here was cheap; nothing was less than choice. The gear was all for trout, and it was the best. I could not quite reconcile it with the heavy saltwater tackle, but that was my fault: the world of trout has seemed mysterious enough to me since I found it, perhaps for a lifetime.

I said nothing for a long time while I carefully laid out the fly rods, cases, boxes, and miscellaneous gear, each separately and in a safe section of the room. Several times I thought I detected Tom's eyes searching mine while I fingered a particularly fine item.

None of the rods were in their cases. One other besides the Dickerson was fully joined, and I began with these first, trying to match up odd tips with mid and butt sections, some of them warped from heat, nicked badly, and otherwise damaged.

"Why weren't these in their cases?" I asked without looking up, as I laid out the three sections of a handsome eight-and-a-half foot Wes Jordan Orvis.

"Well," said Julie, "like Harvey was over and he wanted to see it all . . ."

"Does Harvey fish?"

"Only from the piers at Sheepshead Bay now and then. He drives this motorcycle, see, and he likes to go down there and sit on the piers and drink a few beers on a hot summer evening."

"Why didn't he put them back?"

"Well, a couple of weeks ago we had it all out, every stitch of it, you see, and well, we were having a little fun with the rods and then it seemed like one helluva lot of trouble to . . ."

"Fun?"

"Some of us were . . . a little high, and we were like fencing with the really thin jobbies."

"Like this one?" I asked her, holding up the extra tip to the Dickerson. It had several bad nicks in its finish and one guide had been ripped off, but it looked straight and solid still.

"Guess that's one of them."

"And what's this piece of heavy wool doing on the end of this one?" My God, the fully joined rod was a Payne seven-and-a-half-foot.

"The cat."

Tom had grown strawberry red. "What about the cat?"

"We were fishing for it."

I closed my eyes and rubbed my forehead. Then I disjointed the rod, running my fingers along its smooth red-brown surface. With old Jim Payne gone, his fine rods had recently tripled in value; in ten years they would be priceless.

There were no reels to be found for any of the fly rods: no one knew what had happened to them. And there was one case for which we could find no rod. It had been an Orvis midge. Julie finally admitted she had given it to Harvey.

"The motorcyclist? The guy who fishes off piers?" My voice was high and shrill.

"Look, mister, don't talk that way about him. I can do what I want with Ed's possessions. What did he ever do for me? Clarise knows and she couldn't care less. Who are you to come in here making snide remarks? This is my apartment and my junk and I can do exactly what I want with it."

"Shut up, will you!" said Tom abruptly. "I invited him here to help us. The rod you gave away may have been worth a few hundred dollars or more. And it was Dad's."

"Well, it's not Ed's anymore. I don't care if it was worth ten thousand bucks. Like it was Harvey's birthday and I told him to pick out a couple of things. He liked that skinny little stick and I'm glad he's got it."

"Look, Tom. Maybe I'd better go. This is family business. This equipment was obviously the man's life. It's the very best, and since I take it he wasn't very rich he probably bought it with every spare nickel he had, out of the deepest kind of passion and love. It has financial value. A lot. The demand for a number of these rods—the Dickerson, the Payne, that Garrison—will continue to increase, like blue chips. Make the lot of it neat, get a dealer in, or a couple of them, and get bona fide appraisals. I'll leave you some names. Maybe it will end up in someone's hands who will appreciate what's here."

I straightened my jacket and asked where my coat was.

"Stay a little longer," Tom said. "Julie, shut your mouth for ten minutes, will you?"

The girl balled up her fist and, shaking her head, walked slowly out of the room.

When she was gone I took two or three quick, deep breaths.

"It's a disaster, isn't it?" said Tom.

"It's criminal," I said quietly. "Look at these fly boxes: they've been left on a radiator—they're all rusted and most of the flies are ruined. See this fly-tying equipment? The man probably tied each one of those several thousand flies himself. It's meticulous work. Look closely at this Hendrickson. See how carefully it's made? See how straight the tail comes off the shank of the hook? The neat uprightness of the mandarin wings? The delicate pink in the body? The neatly tapered head knot?"

I held the fly out and Tom took it. He held it lightly at the barb and brought it close and then back a few inches from his face. He nodded his head and handed it back to me.

"And look at these feathers scattered across the floor," I said. "Ripped out of the necks. Look. Blue dun hackle—excellent grade; you can't buy blue dun necks like this today. Mashed. Ruined. The net's broken, but you could bind up the wood carefully with bait-casting line and varnish it; you can't buy another old miniature net like this anymore: it's a beautiful little thing and probably helped the man with hundreds of memorable trout. Broken rods, missing reels, fishing for cats with a Payne! My God, Tom, whether you fish or not, it's absolutely criminal to treat fine equipment like this; it's like trampling on someone's white linen with muddy feet."

Clarise came in then, let her shoulders slump a full five inches, put a strand of hair in her mouth, and mumbled, "Oh, goddamn: this will take months to clean." Then she said, "Look, Tommy, there are a couple of dozen legal matters I gotta talk over with you and Julie since Rena's skipped, and she wants to get out and meet Harvey. So if you can spare ten minutes from all this heady junk, maybe we can get them done. Already it's time to be finished with this lousy cheap stuff—or are you falling in love with it, like Ed did?"

Tom agreed to go in and asked if I'd mind staying alone for fifteen minutes.

"Not at all," I said. "I'd like to look at all this ... tackle carefully."

"Be back soon," he said and walked out the doorway. Clarise went after him, took his arm, and whispered loudly, "Can we trust him?"

"No," said Tom in a full voice.

I picked up a couple of the rods and waved them back and forth, perpendicular to my waist. I popped open a few more fly boxes. *Perhaps,* I thought, *I should make a low offer for it all and try to steal the whole lot. In a week they'll mash it all anyway. It will be worthless. Cats!*

I picked up the vest, carried it over to an armchair, sat down wearily, and began going through the pockets. My wife would be wondering where I was; I had enough trouble breaking away for a few hours' fishing: I didn't much want this disaster to keep me out half the night, in December, when my most family instincts usually emerged.

But the vest was fascinating.

Leader material. Spare leaders, dyed bluebrown. Penknife, small and sharp. Fly dope. Leader sink. Rubber leader-straightening pad. Matted pack of matches.

I put my hand into an inside pocket. *What's this?* I fished out a little black notebook.

I thumbed through it slowly and saw that it was a record of trips, in a neat fine hand. There was a date, the abbreviation of several streams I had fished, a few scattered comments about the condition of the water, an emergence record, and finally, for each day, a list of trout caught and the fly that had taken them.

He had done well.

It was a pleasant, valuable little book—with a wealth of stream information of the kind that would fascinate any hard-core addict like myself. I would have liked to study it carefully, and half thought of taking it. Who would miss it? Who, among his children, would understand it?

Toward the end of the book he had written something else; it took the last six or seven pages. I cannot remember it all, but some words riveted themselves in my brain.

Raining. Sheets and sweeps of it. River growing browner by the minute. River pocked with bubbles and the lines slanting in. So I sit under this ledge, with pipe and pen, with my good Dickerson taken down and lying across my knees. Gulleys of brown water washing down around me. But it's dry here, and there are two nice trout in my basket and I released four more this morning, which started so quietly before sunup, alone, with the mists hovering over the river. Rena would never understand. Never did. Not Clarise. Not Julie. Not ever. Not even the shrill crisp of the morning or the quick disappearance of a dry fly. Not the swallows sweeping down the stream's alley, the stream birds beginning to work when a good hatch gets under way. Not the deep satisfaction of laying down a good cast, several in a row, sixty or seventy feet of line poised in the air and then reaching toward the eddy behind the midstream rock. Not the squirrel who shared my snack a half hour ago. Not the colors of the water or the sharp, sudden tug of a fat native trout. They never did. They never will. I was never able to tell them the slightest small bit of it, not any of them.

And Tom I do not know.

One calls it butchery while she butchers everything private and holy in her and everyone near her; another finds it merely boring. Fine. Each to his own.

Rena tells me I want to be a little boy again.

And Tom, they have never let me know.

Good ladies, I find myself here. The confusions disappear. The sweet mystery of it envelops me. It is full of sweet noises, the air. Perhaps I have failed with you all. You certainly have failed me and perhaps yourselves.

And Tom? I wish to God you could have been here this morning, my son. Whispering while we suited up in the dark before dawn, talking about flies and stream conditions, and a certain, particular trout one or the other of us raised six weeks earlier. He is the one person I would truly have loved to fish with, to communicate the loveliness of being alone with the streams and the trees and the mysteries under the surface. He is the one person I should have liked to tell this morning to, rain and all. Mud and all. Tom, you are my only son and I can give you nothing. You will not call now, now that you are a man. You *cannot* call, you cannot speak to me. I cannot even hope that someday, somehow, you will find me, or this piece of bamboo, or this corner of the world where a man can still husband that sure and gentle legacy that is every man's ...

I closed the little black book and waved it back and forth vigorously. Then I rose, still holding it, and began to walk swiftly to the door.

I heard voices coming toward me. I picked up the vest, slipped the book into its hiding place, and dropped it casually on the heap.

"Well, I've seen it all, Tom, and there's nothing much more I can say. This trout equipment is valuable. The Payne, even though it's been used for catfishing, is probably worth close to a thousand dollars or more; the Dickerson somewhat less; the flies can't be sold; the net and boots, this and that, have no resale value."

"What would you suggest?

I hesitated. "I know you don't fish…"

"I think I'd like to try, perhaps this spring."

"It could be arranged."

"I might have to reimburse my sisters if I took it all. Should I?"

"That's your affair, Tom. But there's something of a man you never knew, who you've wanted to know, I think, in all this."

"Perhaps," he said, looking away from me.

Neither of us spoke for a moment.

"Well, take the Dickerson," I said, "and, if you can get it, the Payne. But if you fish, don't use them for a full couple of years. Learn on a good glass rod and use it until … well, until it seems to be part of your arm. I can show you a little about it this spring if you're really interested. Buy an inexpensive reel for the glass rod, and then, when you're ready, the best reel you can afford—a Hardy or an Orvis. The flies might still be good. Some of them. Go through them carefully some night when you have a few hours. But put away one of each pattern, in cork, for a reminder. The waders are ruined. Keep the net."

"Anything else?"

"No," I said, "I guess that's all."

"I'm grateful to you," he said, extending his hand.

I reached out to him, but drew my hand back. "Oh, yes," I said. "Take the vest." I picked it up and handed it to him. "It has no value," I said quietly. "No value whatsoever. But there are a few items in it that will show you what a proper vest should contain. Your father wore it often, I think, and perhaps you'll find something in it that will help you understand who he was. Otherwise, it has no value."

On the Divide

For three days we fished the lake without a strike. We rose each morning at four, dressed quickly by the bald light of the bulb in the kitchen of the cabin, and then carried our rods and tackle bags silently through the darkness, down the hill to the aluminum boat.

The motor started only once on the first pull of the cord. Neither of us was adept at motors, and we wore our hands raw with frantic tugging. Once, when the winds came rushing along the Continental Divide in which the lake was set like a glittering blue jewel, we pulled anchor, could not start the motor, and drifted half across the lake before another fisherman came after us. I tried to row, busted an oar, and ripped more skin off the palms of my hands.

On the fourth morning the alarm was only a dull ringing far back in my head. The ringing stopped, and then the memory of it woke me. I went into his room to wake him, but he only turned and arched up his body like a cat stretching. "I can't ..." he said. "I can't make it today."

I dressed and gathered up my fly rod and the little teardrop net I always wore fastened to my vest, and the burlap creel in which I carried my reels and flies. I went down to the lake alone, which is how I usually fished anyway. It was better alone, I thought. Then you didn't have to worry if the other person was enjoying himself, whether he would catch the fish you had dreamed of all winter, whether he would see your poor casts. Sometimes with the experts I'd seen fishing turn to fierce competition.

The boy had stopped casting that last afternoon. I had asked him why, and he had answered curtly, "What's the use?"

"They're here," I told him. "Big ones. Up to four, five, even ten pounds."

"Sure," he said.

"They are. Dave told me he hooked a tremendous trout here last September. He had it on for nearly an hour. He said it was actually—"

"—towing his boat. You've told me that. In Cincinnati, Sioux City, Cody, and—"

"Guess I did," I said. "But they're here. I'll swear to it."

"Then why haven't we caught any?" he asked.

"Maybe they haven't come into the channel yet; maybe we haven't found the right fly or lure; maybe—"

"—maybe they're not here," he said. "Maybe they were here sixteen years ago when you say you caught all those monsters."

"Yes, they were here," I said quietly. "I killed a great number of trout when I came to the lake sixteen years ago."

"You said your arms were tired from catching so many."

"They were."

"You said *my* arms would be tired."

I had looked out across the lake, at the surrounding sagebrush flat with its pastures and fences and scattered trees, and at the mountains of the Continental Divide that rimmed the lake, some still snowcapped though it was midsummer. We had fished seven hours without a strike, and the sun was now high and hot.

"Can't we go back," he said, "or run the boat around the lake a couple of times? I like to run the kicker."

The word sounded strange on his tongue. It was a new word and fit him like a readymade suit. We had not been in a boat together before, and I was pleased that he enjoyed running the kicker.

"I'd like to fish," I said.

"For how long?" he asked, turning from me and fingering the rubber covering on the handle of the kicker, turning it slightly several times without pulling the cord.

"We came a long way to fish this lake," I said. "More than two thousand miles. I think we'll get some trout if we'll ... only ... be patient enough."

"Well, I'm tired."

And then he'd put the rod in the bottom of the aluminum boat carelessly, and tucked his head down into his mackinaw jacket though the sun was high and hot. I'd fished for another half hour and had not caught a thing.

On the fourth morning the air was wet and cold. There was a thin drizzle, and I rolled down the rim of the expensive khaki hat I'd bought in the city a week before the trip and lifted the collar of my own hunting coat. This time I pressed the rubber bulb near the gasoline can four or five times sharply before I pulled the cord, pumping it until it grew hard. The motor started on the first pull, and I backed out of the dock and out into the springs.

There were a few lights, and the moon still gave enough light to see by. I eased the boat under the wire that stretched across the springs into which the fish came when the weather warmed and headed out into the channel. When I was parallel to the great clump of willows on shore, I turned left and cut my speed, running the boat slowly until I thought I was in the deepest part of the channel. "Glory Hole" the spot was called, and I had only learned of it the day before from the manager of the cabins. I had fished in the springs the first time I'd come to the lake; there had been no need to fish from a boat. I had caught and killed a great number of them one night sixteen years earlier. It was better that the springs were closed, but I had hoped the boy could fish in them and catch some of the huge trout I had caught. One fish would be enough, if it was the right fish.

I let down the large tin can filled with cement. The anchor chain felt cold and harsh against my torn hands. The barest light was breaking behind the mountains to the east; it came first from the "V" of the mountains, where two pyramids crossed, and then the whole sky to the east grew lighter.

I tied on a long brown leech, with a brown marabou tail, wet it in my mouth, and then began to strip line from my new Princess reel. Soon I had a good length of line working back and forth, and then I laid it out as far as I could and dropped the rod tip to the surface of the water as I'd seen several men do the day before. In a minute or so I began the methodical short-strips retrieve, slowly bringing the fly back through the black waters. It was a rhythmic process and not at all like the dry-fly fishing I had always done in the East. Everything was feel. I had fished the lake with spinning lures that summer after my release from the army. I had come alone and stayed for four days that had stayed pristine these past sixteen years. But now, with flies, I had not been able to induce a strike. Five, six times I cast, and each time waited and then brought the fly back slowly—strip, strip, strip, pause; strip, strip, strip.

It was good, I thought, that the boy had not come out with me. The air grew colder as the mists formed on the lake, and the drizzle grew into a light rain. My hands were already numb, and no one else had yet come onto the lake. I heard unseen sheep baying in one of the meadows.

I enjoyed being on the lake alone, and I enjoyed casting the long line and then bringing back the fly with that slow, methodical retrieve. The years had been long and crowded and hard, and I had watched some of my dreams die and I had not been home enough—not nearly enough—and I had thought all winter and all spring, for several years, of coming back to this lake, where I had once made such a large catch. I wanted to catch some of the big trout very much, on flies. You progressed from worms to lures to flies, and then flies made all the difference. I had wanted the boy to catch some of the big trout, it didn't matter how.

The tip of my rod jerked down sharply. I raised it and felt the heavy throbbing as the line arched out and away. It was a good fish.

The fish moved off to the left and I reeled in the loose line so I could fight him from the reel. Twice he broke water but did not jump. Cutthroat, I thought. I knew that the cutthroat broke water but that the brooks in this lake usually did not. There were hybrids in the lake, too, crosses between the rainbow and the cutthroat, but they would not often jump either.

The fish was not as large as I'd pictured him, and I soon had him alongside and into my little stream net. He was about two pounds. Because we wouldn't be eating the fish, I took the hook out and turned out the net. In the net the fish was bright red. Now as I watched he wavered slowly, his back spotted and the red no longer visible, then darted down and out of sight.

I cast out immediately and after waiting for the fly to sink, began the slow retrieve again. Again the rod tip shot down, and I took another cutthroat about the same size. When I had turned this one out of the net, I sat down on the green boatcushion and took out a cigar. I breathed deeply several times, lit my cigar, and looked eastward. It was still raining lightly, and the sun had not yet broken. It was good to be out on this lake alone, after all the years, after all the changes.

Several other boats were anchored in the channel now, and a man in one of them was fast to a good fish.

"On the leech?" the other man called out.

"Yep. Brown and long, with marabou."

I waited another ten minutes while the fish was brought to the boat. As the man finally lifted it high with his huge boat net, I could see it was a gorgeous male brookie.

The other man had a fish on now, too. The trout had come into the hole. There might be hundreds of them, all staging into the channel that led to the springs.

I cast again, and again took a fine trout. I was in the right spot, in the right hole, and there were many fish, and I had the right fly.

I took two more, about three pounds each, and then, after three fruitless casts, hooked a fish I could not stop. I felt when he took that he was heavy. He did not rush like the others, angling to one side while the line angled up and up. This fish moved straight away from the boat—slowly and steadily; *thump—thump—thump.* Soon he had all my stripping line out, and he began to take line off the reel with the same slow, confident power.

And then he stopped.

I lifted the rod tip to be sure he was still there. There was a heavy weight, but I felt no movement. Perhaps he's sulking, I thought. I lifted the rod again and felt the same dead weight. For several minutes I stood, putting constant pressure on the line but not enough to break it. My chest was beating heavily; my right hand shook.

"In the weeds?" one of the men asked.

"Don't know. Something's still down there. I can feel something."

"Better pull the line with your hand," the man said. "If he's still on, you'll feel him."

I did so and only felt the dead weight.

I gave the line a few more steady pulls, then drew it tight and gave it a sharp tug. When I got the line in, I saw some weeds still attached to it. The fish had wound himself around and around until he was able to break off; I'd never felt the break.

"Tough luck," one of the men called. "Must have been a big brookie—or maybe a hybrid."

"I couldn't turn him," I said.

"One of the big hybrids probably. Eight, maybe ten pounds. Larger even."

I took a deep breath and sat down. My hands were still shaking, so I pressed them against my knees. Then I went into my fly box and fumbled for another of the leeches I'd been given by a neighbor the day before. I breathed deeply again, thought of the boy, and decided to head back to the cabin.

"You really took five and lost a big one?" the boy said as we sat at the linoleum topped table. His eyes were wide, and his bushy black hair, dried by the sun, stood up wildly. He was rested, and I could tell he was excited as he wolfed down a doughnut we'd bought in town the night before. "Five?" And they were about three pounds? Why didn't you keep them? I'd have kept them. Every one of them."

"All the men were getting good fish," I said.

"Why didn't you wake me?"

"I tried to, old man, but you wouldn't be woke."

"Want to go back out? Do you think I can get a couple? *Everyone was getting them?* How many fish did you actually see caught?"

"Whenever you're ready we'll go back out," I said, smiling.

"You're sure I can get some? They're in the channel, like the manager said they'd be this week?"

"Let's find out," I said.

The lake was crowded now. As I moved the boat out of the springs and into the channel, I could see at once that the Glory Hole now had eight or ten boats anchored in or near it. The sun had burned off the mist, and the rain had stopped. It was late morning, and I could see down into the water, right to the bottom in the areas that didn't have weeds. It was a shallow lake and not particularly clear, and in the summer the weeds grew thick and high. I saw several large fish swimming slowly along the bottom and cut the motor. The boy looked over the side as we circled back, and he saw them too. They were large brook trout—four or five pounds apiece.

[93]

"Did you see them, Dad?" he asked. "Did you see the *size* of them?"

"I saw."

"Shall we fish here?"

"Let's head further out," I said. "Near where I got them this morning."

We headed out toward the hole, but several boats were anchored where I had been. I did not want to fish too close to them. I wished there were no other boats on the lake.

Finally, we cut the motor at the edge of the weeds where the hole abruptly ended. I told the boy to cast toward the other boats. His rod was rigged, and he began to cast before I'd fully lowered the anchor chain. He drew the lure back quickly, with the rod tip held high and steady. He made four casts this way; I watched him while I tied on another leech and checked my leader for frays.

"Put the rod tip down and bring the lure back in short jerks," I said. "You're bringing it back too fast."

"Like this?" he asked, and lowered the rod and brought the lure back even faster, still without the short jerks that had worked so well for me sixteen years earlier.

"No, no," I said. "Slower. Slower."

One of the men in my morning spot had hooked another fish on a fly rod, and he fought it noisily with Texas howls. The boy looked over and began to reel his lure in fast again.

In a few minutes another man had a fish on his fly rod, and then another rod bent in that high curving arc, too. I began to cast now, from the bow of our boat, and on the third cast hooked a solid cutthroat.

"This spinning rod is no good," the boy said.

"It will catch more and bigger fish than a fly," I told him.

"That's what you said while we were driving here. All the way across the country you told me I'd have no trouble catching fish with a spinning rod. I haven't gotten a thing. Not a strike."

I put my rod down and took his spinning rod. It was a strange weapon in my hands. I had not used one in many years. I had stopped using a spinning rod after I'd fished this lake the last time and had gone through a long apprenticeship learning the magic of a fly rod. I had caught nothing for a long time, and then suddenly the line no longer whipped down on the water behind me, and the fly no longer slapped down on the water, and my distance grew from twenty to forty and then maybe sixty-five feet.

I flicked the metal lure far out into the hole and let it sink, and then brought it back in short, sharp jerks. I cast three or four more times, drew the lure back with those slow, sharp jerks, and then handed the rod to the boy. He cast again and then again. He imparted a better motion to the lure now, but had still caught no fish. The other men took three more fish on their fly rods.

I cast again and then again. On the fourth cast I hooked another cutthroat. He slashed at the surface several times and then came in without difficulty.

"I can't get a thing," the boy said. "I'm just no good at it. I'll never catch anything."

"You will. I'm sure you will."

"You've been saying that."

"Try a few more casts," I coached.

"Why?"

"You can't catch anything if you don't cast."

"And I can't catch anything if I do cast."

The sun was bright and hot now, and many of the boats were beginning to head back to the dock. I pulled anchor and headed closer to the center of the hole.

But when we'd anchored in the new spot and he'd cast four or five more times, he gave it up and sat down.

"How long are we going to stay here?" he asked.

"We can go back now," I said. "I only wanted you to get a couple of fish."

"I haven't caught any," he said.

"I know," I said.

"Look, Dad," he said. "I like fishing, I really do. And I like being out here with you. But I can't catch anything on this spinning rod. Maybe if I knew how to use a fly rod it would be different. But I don't. And I don't have the same kind of patience you have. I like fishing, but I don't like not catching anything. You don't care. You really don't. But I do. And I'm not going to get any. Not today. Not tomorrow. Not any day this week. I know I won't."

"Well," I said, scratching my head, "why don't you try twenty more casts, and if you don't get one we'll head back to the cabin and maybe visit Virginia City or the Park this afternoon." Perhaps we should head back at once, I thought. I had enjoyed being on the lake alone at daybreak—catching some fish, losing the big fish. Perhaps it had been a mistake to come back to this lake with the boy.

The boy began casting and counting, bringing in the lure much too fast. Thirteen, fourteen, fifteen. Nothing. Sixteen. Nothing.

On the seventeenth cast the little glass rod jerked down in a sharp arc. A good fish. A very good fish.

"Good grief!" he shouted. "Can't hold him!"

"Let him have line," I shouted back. "Don't force him. Keep your rod tip high. It's a good fish, a *very* good fish."

The fish moved steadily from the boat. I could tell by the way the line throbbed slowly that it was a substantial fish, a brookie I thought.

The boy lowered the rod tip and I leaned over to lift it up. The boat swayed and I never reached the rod, but the boy smiled broadly and raised the rod so that the full force of the bend could work against the fish.

Don't lose it. For God's sake don't lose it, I thought.

"He's still taking line, Dad. I can't stop him."

"He'll turn," I said. "Don't force him. *Don't drop that rod tip!*"

The line went slack.

"No. No!" I said.

"Have I lost him? No. I *can't* have lost him."

"Reel quickly," I said. "Maybe he's turned. Maybe he's still there."

"He's there," the boy shouted. "I can feel him. Good grief, he's big. Can you see him yet? I won't lose him now."

I looked over where the line entered the water. I strained to see the fish but could not. It had to be a big brookie.

Now the fish was angling off to the left. He might go completely around the boat. As the line came toward me, I lifted it and let it pass over my head. For a second I could feel the big fish throbbing at the other end of the line. The fish came around the front of the boat, and the boy fought him on the other side.

We both saw him at the same time. A huge male brookie. We saw him twisting and shaking ten feet below the surface, the silver lure snug in the corner of his mouth.

"He's huge. It's the biggest brookie I've ever seen."

"I'm not going to lose him," the boy said. "I can't lose him now."

"You won't lose him. He's well hooked. He's too high and too tired to get into the weeds. You've got him beat, son. I'll get the net." I looked under the seat and came up with the little teardrop stream net.

"He'll never fit," the boy said. "He'll *never* fit in that— whooooa. He's taking line again. He's going around the other side of the boat now."

The fish was close to the boat but not yet beaten. He went deep and around the corner of the boat. I watched for the line to angle out, on the other side of the boat. It never did.

"The anchor chain!" I shouted. "Don't let him get in the anchor chain."

"I can't feel him," said the boy. "The line's on something, but I can't feel the fish fighting any more."

I scurried the length of the boat, bent under the rod, and then lowered myself where the anchor chain entered the water. At first I could see nothing, but then I saw it. The huge brook trout was still on the line. I could see him five feet down, the silver lure in the corner of his mouth. He was circling slowly around the anchor chain, and I could see that the line was already wound six or seven times around the links. It would not come free. Not ever.

"Is it there?" the boy called. "Is it still there?"

"You're going to lose him, son. He's in the anchor chain. There's no way I can get it free."

"Oh, no, *no*," he said.

I put my nose down to the surface of the water. The fish had gone around the chain twice more, and his distance from the chain was growing smaller. He kept circling, slowly, every now and then jerking his head back against the tug of the line.

"I can't lose him! I can't," the boy said.

"There's nothing to be done. If I lift the chain, he'll break off; if I leave him, he'll pull out in another couple of turns."

"What about the net?"

"Don't think I can reach him."

"Try, Dad. *Please* try. I can't lose this fish. Not this one."

I took the little stream net and dipped it far down. The cold water stung my raw hands, and the net came short by more than a foot. The fish made a lunge, and I was sure it would break free.

"Get him?"

"Nope. Too far down. Can't reach him."

"Maybe someone with one of the boat nets ..." But he stopped. The other boats were gone from the lake; we had the Glory Hole to ourselves.

The fish went around the rope again. There was only a foot and a half between him and the chain now. The big brookie was tired. He was half on his side.

I took the boy's arm and pulled him down to where I knelt. It didn't matter if he let the line go slack now. Together we pushed our faces close to the surface of the water and peered down. In the liquid below us, we looked through the reflections of our faces, side by side, overlapping and rippled, and we saw the huge fish.

I reached again, pressing the net down through the water as carefully as I could, trying hard not to frighten the fish again. My arm was in up to my shoulder, and I felt the cold lake water slosh onto my chest. The fish came a little higher this time. I could almost touch it with the end of the net—and I saw clearly now that even if I could get near enough to it, the fish was far too big for the little net, and the lure was almost torn out. There was not chance.

"You'll never get him, Dad," the boy said.

He was holding onto my shoulder now with his left arm and looking constantly through our reflections at the shadow that was his fish.

"It's lost," I whispered.

And then the fish floated up five or six inches. I pressed the net toward its head, felt cold water on my face, saw the head of the huge fish go into the net, saw the line break behind the lure, and lifted madly.

A year has passed, and the etching remains, as if fixed by acid in steelplate: our faces in the water, merged; the tremendous circling trout; the fish half in and half out of that tiny teardrop net; and then the two of us, side by side in the bottom of that aluminum boat, our raw hands clutching a thing bright silver-gray and mottled, and laughing as if we were four days drunk.

The Emperor's New Fly

For years I'd heard rumors about the increasingly good fishing for large rainbows in the Delaware River, and the name Ed Van Put came up repeatedly. As a Catskill-region fish-and-wildlife technician, he was both a knowledgeable biologist and a man with regular access to and understanding of the river. Mike had met him, and we were going to be taken by Ed to one of the best pools on the Delaware. I couldn't miss.

There were a few chores first: to visit a house Mike might want to rent, then over to Len Wright's cabin on the Neversink, to pick him up. By the time we finally met Ed at four o'clock at the Roscoe Diner, I was exhausted; it had been eight hours since I'd officially started on this fishing trip, and though the company was good I was anxious to be on the water—this was beginning to look too much like all those bumbling trips I'd made before I got authoritative advice.

Besides, it had started to rain—first steadily, then fiercely, then not at all, then steadily again. There was a time when I didn't much mind fishing in the rain in early summer, in fact thought it brought better fishing, but I was older now and didn't have a rain jacket with me; about six years earlier when I'd gone outside my apartment to wait for Mike, it had been sunny.

We packed into two cars, and Mike followed Ed north, along Route 17, to the Delaware. It would have been downright unsociable and cowardly of me to ask, but I rather wondered what the bar of the Antrim Lodge looked like at this time of day. An hour later, about five o'clock, we headed down a dead-end muddy road, stopped, stretched, suited up, and headed for the river.

It was still raining—not as hard but steadily. I tried to light my cigar but it kept fizzling out.

What a river! Its huge sweeping turns were more than a half mile long; where we came out of the woods, there was nothing to indicate the hand of man but an old railroad track. Clusters of aspen, willow, birch, and alder graced the far side of the river. Some rhododendron was in bloom. This was a gloriously wild stretch, equal to anything I'd seen out west, and only—at least that day— nine hours from the city. As my eye swept down the length of the river, I saw fish breaking water only a few hundred yards away. They were obviously big fish, in the shallows, and there were a lot of them. Good grief, I'd fish in a hailstorm for creatures like that! They were monsters. I'd hit a bonanza again and was all for trotting down the tracks in my waders to get at them.

"Shad," said Ed. " Probably spent, and almost impossible to catch. They'll be heading downstream in another week or so."

We marched slowly down the tracks in the rain, watching the water constantly. This was as lovely a stretch of river as I could remember ever having seen. Ed said it would be lovelier if the reservoir people let a steady flow of cold water out from the bottoms of Cannonsville and the Pepacton. He said that in another few weeks the water would become so warm that fishing would stop and the fish might die. It sounded criminal.

"What's the drill?" Len asked when we got to the bend Ed wanted to fish. We'd walked about a mile in the rain.

An Adams or Gray Fox Variant, about size 16, would be best; we might pick up a fish or two during the next hour or so, but the real fishing would start at dusk. Ed did better than catch a fish or two. In ten minutes he was into a really solid rainbow that took him into his backing. Then he had another on, then another. He'd earlier told me he'd caught more than two hundred rainbows each of the past two years, most of them over fifteen inches and at least forty or fifty over eighteen. Today, no one else caught even a chub. For me that was not surprising, but I'd expected more of Len and Mike.

I fished from the tail of the sweeping pool up into the run where the current struggled to keep its definition, then into the fast, choppy water, then into the head of the riffle—thinking that the rainbows might go into the fastest water during the day. The trouble was, besides not seeing a fish—except the ones on Ed's line—I couldn't keep a cigar lit; either I'd get one started only to have the rain snuff it out a moment later or I'd spend ten minutes trying fruitlessly to light a soggy cigar with damp matches. I fish better with a lit cigar; some people fish better with talent. But I fished downstream diligently with a large Whitlock Bronze Nymph, which had raised some good fish for me in the West, and watched Ed catch still another muscular rainbow. He casts an immaculately slow and graceful line, and I had the distinct impression that he was also doing something I didn't see, like humming or whistling to these old finny friends to perform for the crowd. He could tell by his taggings that he'd caught several of these fish before; no doubt they were aware that he released every fish he caught and thus had no reluctance to renew acquaintance.

As for me, I sloshed around despondently, bone tired now, whipping the water to a froth, getting wetter by the minute, wondering precisely why I wasn't home reading *The Turn of the Screw* instead of making such a fool of myself. This was strictly regression.

But finally, about eight forty, just after the light grew dim, two splendid events took place: the rain stopped and the fish began to rise ferociously, dozens of them. I promptly lit a new cigar, clipped off my large nymph, and rummaged in one of my fly boxes for a #16 Adams. Well, I was going to make a day of it at last—or at least a fifteen minutes of it. I could *taste* the rise and run of one of those sleek rainbows.

My hands began to tremble. All the old fever and expectation returned, all fatigue vanished. I fumbled with the fly, couldn't get the leader point through the eye of the hook, raised the fly against the dun sky, manipulated the thin monofilament with the deftness of a surgeon, and at last got the pesky thing done.

Eight forty-five, and nearly dark.

The circles—rhythmic and gentle—continued to spread in the flat water where the current widened. Ed was at my left shoulder now, willing to forego these fine last moments of the day so he could advise me. A saint.

"Cast to specific rises, Nick, as delicately as possible. Some of these are really big fish. Over twenty inches. Strike them lightly."

With not a second to lose, I took my dry-fly spray from my vest, held the Adams near my face, pressed the plunger—and went stingingly blind. The little hole had been pointed in the wrong direction. I'd given myself a triple shot of fly dope in the eyes, and even after I doused them with a bit of the Delaware I could barely see.

But, I squinted bravely, puffed with vigor on my cigar— whose tip now glowed like a hot little coal in the dark—and began to cast in the general direction Ed was pointing.

"That looked about right," he said as I laid out a surprisingly accurate cast to one of the inviting circles. I couldn't see the fly but that didn't matter.

"Can't imagine why he didn't take it," Ed said.

When I miraculously repeated the feat, a good cast, he said, "They're awfully picky sometimes. What have you got on?"

"A sixteen Adams."

"That *ought* to do it."

Another cast, my third good one in a row, a record. It was a magical, witching moment, the far bank receding in the swirling mists, the river sounds filling my ears, my squinting eyes seeing only that faint multitude of spreading circles. I could not see my fly but knew exactly where it was by estimating its distance from the end of my bright yellow fly line.

Nothing.

"Strange," said Ed.

"Maybe this time."

Still nothing—and nothing for the next fifteen minutes, when a moonless sky finally pulled the curtain on us and we began to head back up the long stretch of railroad tracks to the cars.

In the headlights I saw a strange sight, which I took the liberty of not reporting to my fellow anglers. There was no fly on my leader! There was only a blackened, melted end, as if, just possibly, it might have been burned through by a cigar.

Mike and I made the long trip back in silence. Had I really fished through the entire rise, the twenty minutes I'd waited for all day, with no fly? No doubt. I was capable of it. My face still smarted in the darkened car with embarrassment, my eyes still stung. I tried to keep my eyelids from drooping, and I tried to talk—because good talk with a good friend after a long day on a river is one of the best parts of any trip. But I was bushed.

I closed my eyes and dreamed of sleek rainbows dimpling to a No. 16 Adams, then skyrocketing out and taking me into the backing. That huge bend of the river was alive with rising fish and each cast was true. I heard Ed say, "They're awfully picky sometimes. What have you got on?"

And I answered, moaning, knowing I had developed a pattern even the experts had never thought of, "The emperor's new fly!"

Grimsa Journal

SUNDAY NIGHT: Salmon. There are salmon everywhere: salmon leaping the falls behind the lodge, their force astonishing; salmon and salmon rivers—this year's, last year's—in everyone's talk; smoked and poached salmon on the table; on the wall, old and new photographs of men with notable salmon; salmon statistics in the log, with pool, fly, and size listed; salmon in my dreams.

And at dinner, at eleven o'clock, after the first evening of fishing, almost everyone said they had taken a few. Schwiebert took one ten minutes after we got to the river—a bright six-pounder in one of the lower pools. Dick Talleur said he was no longer "a virgin": he had taken his first, lost a second. Joe Rosch, who had never fished for them, brought back two—one was over twelve pounds. He said his hands and knees were shaking after it was netted; he said that, from the excitement, he had fallen flush into the river.

The Grimsa is low, but it is filled with salmon. Ten times this afternoon, before we fished, I walked back to the falls, where salmon—some small, some perhaps ten to fifteen pounds—were making their headlong, vital, terrible, exultant leaps at the top of the rush of white water. In the foam and swirl below the falls you could see a tail, a back, flick black out of the white boil. How bright and powerful they are. One four-pounder kept missing the falls and leaping smack into wet lava. I do silly things, too, when caught in the spawning urge.

I have never fished for salmon, but I am catching salmon fever. Perhaps I won't get any. Tonight I was bewildered. I made cast after cast with my #10 rod and double-hooked Blue Charm: across and downstream, then a little half-step and another cast across and downstream. Nothing. Nothing whatsoever. The worst of it was that fish were jumping, coming clear of the water and falling back every few minutes. Big fish. Bigger fish than I had ever seen in a river. Sleek, silver, determined fish. I had not a tick. I went back over my beat four times and moved not one fish.

After a spell, inching downriver along the lava and lava-rubble bottom, watching the crystalline water that appears devoid of all life but for the salmon, you begin to think you will never catch one of these fish. There seems so little logic to it. Sparse once told me: "By God, the beggar isn't even feeding when he's in the river. If a fish rises to my fly, I want to know why." I have not the slightest notion how to get these mysterious fish to move. Even the flies have strange names: Blue Charm, Black Fairy, Thunder and Lightning, Hairy Mary, Green Butt, Silver Rat. In sizes #6 to #10, double-hooked. Which to use?

Still, what a lot of fun we have had so far. We got to Reykjavik at nine Saturday morning, slept, and walked through the closed town (except for Talleur, who is training for the Montreal marathon and *ran* a short ten miles). The city, built mostly of concrete, since there are few trees, is quaint, even charming. Woolens, silverwork, and ceramics are the chief wares—and they're very handsome. Then we had dinner at Naust, which Ernest said was the finest restaurant in Iceland. The place is like an old sailing ship, with round windows and nameplates of old ships at each table. We ate graflax which is raw salmon treated with herbs, buried in the earth, then served with mustard and brown-sugar sauce—and then the others chose grilled baby-lobster tails, an Icelandic specialty; I had British beef and we all drank a lot of wine and then had ice cream and brandy. Ernest told us about the early witch hunts in Iceland, which ended when someone said: "Hey, you fellows are killing off the most interesting girls in town." And Dan Callaghan told one about a guy who ate a couple of stoneflies, washed them down with a glass of wine, paused, and said, "The wine's not right." Talleur was there, and Bob Dodge (who's paired with me for the week), and Bob Buckmaster, who has read and loved Plunket-Greene's *Where the Bright Waters Meet,* and any man who's liked that book I know I am going to like. Anne and Dick Strain, the Perry Joneses, and Joe Rosch, the others in our party, ate elsewhere. We are from Iowa and Albany, New York City and Bellefontaine, North Carolina and Oregon, and we are all in pursuit of this fish bright from the sea, about which I know less than nothing.

The two-hour bus trip from Reykjavik to the Grimsa Lodge this morning wound past the Hvalfjord, which served as an American naval base during the war, and into the Iceland landscape, which is stark, treeless, and curiously beautiful.

Now it is eleven thirty and we are settled into the well-appointed lodge that Schwiebert built and there is still light in the sky and I am exhausted. I am also high-keyed, tense. I know this kind of intense fishing. It will be necessary to catch a fish or two before the edge is off. Maybe tomorrow.

MONDAY AFTERNOON: Got my first salmon late this morning on Beat 3, the Strengir. I had fished hard since seven o'clock, casting across and downstream time after time. Buckmaster had given me a crash course on how to tie and fish the riffle hitch. An interesting technique. Since the fly is visible, the take is more dramatic than when the fly is fished conventionally. After a few hours I tried it and an hour later saw a good fish flash. I held back my impulse to strike, then struck and felt him.

The fish went to the bottom of a heavy riffle, shook its head, and sulked for five minutes. I could not budge it. Then it went a bit upstream, then down into the next pool. And in ten more minutes, Gumi, our gillie, netted it. I was thrilled to get a first salmon, a seven-pounder, but, except for the force of the thing, disappointed in the fight. It had not jumped. It had not taken me into the backing. "Brown salmon," said Buckmaster at lunch. "He's been in the river too long. They don't eat, you know, and lose something every day." This not-eating inspired me. I wished I could learn how to not-eat for three months at a stretch. But the food at the lodge—heaping plates of lamb, halibut, salmon, potatoes, and irresistible desserts—is too good.

I got another fish soon after the first, about four pounds, then struck a fish bright from the sea. It went off like a firecracker, leaped, got below me, let me get below it, and finally I beached it. A good morning. The edge is off.

Fished with Buckmaster this afternoon. What a lot of fun he is to be with. Peppery. Wise about salmon. Full of stories. We were on a difficult pool called, with good reason, "Horrible." Bob uses only a fly he ties called the Iowa Squirrel Tail, in fairly large sizes, with a riffle hitch, and he was determined to get one. He cast long and with great skill and then riffled the fly into the slick before a falls. Nothing. Then we went upstream with Toby, his gillie, and the two of them coached me into catching a small sea trout. Bob went back to "Horrible" and worked hard for more than an hour but caught nothing. Still, we'd found a lot to laugh about and the company was awfully good, so the afternoon was a delight. "There's more to fishing than fish."

"What you're looking for," Schwiebert said, "is a salmon with an itch." I have been looking awfully hard. I don't even know what day it is. My right hand is becoming locked in the casting position, and at night I can feel the thrust of the Grimsa against me and inside me that rhythmic, endless pattern of casting across and downstream, inching forward a half-step, then another cast, then watching the fly rise and sweep across with that pretty little "vee." I've caught nothing in several sessions now, and the wind has become raw, snarling. My casting hand is blotched and swollen from sun and wind and a certain lunatic look has come into my eyes.

Anne and Dick Strain invited me to fish with them this afternoon and I did, on the Strengir again. Anne is avidly looking for new species of birds and is a fount of information about them and about flora. She pointed out the alpine thyme clustered in small patches of bright purple everywhere, cotton-grass, yellow hawkweed, and pink thrift. I can now recognize the whimbrel, with its long curved bill, and the artic tern.

Dick took two good fish in the last of the Strengir runs, then, exhausted from casting my heavy rod into the wind, I lent it to him: whereupon he promptly took a third salmon. I tried for another hour but raised not a fish. Then Sven, their gillie, came by and I lent him the rod: whereupon he promptly hooked a good salmon. They called it the Lucky Rod. I have begun to wonder if my first three salmon weren't flukes. Will I ever get another?

Fishing intensely, you grow not to see yourself. Ernest told me at lunch that salmon fishing makes manic-depressives of us all. I feel low. Is it because Bob Dodge got such a fine bright fish this morning, then another, while I got none? I hope not. I enjoyed watching him fight that fish for nearly a half-hour, then net it. It was about nine pounds and terribly strong, and it jumped and ran and when he finally had it his hands were trembling. We took a dozen photographs of him there on Beat 1, holding the fish by the tail, with the falls and the lodge in the background. His excitement was irrepressible. He went up to the lodge, got some scotch, which we all drank riverside, and said, "If I don't get another fish this week, I'll be satisfied."

But this afternoon I feel low, and it is apparently visible, and I still wonder if I'll ever get another salmon.

More snarling wind and cold but no rain. I got one seven-pound fish, the only salmon of the afternoon by anyone in the party. Is it Tuesday?

Every morning we breakfast, a few at a time, as we get up. A buffet of bread, butter, marmalade, sardines in tomato sauce, cereal, and black coffee is laid out, and we can add two eggs cooked to order with ham or bacon. I always sit facing the window, where I can watch the water and falls. Fewer salmon are leaping now. We need rain.

Then we rouse our partner, head to the wet room, and put on waders and vest. It is cold in the morning and I have been wearing a cotton shirt, a Cambrian Flyfisher's sweater, and an ochre guide's shirt; yesterday I had to add a scarf. Everyone else has felt soles on their waders, which hold well on the lava; I wear my cleated soft-aluminum and felt rubbers, which have proved excellent.

Our gear is virtually what you would use for large trout: a rod for an 8 line (which I have switched to from my 10), eighteen-pound test backing (which no one has needed yet), and a heavy leader, twelve-pound test and up. The best flies have been the Blue Charm, Rusty Rat, Collie Dog, and Black Tube, all on a double hook, in smaller sizes.

You learn to fish the lies, not the rise. You begin to see the line in your dreams as the week progresses and you rotate beats. Fishing until ten, then talking another few hours, then rising early and spending long hours on your feet, everyone gets tired. Joe has started to skip supper. Some of us have skipped part of a morning's fishing, others rest when their turn at "Horrible" comes. Talleur rested by running sixteen miles yesterday.

In the mornings at seven, and then again at four, the gillies wait outside the wet room. Most of them speak English reasonably well; only Ernest, among us, speaks some Icelandic, which someone told me is not a language but a throat disease.

Each day you learn a bit more. The salmon react in a new way, striking in the lower end of the pool, in the slick; you learn the slow and steady Crossfield retrieve for water without sufficient current to swing the fly, or how to vibrate your rod horizontally to induce a take. You cast a bit better and you learn the virtue of careful casting by the increased interest the fish show when your flies land three inches rather than ten from the far bank. When the salmon roll or jump you think of dry flies—but they won't work here any more than you'll find a mosquito: bad trade. You learn to shorten your leader to seven feet, 16-pound test, against stiff wind, and that this does not bother the fish a whit. When a salmon is on, you have a fish with saltwater size and power in trout-stream conditions, and you remember that Earl West told you to play these fish hard, that a half-minute's rest and you have a fresh salmon on again. So you add more pressure and are amazed that you have not yet lost a fish among the five—or is it six?—you've caught so far.

You watch Schwiebert carefully. He is deft, economical, wise about this river. He teaches you the lies and how much skill truly matters. He knows the history of each pool.

And, knowing the river itself more intimately each day, you look forward with greater expectation to the rotation of the beat. You know the beats better and you have more confidence that you can do this thing. This morning we have Beat 5, which has been fishing extremely well. I think about that as I step out of the wet room and walk with Bob toward Gumi's car.

Joe looked shaken tonight. He had lost a big salmon. Very big. He had seen the rish roll just above the falls of Beat 3 and had tied on a small Blue Charm, cast slightly upstream, mended twice, and watched the huge fish take it solidly. The salmon leaped, raced upriver, settled into the pool, then, after ten minutes, leaped again and headed for the falls. Joe decided to try to turn him and the fly pulled free. Now he thinks he should have let the fish go down the falls; he charted the route and thinks he could have followed it. There was much talk and consensus was that this would have been the wisest. The gillie thought the fish would have gone twenty pounds, perhaps more.

Joe was shaken but he has caught an unforgettable memory. I am fishing his beat tomorrow and asked him to map out the spot. Still no rain.

An interesting afternoon with Bob Dodge. We fished a long flat stretch the others call "The Lake." Perhaps sixty or more salmon are stacked up, waiting for higher water, and Dan Callaghan and Perry Jones have taken good fish here. Bob went across stream, inched over to the lip of the bluff, and served as "point man" for me. But I could not, though I cast over the salmon many times, move any of them.

Later we went upriver and each took a good fish in broken water. We are beginning to know a bit more about the river and about salmon fishing, and we have at least some confidence that anyone who can use a fly rod reasonably well can take fish. Iceland is not the moon and salmon fishing is not astrophysics.

A flash of bright silver. The fly turning out of the eddy, buffaloing downstream. The tooled lunge. Up, out of the black near the rock he came, into white water, his back curved and turning. Up and out and then down on the fly as it gained speed and began to zip. I waited. And waited. There! I struck, felt the fish throb, and then he careened off, down toward the rapids. Forty, fifty feet of line. Sixty. The first foot of backing came through my fingers.

Then he stopped, shook his head, started off again, and leaped, smashing the water, shaking, and falling back.

Fifteen minutes later I had him on my side of the river. I looked up and saw a dozen cars lined along the bridge, watching. The salmon jumped again, ten feet from me. Ten minutes later he turned to his side and I led him to shallow water. The fish was ten pounds, bright silver, and bolted off when I disengaged the fly.

It was Thursday.

FRIDAY NIGHT: I tailed my first salmon today, a nine-pounder from Beat 5. Dick Talleur was there and got out his camera.

"No!" I called to him, hiding my face. "I've made my reputation by not catching fish."

"No one deserves a fish like that more than you, Nicky," he said, "after all your family disasters."

"My reputation …"

"I won't blackmail you," he said, clicking off a couple of shots.

When I had gotten a good grip on the salmon's tail, I raised the fish high and kept it high, and kept smiling, long after Dick had stopped shooting.

A little later, upriver, I had four good strikes and could not come up with a fish. Buckmaster kept asking if I was striking too fast. "No," I said, after checking my fly, after discovering that I had busted off both points on the double-hooked fly, "just fishing not wisely but too true to form."

Anne Strain has seen and identified twenty-six different birds, including the gyr-falcon, red-necked phalarope, black-tailed godwit, white wagtail, turnstone, merlin, arctic redpoll, and wheatear. I like the names. I should watch the water a bit less, the sky more. It is strangely beautiful here—spare, the meadows in varying shades of green, spotted, white, and brown Icelandic ponies drinking at the river, the gray streaks of lava everywhere, the snow-splotched mountains, the vast Montana-like space, that little red-roofed Lutheran church on the hillside, the neat farms, sheep everywhere, places where you can look up a valley at four, five waterfalls, one over the other, silver in the sunshine, sunsets the color of salmon flesh, and the light, the light that is always here, even late into the night, making the days longer, fuller.

SUNDAY MORNING: I am exhausted. We leave for the plane in an hour.

Last night Talleur and Buckmaster asked me to go to a local dance with them. Bob wanted to know more about the people. I realized that all I know of Iceland is Snorri Sturluson and *Egil's*

Saga, read in graduate school, and the country had 222,000 people, rampant inflation, gorgeous sweaters, and great salmon rivers. We left at one o'clock at night, in a Land Rover packed with young gillies, the cook, and a couple of pretty girls working at the lodge.

Images: the jammed dancehall and Bob Buckmaster, who is past sixty-five, doing a convincing hustle or rope or robot or whatever it's called; the blinking lights; rock in Icelandic; the young eager faces; Talleur breaking training with a vengeance; the trip back at five in the morning, as the light broke, drinking bitter Brennivin (known locally, and for good reason, as "the black death"), watching thermal geysers and meandering salmon rivers taking the first glints of light, and all singing, at the top of our lungs, in English, "When the Saints Go Marching In."

Then Bob Dodge and I were out at seven, because we had the most productive beat, and I could hardly stand. But I took a good salmon quickly and that seemed a good way to end matters. "Take up your swords," I rumbled, "the morning dew shall rust them," gave my rod to Gumi, and leaned back in the car to dream of the terrible swift strike of the salmon.

Meanwhile, Bob hit into a slew of salmon with an itch, had ten good strikes, missed a few, hooked and lost a few, and took four fish. A better way to end matters.

Now we're packed and ready to leave. It has been a splendid, memorable week. Too brief. Schwiebert and Callaghan caught the most fish, over twenty each, and Anne Strain got a magnificent nineteen-pounder that struck at ten o'clock and fought her until after eleven last night. I got enough.

There is already talk of coming back. The phrase "trip of a lifetime" has been used. There is talk about the effect of this place.

But is Talleur really serious about training on graflax and peanut butter?

Little Wolves of the Weeds

At the far end of the lake, at the edges of the stands of pondweed and lily pad, we stopped catching bass. This looked like fishy water, and Larry said he often caught bass here in the very early morning or late at night, but it was now 10:30 a.m. and another largemouth would be a freak. "Why don't you put on a streamer with a bright Mylar body," Larry said. "Retrieve it as fast as you can."

I found one, cast it flush against the lily pads, as I'd been doing all morning for bass, and got nothing.

"Strip in faster," said Larry.

We were in an old gray rowboat, repainted a dozen times, on a small Connecticut lake, about half a mile around, and we'd had a wonderful morning of bass fishing. One of us rowed and the other cast in against the shoreline, into the varying maze of deadfalls, jutting rocks, coves, and patches of weeds and lily pads. I'd gotten a few and Larry had taken a few; all were chunky fish and their rises to our surface bugs were thunderous. I'd pitch the bug in close to a stump or fallen tree, let it sit for twenty seconds, twitch it, chug it a few feet, let it sit, twiddle it a few times, chug is again, make it gurgle and dip, throw a little arc of water or a splash, then rush it and skip it a foot or two, then let it sit again.

I don't really know whether I'd most enjoyed doing it myself, watching my bug on the water, or watching Larry's bug—full of more surprises—perform on the surface sixty-five feet away.

Bass, with a rise half a foot across, would take the bug early or late in the retrieve; we never knew when. It was great fun, and I couldn't think of any fly fishing I had enjoyed more, though I've yet to find any fly fishing I don't like.

Now the fishing was slow. I caught a fat bluegill that circled and put its weight against the tug of the line, then two more bright orange panfish. This wasn't so bad. I could take an hour or two of it before lunch.

"Retrieve even faster," said Larry, and I did, stripping the line in with short, emphatic jerks. Just before I lifted the streamer out of the water, no more than three feet from the boat, a long, thin fish bolted for it, touched it but wasn't hooked, and set my heart aflutter.

Pickerel. I hadn't fished for them in years, not since I was ten, not since long before I owned my first fly rod. I took my first pickerel when I was six or seven. I had been fishing for pumpkinseeds in a weedy Catskill pond and had hooked a fat shiner of perhaps half a pound. I didn't especially like shiners and was in no hurry to get it in; anyway, it was just heavy enough to let alone for a minute, until it tired, and I remember distinctly, nearly fifty years later, peering down into that twenty-foot pocket within the weeds and seeing it there, three feet below the surface, flashing its silver sides, pausing, flashing again. And then, with electric speed, a great fish shot from the dark water beneath the lily pads, grasped the shiner sideways, and lurched away. I knew nothing better than to lurch back, and the fish, not hooked but holding dearly onto its dinner, flew out of the water and into my rowboat—about four pounds of pickerel.

Later I caught small shiners especially to fish for pickerel and must have taken thirty from that pond over the next few summers. I also caught them in the pool below the dam, on a piano-wire noose I had fashioned. I'd lie stretched out on the top of the wooden dam and watch them for a half hour or more, they as motionless as I, long, thin forms, still and facing the little fall of water over the top of the dam, watching for food. In all the time I watched I never saw them take actual food and never saw them on the prowl. They were always motionless, as alert as wolves, as still as hunting herons.

After I had watched a while, waiting for something to happen, I'd lower the sapling to which I'd attached three feet of fine piano wire, with a slip noose at the end. I'd lower it into the water well behind one of the fish, move it by millimeters toward the tail, pause, let it wait motionless while I watched for any sign of concern in the fish, then with one terrible swift movement bring the noose sideways to the pickerel's gills and up, snaring the hapless fish and hauling it high.

From such low origins do even fanatic fly fishermen start. I don't feel I have to justify my early pleasures by claiming they taught me patience!

The pickerel in Larry's lake averaged about eighteen inches long, with some as small as eight inches and a few that would weigh from two to two and a half pounds. Once I got the hang of it, I caught a slew of them, more than I could count. I stripped in line as fast as I could, until my left hand ached and I could hardly tug faster. I don't believe that you can retrieve *too* fast, either for a pickerel or a bluefish.

The fish were up in the weeds and under the lily pads, in relatively shallow water, facing the pockets among the weeds and the deeper parts of the lake. At first I cast from the deep water in against the edges, as I'd always done for bass. This caught fish, but then it occurred to me that lining up with the edge of the lily pads and casting parallel to them would let the fly tempt more fish. The idea worked. I tried to keep the fly within a foot or so of the pads, and the fish tore out after it and ripped apart the Mylar and bucktail. After a half-dozen fish I had to put on another fly.

The fish came in twos and threes, vying for the kill, snapping and slashing at the fly. Whenever I retrieved slowly, though, they'd follow the fly steadily at a respectable distance and then only streak toward it, mouth open, at the last instant, just as I lifted the fly out of the water. No doubt about it: they craved the chase.

But I found that they also liked a hair frog or mouse fished quite as slowly as you might fish a bass bug. I'd put the fly onto the pads, as I did for bass, then twitch it off and let it lie quietly. The pickerel would come at it with their characteristic mad rush even when it was quite still. They also took a surface lure retrieved as fast as I could bring it in, ruffling the surface like one of those new bass lures that twirl.

Fishing that morning, I was carried back to my childhood, to days less fussy than those I'd spent in recent years on difficult trout streams. It was pleasant not to have such critical inspection of my flies, to see that readiness I remembered from my early days with bluegill, to remember that first huge pickerel taking my shiner. The fish were extremely active (though I have since found them almost so docile that I did not think they were present) and eager. Their requirements seemed simple: something bright and something moving fast. Like a wolf, they did not particularly bother to worry whether the rabbit was gray or brown; so long as it moved and wouldn't bite back, it was dinner.

Spinning, with its faster retrieve and brighter metal lures, would have been more effective; but the pickerel is a lovely fly-rod fish, and a couple of hours passed by with sparks of excitement, lots of action, and not too much worry about why I wasn't fishing to trout on a spring creek. It was fun to see the long, thin fish with the big mouth streak like lightning at our flies.

We kept a mess of them, which Larry assured me was good for the lake; there were simply too many and they would grow larger if we harvested some. Anyway, he said, pickerel were delicious.

I told him I thought they were too bony.

"Just wait," he said.

When we got back to his house, Larry laid four of the largest fish on a cutting board. They were handsome fish, their opalescent green fading now to gray but the black oval markings on their flanks, like links on a chain, still clear.

Larry skinned and cut the fish into three-inch portions, then sliced the bones, halving them but leaving them in place. He soaked all the flesh in milk for ten minutes, then fried them in sizzling oil. The bones must have dissolved, because the little chunks of pickerel were sweet and choice with only the faintest heaviness of bones, like fried smelt, which was quite pleasant.

I always carry some streamers especially for pickerel when I get within one hundred yards of a bass lake these days. Though pickerel will eat insects as well as other fish, frogs, and mice, the streamer is the ideal fly-rod lure for them. If they can be tempted—and some days they can't—that's what they'll take. I like streamers with a hard head and painted eyes, a bright red tag below the head, a firmly tied-in Mylar or other silver body, and white or dyed yellow buckskin. I much prefer kip to marabou, perhaps because I like every part of a pickerel fly to be as durable as it can be made. Two and a half to three inches seems a good size—large enough to interest them, not so large that they'll only snap at it.

I've begun to give some serious thought to eight-inch streamers for their larger cousins, the pike and muskie—but that seems like a major commitment, and for now I'm quite content to have found again the quick little wolves of the weeds.

Largemouth Magic

Green-gray, chunky, with a gourmand's palate and beastly eating habits, the largemouth bass has probably given more pleasure to people than any species other than its little cousin, the bluegill. I am addicted to the brute. I caught my first largemouth in my early teens, on a live sunfish, and they've never been far from my mind, even during some lengthy love affairs with trout.

They're not finicky or fussy or easily scared. They'll eat anything they can catch and get their big jaws around. They mean business when they strike but grow bored—as I do—with the ensuing fight. There is just no freshwater sight as heart-stopping as a truly big largemouth busting up for a hairbug on a muggy night, blasting the surface with the sheer weight and ferocity of its strike, sending a lathed fan of silver in every direction, hustling away like a spooked muskrat when the bass realizes it has been hooked.

I caught largemouth at a summer camp in the Berkshires—first by mistake, while slowly hoisting out a three-inch bluegill, then on nightcrawlers and crayfish, then on minnows caught in a bread-baited jug, then on spinners, spinner-and-worm combinations, Jitterbugs, Pikie Minnows, and finally on big deer-hair or molded-body bugs. The bugs were merely a plump turtle-shaped body with crisscrossed clumps of hair for the four legs. That's still the bug I use most, nearly half a century later.

When I found the fly rod, I never let it go. Even in those early days when I half-tossed, half-slammed a bug out on a level line—sticky from too much grease—I was hooked by the rise of a largemouth to a surface bug. You saw everything. The expectation—as the fly lit, twitched, wiggled, waited, stuttered, and rushed headlong toward you, almost independent of any movement you made— was thrilling. I could barely cast the big thing thirty feet, but when I got it out (and perhaps cheated by nudging the rowboat away from it a few more feet) its presence on the calm surface of the lake mesmerized me. Several times fish struck (and came off) while I looked away, dreamily, and I learned then, for all time, to rivet my eye to that little object on the surface and keep it there for dear life. And once I learned never to look away, I was hooked to the bug, felt its every movement, waited, every moment, for that explosion on the surface, that sudden eruption of calm, that stirring, heart-stopping moment when a great largemouth attacks a bug.

Besides, I liked the way the fishing was done. I didn't have to fish all day, to find fish in deep water, to use hardware of such weight (and number of hooks) that the fight was diminished. I liked an old rowboat that went at exactly the speed I propelled it; I liked the oars making their rhythmic sound against water and oarlock; I liked the constant sight of the shoreline with its myriad shapes and forms: eelgrass, lily pads, old rotted stumps, fallen trees or branches, jutting rocks, drop-off points, rocky flats, coves, islands, channels, overhanging brush or branches, and so much more. Here, you did not fish to a fish, as you did on the flats or for trout; you fished to a spot where a fish might be. Slowly you learned the spots, all of them, not from a book but in the most pragmatic way: you got strikes in certain places, none in others. You did not pitch a fly and let the current take it to a trout but cast to a stump or a patch of weed and then, by wiggle and pop, tried to induce a fish to come and play. It was great fun. It was leisurely—and dramatic.

My friend Mort and I went to the Thousand Islands section of the St. Lawrence River for smallmouths a number of times. We fished for them with live minnows in thirty-five feet of water, below ledge drop-offs. The largemouths were in certain defined channels, not far from the shallows where we caught northern pike, and when they took a plug or live shiner their bulldog fight was distinctive, powerful, memorable. They did not go in for the acrobatics the smallmouths did—angling away from the boat as they came up from the depths and then leaping once, twice, high and wriggling. We'd catch them—largemouth and smallmouth—an hour apart and then talk endlessly abut their differences, about which we liked most. The largemouths were heavyweights, even the smallest of them—one-punch knockout artists—smashing the lure or bait, making their play hard, with bad intentions.

Technology came to bass fishing as it did to everything else, from typewriting to kitchen appliances, and it brought finer reels that didn't backlash, subtler and stronger and lighter rods in a wide variety of patterns, and a cornucopia of whiz-bang lures from spinnerbaits to plastic worms. I listened to their advocates sing their virtues, read about them, watched them work on video, and—at one time or another—tried them all. They caught fish. Often one of them caught largemouth when another worked not at all. Some caught them on the top, others in midwater, still others along the bottom. They were versatile, keyed to dozens of different fishing occasions, often highly effective, always capable of expanding our fishing options. But in the end they did not catch me. As we get older we make choices. We narrow our sporting options because we've found that one route simply gives us more pleasure than another. Isn't that why we're out there? For the quality of the pursuit, the discrete joys the hunt gives us?

I had lost my heart to the long rod, the fly rod. I liked its rhythms; I liked the fact that *I* had to work a bit harder, was more involved; I liked the lighter, more responsive flies and bugs it could cast; I liked the sight of a fly line floating out behind me and then reaching forward. I even liked casting less and being a bit more involved with each cast. And I found, every time I went out for bass, that it filled all my needs. I did not want or need to catch fish all day, every day; I could wait. I had quite enough fishing to try them when they could be caught on the top, at the extremities of the day. And on a long hot summer afternoon on a New England pond, I could take all the pleasure I wanted by easing a rowboat or canoe toward the edges of a weedy cover and casting in against the rim of the lily pads for the odd fish that had squirreled in for a midday rest, with half a hope that an unlucky frog would come its way. I had taken a lot of bass from such spots in the middle of the day, when even bait and deep-water fishermen are having lunch or readying their gear for the evening. If I'm alone I may anchor the boat where I can fan out my casts for perhaps sixty feet of that line that separates open water from the outer edges of a large bed of lily pads. Some bass will be there, even at high noon. I'm in no hurry. It's better than badminton or golf or a gin rickey in the shade on shore. One fish for an afternoon of it will be plenty of reward.

But mostly, the magic of largemouth fishing comes at dawn or dusk, and not only then but the time just before and hours well after dusk. The pond is mysterious, moody, silent then. In the very early morning, after a night on the prowl, big bass can be anywhere. And they're looking for food. I've seen one blast the gently floating plug a friend had left in the water while he untangled a backlash, an hour before dawn. I've seen their streaks and bulges among the weeds; I've had them storm a bug dozens of times, at any of a dozen different moments during a retrieve.

I like to get down to the dock by four o'clock, before there's any light other than the moon's on the water. A loon calls; faintly, a dog barks. The water, what I can see of it, is flat-calm and, in summer, light mist circles above it. I whisper to my friend. Neither of us wants to make the slightest unnecessary sound, even when we leave the car, a couple of hundred feet from the dock. We slip gear into the wooden rowboat, ease oars into their locks, untie the joining rope, and push off. I barely allow the oars to touch the water, just dip their tips gently against the surface. It does not require much more to propel the boat. Only a couple of dozen feet outside the dock area, I bring the oars in and we both scan the dark waters for the best place to cast first. My friend is using a plug, I the long rod. He casts far out into the deep water, toward the center of the pond, claiming the bass will as well be there as anywhere, and I, from the bow, pull line off my inexpensive fly reel, false cast twice, and cast toward the faint outline of the shore. I can see the shoreline brush, a few rocks, but not much more. On my third cast the water breaks and bursts, as if someone has thrown in a cherry bomb, and I feel the hard satisfying weight of a good bass. It does not make a long run, like a bonefish or a salmon; it jumps twice—hard, loudly, with a rude power, and then, against my stubby leader, comes toward me. It's about four pounds. I grasp its lower lip, extract the big hook of the bug, and slip it back into the water. Then my friend has one, a bit larger, on his four-inch jointed plug, and then another. And then we see the first lightening of the sky in the east and head for the other side of the lake, where we take another four fish before the sky brightens and everyone else's day begins.

Largemouth bass are on the prowl in the very early morning hours—and the more you can manage to avoid gentleman's or banker's hours, the better the fishing will be. If everyone gets to the lake "early," at, say six o'clock, I'd get there at five or even four o'clock; there is no hour too early to fish for largemouth bass in summer—and you will find it a different lake, to the eye and for the fishing.

Best, though, is dusk, those great hours when the heat begins to leave the day inchmeal and the lake and the fish gradually become more and more alive. I like to have an early dinner and be on the water about seven thirty in high summer. There will still be some activity on the lake but not so much that you can't find a quiet section where no one will go in for a late swim, where the faster-casting spinners and bait-casters have been and gone. I like to row or paddle quietly, ten or fifteen feet farther out from the shoreline than I can comfortably cast. If I'm alone and the lake is calm, I'll often ship the oars and allow a slight breeze to take me along a shoreline, regulating direction by a brief pull on one oar or the other now and then. This is the time I love best. The sun is off the water, a sunset may still linger in the west, the evening calm has struck the water, and the cool air brings a strange mist to the surface. I can *feel* largemouths beginning to stir, beginning to look for their first meal of the evening.

I have with me the same order of tackle I used thirty-five years ago—as large and powerful a rod (in glass, graphite, or bamboo) as I have at hand, even a #11 or #12, even a tarpon rod. The fight is not my game; casting a heavy air-resistant bug *is*—and it requires a big tool. I use a simple reel with not much backing, for I've rarely had a largemouth run far; I use a weight-forward line (with perhaps two feet of the end cut off, which seems to help casting the heavy bug), a six-foot leader tapered to ten or twelve pounds; and I like a hairbug or a molded-body bug with a big cup, which will pop and throw a lathed wake when I tug the line to manipulate it.

I like progress. But I have found no reason to change—except perhaps the rod, since graphite is so much lighter and has exceptional power. And I'm still blithely content to fish a bug, on the top, where I make everything happen, where I can see it all happen.

I am astonished that more people don't fish for largemouth this way, that they rush around in high-powered boats with huge boxes of lures, that they plunk the lure out and draw it back with a grinding motion, that they need a lot to make them a little happy.

Lengthening my line, I double-haul and send a long cast out toward the fallen branches near the edge of the cove. The bug—that big four-legged one I love so much—lands a foot from the tangle of branches. With a lure I'd have to get it moving quickly or risk it sinking into the possible tangles of branches beneath the surface. But I can let the fly sit. And it does: settling itself from the long toss, rocking less and less, finally motionless. Now the game is all mine. First I twitch it twice, trying to keep it very close to where it fell—thinking that that must be the best spot of all, as near the branches as possible. I am all expectation. My eye is riveted on the bug. I leave the bug there for ten seconds, twenty seconds. Nothing happens. I give it a few abrupt tugs, which make the bug lean underwater a bit and then pop up. Then I leave it alone again, for forty seconds. I barely trust myself to blink. Then I rush it back toward me a foot or so in a steady tug, then pop it once or twice, then twitch it, then strip it back quickly.

I've had fish strike at every moment of such a retrieve: when the fly hit the water, when I was ready to yank the fly out to begin my next cast.

On my next cast I let the stationary bug sit, inches from a stump, for a full two or three minutes. I'm in absolutely no hurry. Then I twitch it slightly and let it sit some more. Then I twitch it again. There *has* to be a bass near that stump. That stump was made to harbor a big largemouth.

And so it does.

With a sucking in and out-rushing of water, a bruiser of a bass takes and bores deep, and then lifts up on sky hooks and rattles its sabres and falls back hard, with a heavy crash. Twice more it is up, into air, and several times it scurries off, with determined force. And then it comes in—five pounds' worth, green-bronze, thick as a loaf of bread.

There is no better freshwater fishing. There is no more delicious expectation than working a hairbug on the surface of a calm lake at dusk. There is no more excitement than the eruption, as if someone had thrown a pig or a garbage can into the water, when a largemouth takes. There is no day when I would pass up a chance at such largemouth magic.

Gray Streets, Bright Rivers

In the evening on upper Broadway, two blocks from my apartment, lynx-eyed women stand near the bus stop as the buses go by, waiting. They wait patiently. Their impassive rouged faces show only the slightest touch of expectation; their gold high-heeled shoes glitter. Their dresses are exceedingly short. One of them hums, and the sound is like a low cacophonous motor, in perpetual motion.

A man asks, with startling politeness, "Would you be kind enough to spare me fifty cents, sir, for a cup of coffee?" Later I see him caterwauling, along with a young tough, eyes wild, waving a pint bottle of Seagram's. Nothing here is quite as it seems.

Four blocks away, only last month, an ex-cop "looking for action" found himself dismembered by a pimp and then deposited, piecemeal, in several ash cans in front of a Chinese laundry I once used.

On a given evening you can see:

The diminutive Arab who every night paces rapidly back and forth in front of the old church, talking incessantly to no one in particular; men rigged up to look like women, with bandanas and false breasts, arm in arm, leering; more lynx-eyed women, one of whom, quite tall and extraordinarily thin, reminds me of a Doberman pincher; a few tired old men closing up their fruit stalls after working sixteen hours; some fashionable people in front of Zabar's or one of the new restaurants, who look like they've been imported, to dress up the place, from Central Casting; the bald, immie-eyed Baptist—his eyes like those little marbles we used to call steelies—his face bass-belly white, with placards and leaflets, proclaiming to all who will listen that the end of all things is surely at hand. Perhaps. Or perhaps not.

Everyone is an apparition, connected to me by eye only. Why am I always looking over my shoulder, around corners, then, to see who's tracking me or what will be? Haunted by ghosts. I want to become part of them, any one of them, to feel their pulse and know their heart, but I fail; some part of me is locked. Bill Humphrey says these people are only ahead of their time: we'll all be there soon.

And sometimes I see, in the early evening, a glimpse of sunset through the rows of stone, catch the faintest smell of salt, and even see the Hudson itself, sullied but flowing water.

I know no more than ten people among the thousands who live within two blocks of my apartment. Next door, for five years, I used to see a grizzled old fart by the name of Mr. Maggid look out of his second-story window now and then. Sometimes he would call to my sons in a high-pitched voice and throw them pieces of candy; at first I half suspected the sweets were poisoned. A year ago, another neighbor from that building came to me one night, his wife with him, and said, "Mr. Maggid is dying."

"I'm sorry to hear that," I said. I didn't know Mr. Maggid. I didn't know what to feel.

My neighbor paused, then added, "He won't leave his room. You can hear him coughing and groaning in there—it's awful—but he won't answer. The door's locked. About a week ago he told me he wanted to die in his own apartment, no matter what happened. He didn't want to die in some sterile hospital. What should I do?"

A moral decision.

Suddenly, in death, Mr. Maggid's life is linked to mine. No more casual encounters by eye; no more candy dropped thirty-five feet down, suspect, never eaten. He is no longer a stranger like that woman who collapsed on the pavement last winter; when I stooped to help her, a passing lawyer told me I'd better keep my distance—I could be held liable for her death.

What to do?

"I really don't know the man," I explain.

"You can't just let him die like that," says my neighbor's wife.

"He wants to die in his own room."

"Maybe he didn't mean it," says my neighbor.

"He meant it," I say. I have known lonely men.

"Maybe not."

"Does he have any relatives? Any real friends?"

"None." The word is absolute.

"The poor man," says the woman. "You can't let him die all alone up there. You've got to call a hospital, or the police. Maybe they can save him."

"That's the point," says my neighbor. "Maybe he's not really dying."

Finally the neighbor calls the police. On my phone. Does that make me liable? And for what? They come, three of them in blue: solid men who will know what to do. They pound on Mr. Maggid's locked door. They shout. There are a few moans, as if some inhuman creature had been walled up in a Poe story and wanted to stay there. Ten minutes later a bright white-and-red ambulance, its top lights turning and flashing, arrives; someone produces a crowbar and brings it upstairs; then I see Mr. Maggid come down the stairs he rarely used, feet first, on a stretcher, an oxygen mask held to his mouth, his eyes wide, then small, darting, then still. An hour later we learn he has died in the hospital. The next day, our neighbor describes to us Mr. Maggid's room. It has not been cleaned in more than fifteen years. Garbage was never taken out. Hundreds of pornographic magazines piled with soiled clothes in the corners and closets. Dust. Dust over everything. The landlord, who had taken legal measures to get Mr. Maggid evicted so he could jack up the rent, can't face the place and takes a year to clean it. A dour bearded guy who edits Woody Allen's movies lives there now. We never speak.

Downtown, where the game for the big green is played, I go to a meeting that lasts eight hours. After the first ten minutes, I feel the tightening in my chest. I begin to doodle; I scribble out a meaningless note and pass it to someone I know across the table, because I've seen executives in the movies do that. I look for the windows, but they're hidden behind the heavy, brocaded draperies so that the air conditioning will take—anyway, we're in the back of the hotel so even if the windows were open, I'd only see the backs of the other buildings. Everyone is talking with pomp and edge; I jot down Evelyn Waugh's observation about New York City: "… there is neurosis in the air which the inhabitants mistake for energy." I drink two glasses of ice water. I speak like a good boy, when spoken to.

Suddenly I begin to sweat. I've been in this windowless room for fifteen years. I have been a juggler, flinging my several lives carelessly into the air, never catching them, barely feeling one as it touches my hand. Nine to five I am here; then a quick trip on the subway and five hours in the classroom; then I am the fastest ghostwriter in the East, becoming a lawyer one week, an expert on Greece the next, then an adopted girl searching for the blood link. When there is time, after midnight, I write high-toned scholarship—on Chrétien de Troyes and Thomas Nashe and William Ellery Channing and Saint Augustine—and shaggy-fish stories; or I prepare a lecture on "The Generosity of Whitman." A smorgasbord, my life. Five hours of sleep and back at 'em again, the ghost who is not what he seems, back at meetings like this one, dreaming.

I say my piece in front of all these important men as enthusiastically as I can. These are the rules of the game. Part of what I say—a few words—has to do with rivers. From my words I catch their briefest warbling sound, like the faint rush of wind among the leaves, or a rushing faucet, and when I sit down, there in the back of the hotel, with the windows covered by heavy drapes and the smoke from cigars (mine among them) thick around our heads, as strategies unfold and campaigns thicken, I see a glimpse of them, inside. Deep within me they uncoil.

Rivers.

Bright green live rivers.

The coil and swoop of them, their bright dancing riffles and their flat dimpled pools at dusk. Their changes and undulations, each different flowing inch of them. Their physics and morphology and entomology and soul. The willows and alders along their banks. A particular rock the size of an igloo. Layers of serrated slate from which rhododendron plumes like an Inca headdress, against which the current rushes, eddies. The quick turn of a yellow-bellied trout in the lip of the current. Five trout, in loose formation, in a pellucid backwater where I cannot get at them. A world. Many worlds.

> ... oft, in lonely rooms, and 'mid the din
> Of towns and cities

as Wordsworth said in "Tintern Abbey," about a nature he felt but never really saw,

> ... I have owed to them
> In hours of weariness, sensations sweet,
> Felt in the blood, and felt along the heart ...

Yes, I owe rivers that. And more. They are something wild, untamed—like that Montana eagle riding a thermal on extended wings, high above the Absaroka mountain pasture flecked with purple lupine. And like the creatures in them: quick trout with laws we can learn, sometimes, somewhat.

I do not want the qualities of my soul unlocked only by this tense, cold, gray, noisy, gaudy, grabby place—full of energy and neurosis and art and antiart and getting and spending—in which that business part of my life, at this time in my life, must of necessity be lived. I have other needs as well. I have other parts of my soul.

Nothing in this world so enlivens my spirit and emotions as the rivers I know. They are necessities. In their clear, swift or slow, generous or coy waters, I regain my powers; I find again those parts of myself that have been lost in cities. Stillness. Patience. Green thoughts. Open eyes. Attachment. High drama. Earthiness. Wit. The Huck Finn I once was. Gentleness. "The life of things." They are my perne within the whirling gyre.

Just knowing they are there, and that their hatches will come again and again according to the great natural laws, is some consolation to carry with me on the subways and into the gray offices and out onto upper Broadway at night.

Rivers have been brought to me by my somewhat unintelligible love of fishing. From the little Catskill creek in which I gigged my first trout to the majestic rivers of the West—the Madison, the Yellowstone, the Big Hole, the Snake—fishing has been the hook. And in the pursuit of trout I have found much larger fish.

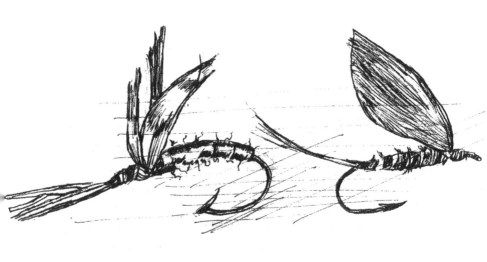

Pilgrimages

I was not born near rivers, and I have not lived my life near them. From the beginning, my fishing has been a matter of excursions. Usually I went for a day, perhaps two days at a fling. For this I would prepare weeks, sometimes months in advance, buying new bits of tackle to meet new knowledge I'd acquired, tying leaders, rewinding guides, selecting the proper flies, lures, or, much earlier, bait.

In my teens these were massive, exhausting treks, beginning in dark basements in Brooklyn at three in the morning, ending when I returned at midnight. Everything was carried in great packs on my back—waders, gear, extra clothing, food, all. Had not some friends got the use of the family car when we were seventeen, I would to this day be humpbacked.

That first day out in April was holy to me. It meant the first break of the year with the gray, indoor winter. I needed it to freshen my eye, to remind me that I can still explore, adventure. It was a beginning and augurs a wealth of days from then until autumn, when the bright rivers will be available, waiting. My feet pick up a quicker pace those first few days in April; my wife says my eyes light up. In my green years I did not miss an Opening Day—but now the season begins somewhat later, under less frenzied, less crowded conditions. I have learned to wait. Another week, another few days will not matter that much. Not now. I could still bear that cold, with the ice freezing at the guides, and no doubt some fish can be taken on a fly. Some fly fishermen I know even make a ritual of the day, complete with a traditional lunch or breakfast at home or at a favorite restaurant; some seek chiefly the celebration—more natural than a Lincoln's or Washington's birthday—of the new year. Who can blame them?

Chaucer begins his *Canterbury Tales* with such a magnificent celebration of the power of spring. When April with its sweet showers pierces to the root "the droghte of Marche," and small birds, too filled, apparently, with the excitement of spring to close their eyes, sing all night, then "longen folk to goon on pilgrimages ..."

It is a pilgrimage indeed. Chaucer's "palmers" come from various parts of England and travel to Canterbury, to seek the "holy blisful martir," who has helped them "whan that they were seke..." Fly fishermen, with little less zeal, seek moving water again. They want to touch that which is awake, alive. All is awake. All begins again. Sometimes, deep in the city, the first touch of spring, a wraithlike dream—green and bright and flowing—seeps through the gray and starts the awakening. Or perhaps, on dark forsythia branches still flecked with snow, bright green buds appear.

All is growing. *Anthony* has grown. I measure him with my eye and see that he is older, calmer, less a child, more a bud about to bloom. Perhaps he is old enough this year. Perhaps. Certainly he's willing. All that winter he had been after me: "Dad. Dad. You promised. Can I go with you and Mike? Can I?"

His older brothers always got the largest piece of the cake; he always wore their hand-me-downs; he always got interrupted at the table. But he is older now, pushing thirteen, holding his own, full of his own mischief and play and purpose. I have tried, with mixed success, to convert people I love to this fly fishing I love; I do so no more. It is, after all, a private affair and must come or not come as it will. But since I talk fishing ad nauseum and find few listeners anymore in my own home, I leap upon Anthony's interest. The addict needs allies.

Would Anthony be bored? Did he know how cold it would be in April? "That doesn't bother me, Dad. You know." Did he realize, his mother advised, that old Dad *talked* good fly fishing but—so it seemed—rarely caught anything? "I'll catch some for him." Did he *really* know, one of his brothers asked, how downright boring it could be? "Dad doesn't get bored." Nope. Not ever. Not for one minute of it.

Well, we would try.

We picked Mike Migel up at eight on a cold gray mid-April morning. Anthony knew and liked him. What twelve-year-old wouldn't like that tall thin white-haired gentleman, with a handshake that gobbles up your fingers with a firm warmth. And he tells stories, too! Wide-eyed and unusually silent, the boy listened as Mike began to tell about growing up in Arizona a half century ago. We began, at the George Washington Bridge, with the Apache massacre in which one of Mike's uncles died, before Mike went to live on the ranch, and progressed quickly to the sheepdog that used to lie beneath the porch on a hot day and nip a bit of the tail off the pet monkey whenever he could; he'd gotten all but a couple of inches of it, during the course of a summer, when we shifted abruptly to the lion hunt. The lion hunt! No sooner were the words out than the boy's eyes widened like a camera lens, catching everything. Mike was only fourteen and went with some men down into Mexico where a lion had been lunching on some unfortunate townspeople. They took guns and mules and tracking dogs. I glanced from the road to the boy's face. The story continued ever so slowly with substories about Mike's first use of a gun, about tracking other wild and dangerous beasts, and we had just picked up the sure scent of this particular cat when we discovered we were two hours upstate already and that it was time for coffee before hitting the river. We hoped the Hendricksons would be hatching. But we were early—they wouldn't be off for another few hours.

In the diner Anthony kept looking at Mike and finally asked, "Well, what happened? Did you get the lion?"

"There's a remarkable story concerning that."

The boy waited.

Mike finished his bite of a doughnut.

"It'll take some time," Mike said "Perhaps we should save it for the trip back, Anthony."

Well ... I'd just as soon hear it now. If that's okay."

I said, "We've got to plan out the fishing now."

"Oh. Does it have to be planned?"

Perhaps not. But that adds to the pleasure. So we talked leaders and flies and particularly choice days in the bright past and, after some debate, chose our section of the river for the day, and after a half hour I could tell that Anthony rightly considered all this trout talk somewhat less important than lions.

Or maybe he didn't.

An hour or so later, Mike and I were a hundred yards apart in a cold, deep riffle below the Big Bend. It was far colder than we'd thought, the water in the high thirties, the air not much warmer. There was still no sun. It had begun to drizzle steadily. At the bend, a long flat glide turned with deceptive speed into a treacherous, sweeping rapids. I was fishing a Red Quill upstream, a bit too quickly, without great expectation; Mike, from a fixed position below the bend, where the pinched flow began to widen, was fishing a wet fly in the currents, casting slightly upstream, mending, letting the fly work as slowly and deeply as possible. We'd been at it for an hour and the signs were not good. The water was too heavy and too cold; no flies had shown—and wouldn't; we were too early for this run to produce. We shouldn't have chosen a river so far north.

But it was the first day out and I could feel a deep stillness inside me. I enjoyed casting; I enjoyed watching Mike cast. But we were too early, much too early; the green was still sleeping in the alders and the trout were slow.

While I worked rapidly upstream toward Mike, I could see Anthony fishing along the bank above us. His white face glistened out of the dark low alder branches and surrounding grasses.

"Anything at all?" I asked Mike.

"A tap. Maybe two."

"Any size?"

"Couldn't tell."

"I don't think any flies will show."

"I saw two. Exactly two. Quill Gordons, I suppose."

"It's a start. We're a week early. By Thursday, if it warms, they should ... Anthony!"

The boy had waded out into the glide in his brother's baggy chest waders. He was coming toward us. "Anthony! Go around! The water's too deep there. Too fast. Don't try to wade! Go through!

Had he heard me?

The sound of the bend rapids was a steady rush in my ears. Mike started to move brusquely upstream. I followed, rushing now against the heavy press of the current. I knew that stretch. The boy was not going to make it. I waved him back frantically. I shouted. Didn't he hear me? Mike kept moving quickly around the curved edge of the bend.

Then, while we were still fifty yards from him, hopelessly too far, I froze, then lunged forward again, up to Mike, past him. Anthony started to lose his balance as the current quickened. We could tell his feet had slipped; we could see his small body twist and struggle against the greater force of the water. He slid forward now, almost racing at us, weirdly, as the water leaped toward the turn. Then he was off his feet and under, all the way under, over his head, splashing, flailing out, his feet out from under him now, then up, fear in his eyes for the first time, his movements jerky, wild, as the water deepened and sped out toward the fastest white-capped broken water where we'd never be able to reach him.

"Anthony! No! No!"

But then he was up somehow, with a toehold and we breathed deeply as he lunged toward the bank, *willing* himself there—slipping back, forcing himself on, safe.

In a small covert among high dead grasses, in the cold wet air, we stripped off his jacket, slacks, shirt, undershirt, underpants, socks, everything. He stood stark still and wide-eyed, unashamed, shaking only slightly, as we wrung out each bit of clothing: silent, white, like something sprung suddenly from winter earth on a spring afternoon.

An hour later I was still shaking.

It had been as close as it can get.

In the warm car, heading home, with my old fishing coat snug around him, Anthony sat like a prince. Mike and I talked about the two flies he had seen, the one I saw later and positively identified as a Quill Gordon, and then Anthony heard all about the lion, in effusive detail, and he said, "You guys don't catch anything but you sure have fun out here."

He and I fished together on brisk, misty mornings in May; and then in June, standing by my side in the Esopus River, he caught his first trout on a fly. And last week, as the time for another pilgrimage approached, he came over to my desk one night, hung on my shoulder, and said, "About this book you're writing, Dad. I mean, you'd better get it done in time, by April, so we guys don't lose any of our fly fishing time."

Adventures in the Fur Trade

Walking to and from my old office, I had to pass every day through New York City's fur district. This is an area roughly between Sixth and Seventh avenues and Twenty-seventh through Thirtieth streets, at least a lot of it is there; and some buildings—first through thirtieth floors—are wall-to-wall fur cutters, fur merchants, fur storage firms, fur designers, and fur wholesalers. The significance of this concentrated marketplace eluded me for more than four years.

But not even I can be that dumb for that long.

One day last winter I passed a huge dump-bin in the middle of West Twenty-eighth Street; it was swarming with dumpbin scavengers. Thirty or forty people, men and women, were tearing at cardboard boxes filled with mink scraps. They were silent but intent about their business, and they were quite particular: they chose only the larger scraps, a foot or more in length. The rest of the stuff—slim cuttings of irregular size and shape—they simply threw back into the dump-bin or onto the street. In all, there must have been a ton of mink, mostly the smaller scraps that nobody wanted. It was everywhere.

I had been tying some small caddis flies and vaguely remembered a British friend who used mink for his wing material. So, nonchalantly, aloof from the serious picking, I picked up a few small cuttings, enough to tie a couple of dozen mink-wing caddis flies. Then I shook my head sadly at the hive of disreputable scavengers and headed home.

But in the night, while it poured, I dreamed of mink. I saw the dump-bin and the horde of silent vultures; but mostly I saw the scraps of mink that no one else had any use for. I woke early the next morning, forgot to shave, and rushed downtown an hour early, full of great expectations. I'd collect up a barrel of the stuff; I'd trade it for other materials; I'd swap it for flies; I'd sell it; I'd corner the mink market; I'd be rich; I'd retire to Montana.

But the dump-bin was gone and the efficient New York street-cleaning machines had left only a few scraps, which I picked out of the wet streets and stuffed surreptitiously into my pockets.

When you are unaware of a thing, you do not see it. I fished for years during leaf-roller "falls" before I saw them. And when I finally noticed those delicate green worms, I wondered how I had missed them for so long. They were everywhere: on the branches, on the leaves, dropping down to the surface of the water on spidery threads, on my rod, on my neck, on my vest, in my waders. How could I *not* have seen them?

I dreamed of mink and searched every morning for mink—and thus began my strange adventures in the fur trade.

Early and late I hunted fur.

One day I found a truck hauling out rabbits' feet—millions of them—and plucked a dozen out of the garbage and wedged them into my always crowded pockets. One night I found a small quantity of some exceptionally soft chinchilla cuttings, packed them up carefully, and sent them to Craig Mathews, the superb West Yellowstone tier. He tied me up a couple of mini-streamers that were bound to be lethal, and from then on I could not keep my nose out of the gutter. I'd shuffle down Twenty-eight Street, tipping up garbage-pail tops, poking into green bags, walking off the curb and into alleyways. I found beaver cuttings, some mink, a bit of sable now and then, a couple of fox half-tails, some Australian opossum. One night I almost got hit by a truck backing up in the dark, and I must surely have been taken for one of New York's lunatic street people. Frankly, I didn't notice. And if I had, I wouldn't have cared.

I'd heard about road kills and the fine pelts that could be found on highways—from Eric Leiser's versatile groundhog to deer. But this was ridiculous. There was gold in the street, just for the picking, and it was clean.

Off the stuff went to Craig and back came some of the most beautiful little mink caddis, #22, you've ever seen—and an enthusiastic letter saying that he'd take all I could find. We called the flies—in case you care—the Lyons-Mathews Seventh Avenue Specials. Not only my fortune but also my fame was assured.

My family, my business associates, and anyone else who saw me with all those fur scraps tumbling out of my pockets surely thought me mad. I was in ecstasy. I neglected my business and my friends; I ate lunch while walking and searching; I did not think trout, I thought chinchilla.

And then the flow stopped. For two weeks in January and early February, with snow and slush spoiling the streets, I found no more than a piece of rug and a hank of lamb's wool. Was the cutting season over? Should I go directly to the dealers? Somewhere out there, in the labyrinth of the fur district, was a fortune. Scrap fur—which must exist by the carload, which was being thrown out somewhere, by someone down there, every day—must have a yearly street value, if converted into flies, of at least twenty-four million dollars.

I couldn't leave my business during the prime hours of the morning and afternoon, much as I longed to do so, so I enlisted the aid of my good friend Justin. Ah, Justin! Never was there a more passionate fly fisherman or friend. On a perfectly grizzly March afternoon, he called me from a pay phone in the street and said he'd found the mother lode. Our fortunes were made. The phone connection was poor so I told him to rush over and we'd huddle on it. Minutes later he was there, wet as a Labrador retriever. I dropped a mess of insignificant contracts and manuscripts in a heap on the floor and he gave me the dope: there was a scrap-fur broker, in fact a couple of them. He had been to a dozen cutters and dealers, and they all said they sold their scraps by the pound to a broker. Justin had found him, in a ground-floor cement-floored room, surrounded by mountains of fur. "You never saw so much, Nick," he said, his voice rising. "There are bales of it, hundreds of them, up to the ceiling, all over."

So I raced out. It was three o'clock in the afternoon on a Tuesday. Justin was right. Nutria, Polish nutria, mink, ermine, beaver, sable, chinchilla, five kinds of fox, Australian opossum—butt ends, tails, body fur, thin cuttings, fat cuttings, head pieces, belly slabs: you would not believe the amounts. It was a fly tier's Valhalla. And it was all dirt cheap. The broker filled a three-foot-high paper bag with Australian opossum and said, "Give me three bucks, make it two—you look like a nice guy." And Justin and I took all we could carry, enough to make fifty million flies, hauled it all, struggling, both arms full, up the wet streets to my office. We were too excited—or exhausted—to talk.

Then I spent a couple of hours packing it up in cardboard crates and shipping it west, in trade for flies. In all, by the time the trout season opened, I'd spent dozens of hours hauling, packing, and shipping box after box of that stuff to tiers; and bits and pieces of it stuck to my clothes, spread out over the floor of my office, would not be extricated from the rug, nearly lost me an employee who shrieked when she saw a fox head in my pocket, and very nearly drove my little business into bankruptcy. Worse, we glutted the market and turned my little gold mine into a pig's ear. And I grew bored by it—oh, how bored I was by April after all the lugging and packing, with nutria coming out of my ears, after shipping all those dozens of cartons of fur cuttings. Justin was, too.

I might have continued my madness for months longer but the fates were with me: our lease was up and we had to move. Fortunately, we moved to the paper and printing district, where I have yet to find a use for the cardboard crates and boxes of paper scraps I pass every day.

It is months now and sometimes I get an itch to get my hand back into the fur trade. Now and again I'll get off the subway a few stations early, in my old stomping grounds, to check a few of my favorite haunts. They're still there: the garbage pails two doors from the corner of Seventh Avenue and Twenty-eighth Street where I found all the sable; the rutted corner of Seventh and Twenty-seventh, where I could *always* get a pocketful of chinchilla in the morning; the alleyway up Twenty-seventh where they dump the rabbits' feet. I still pick up a few choice scraps when I go, for old times' sake, but my heart isn't in it anymore. It's May, and I'm working a bit harder and longer, so I can take off the odd Friday and head for the mountains. I happen to prefer fish to fur.

But the gold's there, and Justin and I will tell you where it is—if you promise not to get us involved in the fur trade again.

Hemingway's Many-Hearted Fox River

Late September in Michigan's Upper Peninsula can be a time of gray mists and steady rain. The deciduous trees—maple, aspen, crabapple, birch—have begun to turn; but in a wet year their colors are less brilliant, more muted: umber, ochre, russet, mustard yellow rather than gold, gaudy orange, and vermillion. At gas stations you see fifty-pound bags of carrots, dried corn, and rutabagas, piled five or six high, used for baiting black bear and whitetail deer. The blackflies of June and July are gone; the few mosquitoes near the river are enough to verify that reports of their size and ferociousness were not far-fetched. After a year of heavy rains, the trees were only beginning to turn when I came; it rained all week; the rivers were still high, some as much as several feet.

The Fox River near the town of Seney is several feet fuller than it should be in September and the fishing has been slow. Anyway, the bear and grouse seasons have opened. In more than a week of driving every day from Seney to the blackstump fields of the Kingston Plains, to Stanley Lake at the head of the Little Fox River, the sky has rarely changed from its somber Payne's gray, but I have watched the maples and birch along the Fox

River Road turn slowly, the sweetfern grow from faded green to tawny red. I have seen Canada geese silhouetted against the ashen sky, two bald eagles, a couple of ruffed grouse, and a dozen whitetail deer—always at dusk, one fording the river. No fly fishermen. Only a handful of men who use spinning rod and bait, all concentrated at the eight campsites and state access points on the main river. Two Fox regulars, Howard and Dean, brothers who live downstate, have been taking brook trout on worms; they come up every year, camp in the grove of sleek recreational vehicles at the Seney Municipal Campground just north of town, and love to catch native brookies. It is a happy ritual for them and they tell me that they can take their limits anytime they choose; they are forthright, workingmen, not the kind to brag.

Over the years I have heard of a dozen young writers who made the pilgrimage to fish the river Ernest Hemingway fished, and used for his remarkable story "Big Two-Hearted River"— taking the resonant name of a nearby river to suggest life and death, perhaps, and also, I think, a generosity of spirit. A few pilgrims, including Hemingway's eldest son, Jack, fished the main stem of the Two-Hearted River, thirty miles northeast of Seney, in error; those who have come out of curiosity or homage to the Fox, as I first did in the late 1950s, have been less impressed by the trout than by the blackflies and mosquitoes. From June through August the blackflies and mosquitoes are prodigious, legendary.

In a week of hard fishing I caught more nostalgia than trout. One look at the tangled river above Seney, choked with tag alder trees, and I glumly put my fly rod back into its aluminum case and set up a spinning outfit. I tied on a favorite lure from my teens, the silver C.P. Swing, size #3. With it, I cast into the deeper pools at the few pullouts, where the state has built fences and paths to stabilize the soft sand banks; in the flat below the old railroad bridge; as close always, to the many deadfalls as I dared. I lost a scant seventeen lures and caught a handful of wild brookies—all with parr marks, bright as jewels and not much larger. Then I found a place where a grassy bank left room for casting a fly and began to fish with my long rod and Jay-Dave Hopper tied by Jay. I'd cast up and across, against the omnipresent tag alder branches on the opposite bank. I'd try to find slight indentations into which I could pitch my fly, allowing me to float the hopper into the trouty shade, out of sight, and keep it free-floating until it dragged in the slick glides. I liked having the fly rod in my hand again, and I cast well and fished the water well but took only one eight-inch brookie.

As the week wore on I learned more about this difficult, even inhospitable river, of a kind I had not fished in many years. And I tried—in the steady, cold rain—to scrape the patina of time away to find the underpainting, a river and a young man more than three-quarters of a century ago.

Seney, the town through which the Fox flows, and the place name that positively identifies the river Nick Adams fished, has 185 residents these days. There are a couple of gas stations, motels, a bar, two family restaurants that serve pasties and good plain food with lots of gravy, stores only sparsely stocked in September. A Mennonite family runs the Golden Grill and the grocery attached to it, and sells, with the necessities, inspirational books, cards, and key holders. Welding, truss business, woods work, and tourism are how most people earn their living here. Seney is now mainly a brief stop on the arrow-straight M-28 that bisects the Upper Peninsula. It is hard to imagine that a hundred years ago it was a notoriously rough and lawless town, officially founded in 1881, growing like "an ugly and poisonous toadstool," the fulcrum for fifteen lumber camps that cut the great white pine forests and floated logs to Seney or, down-river, Thompson and Manistique. Much of the lumber used to rebuild Chicago after the Great Fire of 1871 came from the Seney area.

The town had twenty-odd saloons, two huge brothels and smaller ones at the outskirts, and it catered to tough lumbermen with names like Snag Jaw, Pig Foot, Pump Handle Joe, Wiry Jim, and Silver Jack. It was a raw, violent place, where an ear sometimes got chewed off in a fight, with 3,000 permanent residents and double that number in the spring.

While the lumber companies were decimating the great white pine forests, the town burned in 1891 and then again in 1895. Little remains except the contents of a one-room museum assiduously assembled since the early 1970s by C. R. St. Martin, the town supervisor, and his wife, Myrtle, and pilings in the river from dams built to store water that was later used to run logs downriver. Only in the little graveyard just south of town is there one of the last hints of the town that was. It is a simple inscription on a white wooden gravemarker:

CHAS DEWEY
Killed Age 33 Fighten

Seney and its history of violence and eventual demise are important to Hemingway's story; he starts there and the burned-over country reflects Nick's nearly bankrupt emotions. But the river is the heart of the story and I went directly to the iron railroad bridge, even as Nick Adams did, as soon as I reached the town. I knew the river would not be the same long before I stood where Nick stood more than seventy-five years earlier and looked down at the "clear, brown water." You don't even wade in the same river twice on the same day. The river was smooth and quick, still tea-colored from the tannic acid it picks up in the bogs, from the decomposition of pine and cedar needles, and it brushes up against the same black bridge pilings. I stood for a long time but could see no trout holding on the sand-ridged bottom. Surely the water—even in this month of high water—was not deep enough to hold the head of trout Nick describes, no doubt because sand and silt had filled it in, a process begun in the 1890s; when timbering sent the soft sand banks crumbling into the river. And the process had been accelerated by poor management in the 1950s, a period when motorboats were permitted on the river. I doubt if the boulders and pebbles Nick saw were ever in this sand-bottomed river; he plucked them, as he did whatever else he needed, from other rivers he had fished. Looking down from the bridge I was looking at several rivers—the one Hemingway fished, the one fished by Nick in the story, and the one below me; only aesthetically was it of less importance where Hemingway had been than the discrete world he created in his story.

In a few moments I took one of the five grasshoppers I had caught by hand in the high grasses between the road and the bridge and dropped it into the river below the bridge. The hopper kicked and twisted on the flat surface, floated without movement, kicked a bit more, and then drifted the length of the pool, undisturbed. The others followed it and went downstream equally undisturbed; another dozen went into the Fox at various points upstream, and not one was taken. For those first few hours I thought I was fishing a halfhearted little river.

In September 1919, Hemingway fished the Fox with two friends, Jock Pentecost and Al Walker, for a week. Though there are a dozen theories about where they camped, their base was probably no more than a mile or so upriver and from there they ranged above the confluence with the Little Fox, eight miles northwest. In a letter Hemingway wrote on September 15 describing the trip, he says that the three of them caught some two hundred trout, mostly on live grasshoppers, wantonly shot at deer with a .22, and that he lost a fish big enough to break his hook at the shank. And then, late in 1923 in Paris, he started a story called first "Black River," then "Big Two-Hearted River."

"We got off the train at Seney," that first draft began, and then he changed the "We" to "They." Jock and Al are in the fragment, by name. They lift "the bundle of tents and bedding out of the cinders" where the baggageman had thrown them, and look around. Hemingway describes the burned remnants of the town, the hotel "almost level with the ground," its limestone "chipped and split by the fire," the ironwork melted. It is good reporting, but he cannot find the imaginative energy to leave Seney and after several pages stops this version. Then, in a 100-page handwritten draft of the story he wrote on and off in 1924, finishing it in high summer, he came to the river at once and, despite some long false sections that he eventually cut, never left it. For the river is the great heart of the story. But is it the Fox? "I made it all up," he told Gertrude Stein in August when he showed her the draft, "so I see it all."

In brief, the story is a vivid, detailed drama in which the young man, quite alone, gets off the train at a burned-out town called Seney, takes a day-long walk upriver, camps, and the next day, with ritual care, fishes with live grasshoppers. He catches a small trout that he releases, two decent fish that he kills, and loses a big one—the "thrill of the loss" too much for him. Then he decides that to fish in the swamp would be a "tragic adventure," and heads back to camp. Nothing—*and everything*—has "happened."

By his deliberate movements, we realize that the young man has come to the woods—as many fishermen do—for some form of rejuvenation; we realize he is carrying some unidentified mental baggage, dislocation, and that, by slowly setting up his camp, preparing his own beans and spaghetti, and the next day rigging his fly rod and fishing, he is regaining some measure of control over himself, imputing order to his life. He brings certain skills: how to read a river, the techniques of fishing. He loves to fish. The story starts late, after traumatic events have happened to Seney and Nick, and ends abruptly when he decides he will not fish the swamp, where he has less control. "There were plenty of days coming when he could fish the swamp." He knows his limits.

It is a remarkable story—fresh, understated, crisp, elliptical, earthy, full of innocence and love of country, and oddly as suspenseful as a good detective story. Much later, in *A Moveable Feast*, Hemingway said, "The story was about coming back from the war but there was no mention of the war in it," and still later (in an essay, "The Art of the Short Story") "there were many Indians in the story, just as the war was in the story, and none of the Indians nor the war appeared."

Though Hemingway changed the Fox River, along with the country around it, to fit the precise needs of the story, a river called the Fox very much remains and it has the raw and mysterious spirit of the river Nick Adams fished. The whole Upper Peninsula still contains pockets of wilderness, vast stretches of raw and barely compromised country.

The Fox today is still the color of tea, from the swamps it drains. There are still old logjams, with velvet moss and grasses growing from them, plastered with maple leaves. There are jack pine deadfalls everywhere, their spiked branches like a Maginot Line to protect the river from cannoers, float-tubers, even fishermen. Often, the bottom and midwater of pools are booby-trapped with tangled branches and snags—or are too soft with silt to dare wade. The quick river plays against the tangle of trees and creates riffles and eddies, and so do the pilings from old dams, bridges, and conservation deflectors the river has mostly reclaimed. In the distance you can see stands of yellowing birch and aspen, the brighter red of a few maples; and you can always see random clusters of conifers defoliated by insects or fire—skeletal, ghostly, still straight. The land is mostly sand-loam plains, with pockets of muck or bog or hardpan, covered with pine and tamarack needles and sweetfern, dotted with an occasional late black-eyed Susan, high grasses, sweetgale. There is not one swamp, as in the story, but a hundred of them, each dangerous, each—for Hemingway's purposes—a "moveable" swamp, each as threatening to a sixty-four-year-old writer as to a twenty-one-year-old boy back from the war. And everywhere there are the tag alders, the lowgrowing, weedlike trees that proliferate after the cuttings and burnings brought sun to the moist plains near the river; often they extend three or four feet into the river, making wading and casting impossible. The river runs under the branches and then, as it bends, the river appears to vanish into a maze of browning alder leaves and angled pines. It is a difficult, overhung, and very trouty river.

Eventually I fished hardest well below the town, where the river is wilder, shallower, as it flows through cattail bogs and tamarack swamps, dotted with maples and elm. There I found several worn spots in the marsh and thicket where bait fishermen have set up shop. There was barely room to lean out for a quick underhand cast, a single thrust directly across and slightly upstream. It was an old skill for me and I could soon send the lure to the opposite bank with some ease, flutter it back a foot, reel backward a turn or two so it dropped lower in the water, flutter it again. I had switched, on local advice, to a Panther Martin; on the same local advice I soon affixed a small worm I found by lifting a log. On my seventh cast a fish flashed at it in the deep water downstream and against the near bank. I could see little more than that the fish was large. I cast again, to the same spot across the river, and negotiated the lure so it went back into the same eddy. There was no response this time so I lifted the lure with a swift movement for another cast. And then, a foot below the surface, coming quickly, I saw a head emerge from the undercut bank and one of the largest wild brookies I have ever seen, nineteen or twenty inches' worth, lunged at the lure and nicked the worm. I saw the whole of it—its sold girth, dark flanks, huge head. And then it was gone and, on repeated casts, would not come to the lure again.

I sat on the wet bank, shaking a little, smiling, and listened to the sussurant hum of water against the deadfalls, of the riffles as the smooth river bent and went out of sight.

There are tales told at the Seney party store of secret pools and trout measured by hands spread half a yard apart. Local young men, rugged and evasive, walk far back into the tag alder swamps, camp for several nights, and come out with their limit of wild brook trout, twelve to twenty inches—plump wild brookies, their flanks a smooth dark silver gray, with mottled back and bright red markings. Clearly the river can provide excellent fishing, but only to those who have private routes in—below Seney, upriver from the town, through the swamps that protect the "spreads" on the East Branch and below Seney, up the East Branch, which may hold the better fish. The best fishermen take faintly marked trails or make their own, often through high grasses, marshland, and bog. They are rightly covetous of their hard-won knowledge and they rightly resent those who blaze trails, cut the tag alders and fallen hardwoods that make penetration by foot or canoe difficult. It is not a river to be fished quickly.

Howard and Dean tell me that they caught bigger trout in the 1940s when they first came up, that the fish were smaller and fewer in the 1950s, and that it is better now than it's been in twenty years. They use flies downstate, only live bait here. They come for the wild brookies. And there is one man in his late eighties who fished the Fox before Hemingway came; his father tied him to that same railroad bridge in 1913 and he caught his first fish, eight brook trout, on a cane pole in no time at all. He used to get nine or ten fish out of one hole, he reports; now he's lucky to get one. He still fishes when he can but he thinks the river has been raped too often.

But the fish are there, thanks to friends like Dick St. Martin, who pressed the state to make the Fox a Scenic Wild River recently, and thanks to sensible, well-educated men like Steve Scott, a biologist and the district fisheries program manager. He has seen photographs of tables loaded with sixteen-to twenty-inch brook trout, from the turn of the century, and he knows that a few of the better fishermen today can still take a limit of twelve- to twenty-inch trout. He broods about the river, about whether the limit of ten fish is too great (he and I think it is, even for an area where local folk still insist on living off the land), whether boats ought to be allowed on the river, how to prevent (with sediment traps) more sand from collecting on the bottom, how many fish to stock; though there is an excellent natural reproduction, the state does supplemental stocking of Assinica brook trout in the main river—12,000 in 1996. It all costs money—and there are limits to that. Scott is pleased that, since 1989, the Fox has been part of the Michigan Natural Rivers Program. He is pleased that there is enough gravel for natural reproduction, enough sculpin, minnows, crayfish, caddis, mayflies, and stoneflies for food, that there is no winterkill. The river has a lot going for it—the groundwater that feeds it, which keeps the temperature under sixty-eight degrees Fahrenheit; the deadfalls that provide cover; even the tag alders that provide shade and make access so difficult. He is pleased that the Fox, in both of its branches, but especially the East Branch, is a river capable of yielding quality fishing for wild brookies, decent numbers of big fish like the three-pounder he recently shocked. He worries about use and overuse, crowds and publicity, and the mandate to provide quality fishing against the conflicting demands made on it. He says, puckishly, that "the best fishing is in May and June—when the mosquitoes and blackflies are worst."

Each day there was a bit more gold and crimson in the birch and maples along the Fox River Road. On my last day, looking out across the burnt-over Kingston Plains, littered with black stumps a hundred years old, preserved when fire struck green pine and pitch preserved them, I thought about the old railroad bridge, the logjams and deadfalls, the stands of second-growth pine, the grasshoppers. It was not hard, beneath the patina of the years, to imagine Hemingway up here with Jock and Al, finding the Little Fox "lousy with them," camping out, ranging over country just as wild now as it was then—and Hemingway being brawny young Hemingway with youth to burn, which he did, and Nick Adams being skittish of swamps. Nor was it hard to imagine the young man in Paris who had not yet (in his words) begun to trade on his talent, writing about what he knew and loved best, trout fishing in wild country.

In front of me, next to a stand of blueberries, there is a black stump, stark against the failing vermillion sun in the west. It looks solid as oak. I touch it gently. The crust is firm, the century-old cinders soft beneath my fingers. I touch it again and the stump, like an old memory or stale cake, crumbles in my hand into black dust. But inside is a core of fresh pine, preserved all these years by the pitch.

mari lyons

French Pike

The fly fishing in Paris was extremely poor. I could find no trout in the Louvre; there were none in the Orangerie; only the Musée d'Orsay had one—in a Courbet. Nor were there any fishermen with their long rods along the Seine. I walked the quais and looked but saw only one fish in four or five miles: amid the floating debris, among the heavy shore weeds, a carp, belly-up.

I did find two shops, one of which was surely my kind of place. It was called La Maison de las Mouche, on the Ile de St. Louis, and it was crammed with flies, rods, reels, and all the delicious paraphernalia that drives us nuts. The proprietor spoke little English, and I speak less French. Our conversation amounted to a muttered "Ritz" and a "grand mouche" and a "cad-ese" and a couple of "cul de canards." I bought several of the latter, blond, in #18, which reminded me of some Pale Morning Duns I'd once seen, in another country. And later I packed them up carefully and sent them to my friend Herb, well west in that other country. I told him to run them by some large speckled friend we knew in a certain pool called Paranoid. I told Mari: "We've come to the wrong place. The fishing's lousy here."

Matters picked up considerably, though, when Pierre returned from Portugal.

He had been at the beach with his family, far from rods and flies and any chance to fish, and his frustration had swelled to a fine frenzy. He wanted to go out right away. At once. The next morning. We could fish the upper Seine; we could fish for carp below the Pont Neuf—at four o'clock in the morning; there was the chance of a helicopter ride to a chalkstream only fifteen minutes as a fast crow flies; there was a pond with big pike on the border of Normandy and Perche.

I looked at the big pike on the wall of Pierre's Left Bank apartment. It was a considerable fish, better than thirty pounds, and it had come out of the big-pike pond about which Pierre had spoken.

My friend pushed the chalkstream option; he said it had a good head of wild browns and had been fishing very well—the big mayfly was on. I'd never fished a French chalkstream and the idea appealed to me. But the pike on the wall, with the mouth of an alligator, had put the hex on me. I asked Pierre lightly if that was the largest fish to come from that pond. No, there had been forty-pounders, and one day the previous October he had seen something that suggested some were much larger. He had been on the lake alone, during bird-shooting season. Now and then he heard shots. After one cluster of blasts, a pheasant came rocketing out of the woods, fluttered, and fell to the surface.

"Don't tell me the rest," I said.

"It lay there on the surface, Neek ..."

"I don't want to hear about it."

"It lay there for a few moments, and I watched its wings struggle, and then I had to turn the boat a bit and for a moment I couldn't see it."

"I don't believe this, Pierre. It didn't happen. Not a whole pheasant."

"I turned away and then there was a tremendous splash ..."

"No!"

"... and when I turned back, there was just ..."

"No, Pierre!"

"On the surface, Neek …"

"Stop it"

" … there were only three feathers. Fifty pounds. Fifty pounds that pike was, min-e-mum."

The pond, leased by Pierre's friend Alex from a duke, is two hours from Paris, if you drive over one hundred miles per hour most of the way. We stopped for coffee and then for the makings of a sumptuous lunch, and made it in 121 minutes.

Wobbling slightly, bundling myself against the rain and chill, I allowed myself to be ghillied by rowboat to an embankment where the water dropped abruptly to fifteen or twenty feet. At least seven twenty-pounders—if I kept the various pike distinct in my mind—had come from that very spot. Even one of Alex's girlfriends, out for the first time, had caught one that size. Twenty pounds seemed the size at which serious counting begins.

I could see this was a remote, modest-size pond, perhaps twenty acres, surrounded by forest, with weedbeds in the coves, some deep channels, and the embankment drop-offs. Alex leased it very cheaply, with a house and some incidental buildings, and since I'm restless and always looking for a "home," I considered that option and concluded that I could live in this place forever and write shaggy fish stories, especially if I could get a twenty-pounder every couple of days.

The three fish Alex and Pierre caught were one-quarter that size. I caught nothing but a running nose and a rather large, full branch, well beneath the twenty-pound class but of a much more complicated species. That and the rain did their best to discourage me. I thought briefly of the warm museums in Paris. Then Pierre hooked one a bit larger and handed me the rod. I told I didn't need his pike—in the fullness of time I'd get one of my own, thank you. Alex caught another, and I had one flash at my lure and struck much too fast and hard. Then Pierre jumped one on a big popping plug, and I got out a fly rod and began to flail away. The rod was light—only a six-weight—and the bass bug, with wire tippet, was unwieldy. In the wind the rig jerked around spasmodically, and I could not help noting that my companions had stopped fishing; they were now low in the boat, head tucked into chest, arms in protective embrace, strong French words emerging rapidly from each pile of person.

In the candlelit camp building we built a fire, had charcoal-roasted steaks, country pâté, warm local bread, and a pleasant beaujolais—and my spirits picked up considerably. Then we walked back to the lake, and in a steady rain, rowed to the opposite side.

The water there was dotted with tiny rock islands, each fitted with one of the duke's duck-nesting structures. Each structure had a neat little metal ramp leading to the water. We saw one week-old duckling totter out to its ramp and then, wisely, have second thoughts and scurry back, for the pond looked very nervous where the ramp entered the water.

Though we did not have duckling or pheasant imitations, we fished near the ramps a couple of times, and Pierre had one good pike leap right over his big popping plug. He is one of the great fishermen—a former champion caster with several kinds of rods, a demon-pursuer of all the great gamefish. He once told me, "All I want to do, Neek, is fish. I want to fish for every species in every part of the world. I want to fish all the time, everywhere."

This is a sort of large commitment, and my little passions pale before it. Pierre also finds fish and eventually, late in the afternoon, when hope had almost metamorphosed into despair, he found one for me. "There, between the two weedbeds," he told me, and I cast the big frog bug in, chugged it, rushed it, let it wait, chugged it some more, and began to lift it out when my first pike struck—and missed.

"Back, back!" shouted Alex.

"Quick!" shouted Pierre.

I was quick and sure-handed, the bug bounced once, there was a heavy splash, I struck, I felt a heavy rush, and four minutes later I grasped my first pike behind the gills and lifted it into the boat. It may have been French but it sure looked like a Northern to me.

The fish was shy of twenty pounds by about fifteen and could not have fit more than a couple of furry ducklings into its maw. But I felt very happy about the outcome, got my picture taken a dozen times with the grizzly thing, then chucked it back.

The fishing in Paris is generally poor. Go for the museums, the food, the history, the culture, the ambience, the picturesque winding streets. Go if you want to try to regain your youth, even though you won't. The fishing isn't much, but if you know Pierre, you can do all right.

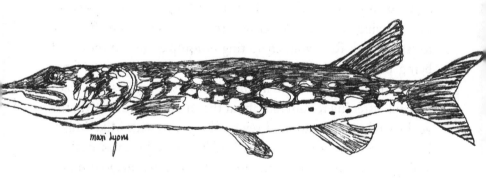
maxi lyons

In the Car

Some of my most pleasant times on fishing trips have been in cars: driving with Les Ackerman the two hours from Big Sky to Island Park Reservoir, chattering nonstop about business and being past fifty and fish; in the car with Thom Green, from Denver to Utah, where we intended to pursue rumors of goliath bluegill, listening to him talk about the structure of the earth, the geology of oil exploration; dozens of long trips with Mike Migel, hearing stories about a hundred of his crazy business deals—selling grass-making machines to the Arabs, leaching gold mines in Ghana, peddling cement to Nigeria. None of Mike's deals ever flew. The machines dried up, there was never, anywhere, enough gold, the cement ended at the bottom of a bay after a coup.

The stories went on for years, as we drove to the Catskills or the Connetquot or the Battenkill. Two new ones began before I'd heard the sad end of one I'd been following for two full fishing seasons. Deals came so close to a handshake, there even was a handshake, that I expected our forthcoming trip to the Ausable to be with a multimillionaire. And then they deconstructed. Every last one of them. We'd get into the car in front of my apartment and they'd start at once—interspersed with reports he or I had heard about the river we were going to fish, fish caught or lost ten or thirty years earlier, fly talk, rod talk, family talk, and then more elaborate business schemes and reports.

I loved the man and miss him and wish, somehow, one of those deals had flown, that he had not died dreaming that one last gold mine, with just another few days of search, would reveal its treasure, which Mike proclaimed—almost with his last words—to be there, absolutely.

We had lunch only a few times a year, rarely spoke on the phone, split when we fished; so those hundreds of hours in the close contained box of the speeding car, cigar smoke practically choking us, rocketing toward or from trout country, were (as I think back on those dozen or more years) the heart of our friendship.

And of my many trips with Mari, car time was always best—especially when I was at least an hour from the river, especially when I did not get lost and then come unglued.

We had driven from Bozeman toward the Big Hole, where we were invited to meet some new friends, Dick and Ann. I had left especially early so we could drive to the upper river, near Wise River, where I had once fished. I wanted to show Mari that gorgeous upper valley and then drop down to Glen and meet our friends at their place about one o'clock.

At eight thirty we got off the main highway for coffee and seeing a sign to Twin Bridges, decided we had time to take the long route, through Dillon. We were chattering blissfully, devouring every feature of the moving landscape. We passed through Twin Bridges about a quarter to ten and I noted that there was a road nearby that led to our friends' ranch. I loved the Big Hole. I had had some spectacular days fishing it with Glen West and Phil Wright. Perhaps we should call and come early. I'd trade a day of even happy sightseeing for a day of fishing any time.

By one thirty we'd been upriver and then down, and had barely gotten out of the car. We were already late. I looked at my scribbled notes and saw that Ann had indicated a road half a dozen miles from Glen as the back route to their place. So I got off the main highway, turned left then right onto what had to be old Route One, and headed back toward Dillon. I looked carefully but found nothing that resembled the road she'd described. In fact, when I looked at the mileage gauge, I realized I'd driven eighteen miles already, not the six she'd indicated, so I backtracked, stopped at the Glen Post Office, and asked instructions.

The postmaster did not seem to have talked with anyone for the past six months. He was in no sweat to see me leave. He got out a map. He got out the telephone directory. He laid them on the counter. He had never heard of the road I'd mentioned. "It's only six miles away," I advised him. He had never heard of my friends, though they could not have been ten miles away.

Baffled, tense that I'd miss the afternoon Pale Morning Duns, I called Ann, verified my location, apologized for being so late, listened to my voice—disembodied now—promise to be there in fifteen minutes. It was two thirty by now and we were clearly very close. "We're very close," I assured Mari. "Very close."

Mari told me, in her great wisdom, that I had been driving too fast and must have missed the road, so I went no more than thirty miles an hour for about ten miles, then picked it up to forty, then fifty-five, then sixty-five. There were no markers or signs on the road. I was now not even sure that we were on old Route One.

Twenty-five miles down the road, my nerves began to race faster than the car and I listened to Mari's third sensible suggestion that we "ask someone."

I had been up and down this road now twice. I was on the verge of heading directly to Dillon and calling Dick and Ann and reporting a seizure, or something.

The only someone I could find was a fellow on a tractor. I jolted the car to a stop at the rim of a side ditch, jumped out, and asked the fellow where our mysterious road was. He shrugged and replied in Spanish. I told Mari I did not think we had gone clear to Mexico but that we were clearly too far and ought to head back to Glen for the third and last time, for one more try.

I raced back at seventy-five miles per hour, decided not to stop at the Glen Post Office again because the fellow might have me arrested for lunacy, and pulled alongside an old fellow in a pickup truck. "Is this old Route One?" I asked, my body pulsing like mad, my foot ready to pounce on the pedal and be off, so we could at least catch a bit of the evening fishing.

"Wal, son," the man said slowly, "What's that you wanted to know?"

I repeated my question.

"I've been driving this road for fifty years," he said.

"Yes," I said.

"No. No, that's not right, son. It's fifty-seven years, exactly fifty-seven years come October since Martha and I came over from Townsend ..."

"Yes."

"... and I drove it every day for fifty-seven years. Most every day."

"Is it in fact Route One?" I asked.

"It used to be the only road, of course, until the big superhighway was put in ..."

"Yes."

"... and I guess I drove it every day so I ought to know what it's called."

Ten minutes later he admitted it was Route One, I raced back to Glen, barely speaking to Mari—who was the only person I could blame for all this, since she was laughing wildly now—got out, kicked the car, which might be responsible, went into the bar, got exact mileage from a man I owe my life to, and sure enough found the road and arrived at Dick and Ann's at five thirty, only four and a half hours late. On the way out that evening, I noted to Mari that it took us exactly thirteen minutes to reach

Twin Bridges, where we'd been that morning. The fishing had been fair, the driving awful.

The car is not merely the source of good talk and torment of course. Mari and I once drove with my friend Pierre from Paris to a pike pond near Normandy. It was a long, happy day—but a wet one; and in the evening, having started at five o'clock that morning, Pierre, who has boundless energy, said he wanted me to fish a small chalkstream an hour closer to the city. When we got there it was pouring like mad—steady and very hard. Mari said gently that she'd rather read then have the great honor of watching me catch my first French chalkstream trout. Pierre got out an old blanket and she put it over herself, covering all but her head. She seemed very warm and content as I looked back at her through the wet window.

Then Pierre and I marched a half mile through very wet three-foot-high grasses. I was exhausted from the long day and, without boots, wet to the skin, chest to toes—and cold. The sight of a couple of Green Drakes fluttering above the water and trying to avoid the cold raindrops perked me up a bit. So did the first little slap rise I saw.

Twenty minutes later, fishing to that rise, I caught a happy little seven-incher, got photographed with my first French chalkstream trout, and fled back to the car. I had no itch to glorify or prolong my misery.

Mari was in the backseat, still huddled under the old blanket. She had put down her book.

"You ... all ... right?" I asked.

"Fine, fine," she said. "But back so soon? And I thought you boys loved to play in the rain. Isn't the fishing—"

"Had ... enough." I said.

"Oh, dear. You're chattering," she said.

I grabbed a piece of the blanket for myself and my wife of thirty-five years sat up and hugged me tightly and in a few minutes I felt amiably warm. In a little while my teeth stopped knocking together, I felt no more chills, and was able to talk.

"All these fishing trips," I said. "All these years."

"Yes," she said. "Are you warmer now, dear?"

"Fine, fine," I said, and then feebly: "And I always thought it was so awful for you ... back in the car."

Where to Go

I was in Vernal, off US 40 in northeastern Utah, pursuing with my friend Thom Green rumors of gargantuan bluegill—which, from where I come, is a long way to go for bluegill—when Thom told me: "You realize, Nick, that you have an obligation to your readers to tell them exactly where you've been."

I was not so sure.

"Let them find their own bonanzas," I said.

"That's the wrong attitude. That's what they're buying the magazine to have you do for them. That's what you're paid to do."

"Not that I've found so very many hot spots," I said reflectively.

"Still, when you do ..."

"But you know what happens when someone announces such a place in a magazine with one hundred thousand or two million readers? Such publicity can wreck a river or a lake over night. Someone goes there a year later and they think you've lied; but you've really *caused* the disaster. There are places, Thom, where you can get trampled to death during a Green Drake hatch because someone has been just a little too explicit about his where-to-go."

Thom knew that. He had seen it happen. But he insisted I had an obligation.

"The first thing," I said, "you get none of the solitude that brought you there. Everyone and his mother-in-law are suddenly flogging the river to its doom. Then the size of the fish goes down. One year the average size is five pounds, the next it's three, and then you're fishing for guppies. If someone's subscription is a month late, they're liable to find something that looks like a New York street after a blackout." I was becoming hysterical; nothing looks quite that bad.

"Still," Thom said, "that's what you've been paid to do; that's what readers want. They get two weeks' vacation and they want reliable information, not mystery lakes. You shouldn't take an assignment if you don't expect to produce hard facts."

"But does everyone want to vacation where everyone else is vacationing? If you tell everyone about a posh lodge in Canada that costs three thousand dollars a week, you won't get many takers, not with taxes what they are, but if you mention a public river, you'll spoil it. No. I'd rather go into the worm business than become a popularizer of secret spots. Some writers even make a profession of such discoveries, to the loss, Thom, of their immortal souls. I saw one writer photographed on *four* different rivers—all of which are now on the decline—with the same eight-pound brown trout!"

Thinking of photographs of big fish, we could not help noting, as we walked in and out of several Vernal tackle shops, that all had dozens of unique shots pasted on the walls near the cash register. They were Polaroids mostly, with one unusual feature in common: they were of positively gigantic trout. Eight-, nine-, and ten-pound fish. We had not come for trout, but these were irresistible. Were they from Flaming Gorge? Perhaps we could catch some on a fly designed to imitate the reservoir's principal trout food: Rapala lures. No. They were from Jones Hole Creek.

Anyway, we were in a regional storm and the lake we had intended to fish was unfishable. Perhaps we could amble over and snoop around this new discovery.

Jones Hole Creek. What a lovely mysterious name. And true. You can find the place on any local map. And those big trout, dozens of them, had all come from Jones Hole Creek within the past two weeks. No question about it. Here was an unexpected story: "Lyons Clobbers Trout in Unknown Bonanza." I had written some stories on which bored Madison Avenue editors, in a fine frenzy, had slapped such a title—but I had never found more than two cents' worth of a bonanza in my life.

Nor was there any mystery about the place. Not only would the tackle dealers readily tell of the creek, but the Vernal Chamber of Commerce had a printed map of how to get there, which looked simple enough. How to get there. Ah, dear. Not only "where" but "how." The ultimate sin. Well, this time I would see and catch and tell. The townspeople, photographed in flagrant numbers and in flagrant pride with their monster trout, did not seem shy or secretive. If they did not care, why should I? Let Jones Hole Creek be damned.

So we started out, Thom and I and also W. Earl West, Jr., and Dr. Ed Reasoner from Casper, Wyoming, in Ed's van—and I swore to them all that I would tell everything this time, the whole truth.

It was only a forty-mile drive, mostly over paved road (except, the brochure mentioned, from mileage 16 to 25.5). For my readers I want to be very explicit about how to get to Jones Hole Creek. At mileage 2.9 there is a junction, at which you take the left road. You take the left road again at 7.8 and then the right road, across Brush Creek, at 10.0. At 15.7 there is another junction and you must keep left; the right road is a dead end. The sagebrush begins to give way to cedar and piñon pine here, the brochure says, but frankly I did not notice; we were climbing slowly upward now, hitting the unpaved section (which I did notice), and executing a series of sharp horseshoe turns on a dirt road with no railings. Actually the road is not dirt after a rain. It had rained quite heavily that particular morning. We squooshed our way up the sloshy, muddy ruts, looking down into an eight-thousand-foot drop. My stomach felt approximately that deep.

"Put the car into low gear," said Earl.

"Mind your own business," said Ed.

I was not particularly in the mood for bad Casper, Wyoming, jokes and elected at 21.2 miles not to look out the window anymore, not even when Earl pointed to Diamond Mountain and told the story of how two 1870s hustlers named Arnold and Slack salted it with diamonds and got a San Francisco syndicate to raise ten million dollars; those investors must have been as light-headed as I now was. At least not many people could travel a road like this; Jones Hole Creek was surely loaded with lunkers. Those in the pictures were the size of baseball bats.

After having not spoken for fifteen minutes, nor done anything but pray quietly, I launched compulsively into a story I once heard about a man who came back to an eastern hotel with several outsized brook trout. When asked where he got them, he gave detailed instructions ending with the general caution: "One small problem, though. Rattlesnakes. Once you get past the fallen oak and the quicksand, if the mosquitoes—they're the size of hummingbirds—don't get you, the rattlesnakes will. They lie on the rocks, dozens of them. I've seen them hanging from the trees. But those brookies! You really ought to try Rattlesnake Creek."

I finished the story and Thom said, No. Jones Hole Creek could not possibly have rattlers. The Chamber of Commerce recommended the trip for little kiddies, along with Dinosaurland. It had to be safe.

At 22.3 we passed Diamond Gulch Junction on the plateau. At 22.5, hallelujah, we reached paved road again; but at 31.0 we began a severe descent into the narrow and rugged canyon that I was quite sure would be my final sight. It was not. At 40.0 we finally reached the Jones Hole National Fish Hatchery that stood at the head of the creek. The forty miles had taken nearly two hours. I was limp. Had I traveled all this distance to fish in a hatchery?

Now the sun suddenly made a bright appearance; the wind stopped. We saw dozens of birds working in the pit of the canyon. Not only had we found a bonanza, but we were surely there at precisely the right time—there was a gigantic hatch in progress—and not one car in sight!

Unfortunately, a few people had found Jones Hole Creek before us, which was where they fished, not in the hatchery. An old Fish & Game hand with a narrow, bumpy face and the scratchy voice of truth said: "Well, there was some big fish in the crik. Mighty big fish. They come up from the Green for a couple weeks in the early spring. But there ain't none anymore. No, sir. You bet."

"Have they gone back down?" I asked.

"Didn't have no chance to," he said. "We had three hundred people a day up here for two weeks. They got about every one of them trout, you bet. There ain't none anymore. All fished out. Not a one left. No, sir. All gone."

We spent an hour verifying his story. Jones Hole Creek proved to be a spritely little brook, spring fed, clear as fresh tap water, filled with watercress and rich in streamlife. Mayflies and caddis were hatching profusely. But the old guy was danged right. You bet.

A couple of days later we pursued a rumor that Ray Lake in Wyoming was yielding ten-pound brown trout. The lake had been closed by the Indians of the Wind River Reservation for four years, and it sounded like a sure bonanza. But we discovered, five hundred miles later, that it was infested with carp. Thom got a couple on flies, big ones, three- or four-pounders, and they were rolling and jumping out there as if it was a hustlers convention.

I could tell you exactly how to get there from Jones Hole Creek. But that might be more than you want to know.

On My Brave Wife

The other night, sitting with fly-fishing friends, addicts both, who had come over to see my new seven-and-a-half foot Kushner rod—an extraordinary instrument—I mentioned a trip I'd taken with my wife and oldest son to a remarkable valley in Colorado. My voice beginning to rise, I recalled the long haul over dirt roads, the frequent false trails we'd followed, following the briefest hint, from a friend's letter, that at the end of our trek we'd find one of those rare untrammeled corners of the trouter's world.

I have followed slenderer trails—and usually found less than I'd sought. It is the fisherman's way, exploring, and I shall follow such slim promises until I follow no more trails at all.

I spoke of that first sight of it—bright and silver through the trees, the river—after three hot summer hours on dusty roads, and of how we found a pleasant ranch along the bank, paid a modest rod fee (I had only enough money with me for one rod, so Paul and I would share), and went down to the water.

Mari came in with coffee, smiled, and stopped to listen patiently. My voice was quite shrill now, my eyes huge. Having made conspicuously little headway in interesting her, ever, in any matter piscatorial, I rarely allow the fevers to take me when she is present anymore. Still, we had found a happy truce. I lived that part of my life a bit more inwardly and she began to take her watercolors to riverbanks, perhaps because the mosquitoes seemed to bite less when she was working.

I knew she loved this valley. We'd spoken often of it. We'd even asked whether there might not be a few acres for sale along the river. It is an isolated place, desolate for some, far from any town, far from any of the modern world's entertainments. One defiles such a valley by bringing anything but oneself. If one brings enough, the valley provides all else. Its long sloping and overlapping hills, spotted with small pine and hemlock, give way to broad, lush meadows; snow-blotched peaks reign at a great distance; cows grace the fields with their slow, heavy grace; and a bright dancing river runs through the heart of the place.

Peace, I'd never been to a place so peaceful.

Deep, quiet, lasting peace. Like a rare elixir.

Mari felt that way, too: I knew it.

In the winter, we learned, the snow was ten feet deep and the elk herds raided the cow barns; in late spring, the river was high, unfishable, but already the meadows were spotted yellow and purple with wildflowers. Then, in August, when we came, the waters came down and the river was a mecca: quick glides, riffles, bend pools studded with boulders and fallen trees. The water was emerald. The river was just small enough for the fly fisherman to touch its hiddenmost secrets, large enough for demanding casts and large trout. We saw no other fishermen along twenty miles of it.

And it was gorgeous.

"The whole valley was gorgeous, wasn't it, Mari?"

"Absolutely," she said with genuine enthusiasm. "I'd move there tomorrow."

Emboldened by her interest, I let my voice touch a wild note or two and went on to tell how Paul and I had gone upstream to the fist great bend pool while Mari got out her watercolors. It was late afternoon, and the valley was hushed. I was going to ask her to verify what happened next—how we'd seen a good trout turn in the current, fished for it with a Rio Grande King, taken it, taken three others in rapid succession, first Paul, then I, all fat wild rainbows, fourteen to eighteen inches—but I remembered suddenly, three years later, that Mari had not showed. We'd met her back at the car, after dark.

I squeezed my memory and it came up with roses: she hadn't been bitten to shreds by no-see-ums, there had been no visible scowls on her face, she's seemed positively beatific.

At the time, I'd asked her nothing. Paul and I had been in a state of acute neurotic joy: we'd finally taken fifteen or so fish, all over fourteen inches, all spectacular jumpers. We'd never budged from our position just to the left of a boulder where the current broke and swirled. We'd said little. Mostly we'd smile when another fish rose and was properly stuck, each turning to the other with an electric jerk, knowing and feeling together. His line went out more deftly with each cast; his reflexes were better than mine.

On the way back we relived it a dozen times, saw a slew of deer in the headlights, and were still in a trance when we returned to our cottage.

"Did they really get that many? That size?" one of my friends asked Mari. They were no worse than me: off the river, I rise regularly to such tales, demand proof and detail.

"Ask Paul," I said.

"He's just another fisherman."

I asked Mari. "They said so," she said.

"You didn't actually *see* it all?" the other asked. "There are rumors that Nick *never* catches any fish."

"They may be true," I muttered, taking back the Kushner and simulating a little side cast toward the pocket between the couch and the bookcase.

"No. I was busy," Mari said placidly.

"Painting?" I asked.

"No."

"You didn't spend the whole time in the car, did you? The sunset was incredible."

"No, I saw it I got a good long look."

"Maybe *she* caught more trout herself, downstream," one of those jokers said, "and didn't want to embarrass you."

"Not hardly," she said, laughing.

"Well, what did you do?"

"If you must know," she said, "I got out my watercolors as I'd planned, went through the barbed-wire fence to the bank of the river, and sat down to work."

"I never saw that watercolor," I said. "I'd like a watercolor of that spot."

"I'd made a good start—a rather greenish landscape, of the river and some willows on the far bank, with a few cows off in the meadow, when I saw a black bull on my side of the water rear up, lower its head, and start toward me at a trot. I dropped half the paints, smeared the painting badly, and got behind the fence just in time. It was after me, all right. I ripped my dress and put a bad gash in my left ankle—"

"I don't remember a cut on your left ankle," I said.

"On fishing trips you don't often look at my left ankle. Anyway"—she was speaking in a perfectly normal, mild-mannered tone, and there was even a Madonna-like smile on her face—"I put the watercolors in the car and sat at the base of that huge rock hill a little downstream. You remember. The one about eighty feet high, of crushed boulders. The valley was exceptionally beautiful, so peaceful, and I was watching the way the hills changed color as the sun dropped, thinking of Turner, hoping you and Paul were having a good time—you'd dashed off so quickly I didn't have a chance to wish you good luck—when I saw something move out from one of the rock crevices just below me."

"Good grief."

"It was a snake. About six feet long." She held out hands, but they didn't go far enough. "Black. Making a rustling sound. Flicking its tongue. Slithering toward me."

"No!"

"Oh, yes. So I fumed and scrambled right up that huge hill of rocks."

"You can climb rocks?"

"You never saw anyone climb them faster. I shot up, bruising both knees, one elbow, my jaw, scratching my—"

"I never noticed," I said quite sheepishly.

"You never noticed!" said my friends, the Andrews sisters.

"It was dark when we got back," I explained.

"Anyway," Mari continued, her voice like honey. "I finally got to the top, looked back, almost fell down, and then turned at some noise and saw the hugest, shabbiest, fiercest wolf of a dog I've ever seen. It was growling in a low, steady growl and gnashing its huge teeth, and I almost fell down ...where the snake was."

I couldn't say a word.

"That dog kept gnashing and growling for a full five minutes while I stood shivering with absolute terror on the top of the rocks. Oh, yes, I could see clearly. All the time. The sunset was exceptional."

I looked at my friends. They were on the edges of their chairs.

"But then," Mari said, "a young boy came along."

I breathed deeply.

"He was quite young, but he was whittling on a stick with a ten-inch knife and looked like he'd come from the nearest reformatory—and he had the short butt of a cigar in the corner of his mouth, and his eyes ..."

And the story went on, another ten minutes of it, interrupted by the chorus chanting, "Peaceful valley!" "Brave woman!" "Brute."

When she was done, she smiled pleasantly and excused herself, she was rereading Henri Focilon on "The Life of Forms in Art."

My friends shook their heads in unison; they positively refused to look at my new fly rod, though I'd especially wanted them to feel how much more power the second, heavier, tip gave the rod, Finally, one of them said, "And she didn't say a thing until now? Three years later?"

"First I've heard of it," I said glumly, beginning to put the rod into its cloth bag.

"Remarkable."

"A brave, wise woman."

"All that ammunition and she's never used it. Jean would have …"

A few minutes later, they got up to leave. But first they went into the dining room where Mari, demurely, was reading.

Reverently, as if she was the sainted herald of a world that might be, they placed kisses upon the forehead of my brave wife.

I noticed, for the first time, she had a thin, white scar on the tip of her chin.

The Metamorphosis

My friend Clyde awoke one morning from uneasy dreams to find himself transformed in the night into a gigantic brown trout. It was no joke. He looked around him, hoping to see his pleasant little one-room apartment where he had lived a hermetic life since his wife cashiered him. Its walls were papered with color photographs of rising trout and natural flies the size of grouse; each corner held three or four bamboo rods in aluminum tubes; the chests of drawers were crammed with blue dun necks and flies and fly boxes and his thirteen Princess reels, the windowsills and bookcases were packed solid with hundreds of books and catalogs and magazines devoted to the sport to which he had devoted his life. They were not there. Neither were his hands, which were fins.

Instead, he was suspended in cold moving water under an old upturned maple stump. From the clarity and size of the water, he deduced he was in Montana, or perhaps Idaho. That was fine with Clyde. If he was going to be a trout, and he had often meditated on what it would be like to be a trout (so he could tell how they thought), he'd just as well be one in Montana and Idaho.

"Well, this love of fly fishing sure takes me places I otherwise wouldn't go," he thought.

And as soon as he thought this, he realized, since he was thinking, that he had resolved an age-old problem. If he, existing under that old tree stump could think, he could analyze his own thoughts, and since what was true for him would have to be true for all trout, he could learn what any trout thought. He was glad he had read Descartes and Kant before he went on the Halford binge.

Curiously, his esoteric studies had led him closer and closer to this point. Only the night before he had been sitting in the dimly lit room, sunk deep into his armchair in front of the lit fish-tank in which swam Oscar, his pet brown. He had been staring intently, reciting a mantra, meditating, as he did every night for four hours, when, for a moment—no, it could not be true—Oscar had (at least he thought so) told him that Foolex dubbing was the ultimate solution to the body problem. "Not quill ribbing?" he had asked audibly. "Definitely not," said Oscar. "I like you so I'll give you the straight poop. Foolex is where it's at. Anyway, tomorrow it … oh, you'll find out."

And so he had.

He had a thousand questions and worked his way a bit upstream, where he saw a pretty spotted tail waving gently back and forth. The trout, a hen, about three pounds, shifted slightly as Clyde nudged her and eyed him suspiciously: it was still three weeks before spawning season and she was feeling none too frisky. He opened his mouth to ask her about Foolex bodies and careened back in the current. The henfish, named Trudy, thought he was a dumb cluck and that she ought to work her way quickly past the riffle into the upper pool. Maybe this bird's clock was wrong. She had a rotten headache and feared he might even attack her.

Clyde, ever watchful, immediately deduced from her defensiveness that communication among trout, like communication between fly fishermen and bocce players, was impossible. He'd have to answer his questions by himself. This is never easy, particularly not on an empty stomach. He had not eaten anything since the pepperoni sandwich fifteen hours earlier, and he was not dumb enough to think he could soon get another, since the Belle Deli was two thousand miles away.

There was a silver flash and Clyde turned and shot up after it, turning on it as it slowed and turned and lifted up in the current. But he was too late. A little twelve-inch rainbow had sped from behind a large rock and grasped the thing, and it was now struggling with ludicrous futility across stream, the silver object stuck in its lower jaw.

"Incredible!" Clyde thought. "How could I have been so dumb?" He had not seen the hooks; he had not distinguished between metal and true scales. If he who had studied Halford, Skues, Marinaro, and Schwiebert could not distinguish a C.P. Swing from a dace tartare, what hope had any of his speckled kin? He shivered with fear as he asked himself, "Are *all* trout this dumb?"

He worked his way back under the upturned stump, into the eddy, and sulked. This was a grim business. He noticed he was trembling with acute anxiety neurosis but could not yet accept that *all* trout were neurotic. He was positively starved now and would have risen to spinach, which he hated.

Bits and pieces of debris, empty nymph shucks, a couple of grubs swept away into the eddy. He nosed them, bumped them, took them into his mouth, spit some of them out. By noon he had managed to nudge loose one half-dead stone-fly nymph, *Pteronarcys californica*; he had nabbed one measly earthworm; and he had found a few cased caddises. Most food, he noted, came off the bottom; that's where it's at. The lure had come down from the surface; he should have known. He was learning something new every minute.

By now he had recognized that he was in the Big Hole River, below Divide; he was sure he had once fished the pool. Settled into that eddy under the stump, he now knew why he had not raised a fish here: the current swung the food down below the undercut bank, but his flies had been too high up in the water. The way to fish this run was almost directly downstream from his present position, casting parallel to the bank so the nymph would have a chance to ride low and slip down into the eddy.

He was trying to plot the physics of the thing, from below, and was getting dizzy, when he realized he could starve flat down to death if he didn't stop trying to be a trout fisherman and settle for being a trout. His stomach felt pinched and dry; his jaw ached to clamp down on a fresh stone-fly nymph or, yes, a grasshopper. That's what he wanted. He suddenly had a mad letch for grasshoppers—and there was absolutely nothing he could do to get one. He was totally dependent upon chance. "A trout's lot," he thought, "is not a happy one."

Just then the surface rippled a bit, perhaps from a breeze, and a couple of yards upstream, he saw the telltale yellow body, kicking legs, and molded head of a grasshopper. It was August, and he knew the grasshoppers grew large around the Big Hole at that time of the year. It came to him quickly, he rose sharply to it, then stopped and fumed away with a smirk. "Not me. Uh uh. A Dave's Hopper if I ever saw one. Not for this guy." And as he thought this, Trudy swept downstream past him, too quick for him to warn, and nabbed the thing in an abrupt little splash. Then she turned, swam up by him, seemed to shake her head and say, "How dumb a cluck can you be?"

So it *had* been the real thing. Nature was imitating art now. Oh, he could taste the succulent hopper.

Another splatted down, juicy and alive, and he rose again, paused, and it shot downstream in a rush. He'd never know about that one.

Oh, the existential torment of it! "And I thought deciding which artificial fly to use was hard!"

Two more hoppers, then a third splatted down. He passed up one; lost a fin-race with Trudy for the third. She was becoming a pill.

He could bear it no longer. He'd even eat a Nick's Crazylegs if it came down. Anything. Anything to be done with the torment, the veil of unknowing, the inscrutability, which was worse than the pain in his gut, as it always is.

And then he saw it.

It was a huge, preposterous, feathered thing with a big black hook curled up under it. Some joker with three thumbs had thought it looked like a grasshopper. The body was made of Foolex. How could Oscar possibly have thought that body anything other than insulting? Clyde's hook jaw fumed up in a wry smile; he wiggled his adipose fin. The fly came down over him and he watched it safely from his eddy. And it came down again. Then again. Twelve. Thirteen times. Trudy had moved twice in its direction. He could tell she was getting fairly neurotic about it.

Foolex? That body could not fool an imbecile. It *was* an insult!

Eighteen. Twenty times the monstrosity came over him. He was fuming now. How *dare* someone throw something like that at him! Had they no respect whatsoever? If that's all fishermen thought of him, what did it matter. He was bored and hungry and suffering from a severe case of *angst* and humiliation. Nothing mattered. It was a trout's life.

He rose quickly and surely now, fuming as the thing swept down past him on the thirty-third cast. He saw it land in the surface eddy for a moment. He opened his mouth. Foolex? It infuriated him! It was the ultimate insult.

He lunged forward. And at the precise moment he knew exactly what trout see and why they strike, he stopped being a trout.

mari lyons

Very Minor Tactics on an English Chalkstream

An English chalkstream is a gentle, pastoral part of this frantic world. Limpid green and translucent, the river glides clear and steadily over flowing waterweed. Here and there a swallow or marten or finch dips and glides. Herefords graze in the lush meadow. Protected for centuries, guarded by riverkeeper and rule and club fiat, the water and its world are much like they were a thousand years ago. Yet on such gentle waters, within the frame of carefully fashioned codes, mighty dramas often transpire.

From a busy week in London, an American went one morning recently to the "Wilderness" section of the River Kennet in Berkshire, one of the noblest of the chalkstreams. The Kennet, carefully tended by the good riverkeeper Bernard, grows lusty trout to test the highest art of skilled fly fishers. John Goddard, who has taken three- and four-pound brown trout from these noble waters, usually passes the stern test. The American could not have had a better guide. And he had the company of Timothy Benn to advise him wisely about tactics.

The American had been to this river before. He had fished the Kennet several years earlier, for twelve hours. There were good trout in the Kennet—two- and three-pound browns—and he had seen many of them that day. You had to be careful to see the fish before the fish saw you, and the fish should be "on the fin," feeding. That was the code. You fished to the fish; you did not fish the water. And you fished only upstream, with a floating line. Often you had to kneel so that the trout would not see you, and the American marveled later that he had spent most of that day in the praying position, although, perhaps mistakenly, not for spiritual guidance. Often the casts had to be guided with deft skill through the maze of low branches, back branches, and high border weeds; the American only sometimes managed this but felt his flies lent a festive touch to the trees. And the trout spooked easily. The American had not gotten one of those large Kennet browns to move toward one of his flies.

But for two years he had dreamed of the river, and his dreams were mingled with the most cunning scheming. This time he was not without strategies. He had studied the minor tactics. He had learned the puddle cast. And he carried his lucky net.

But then, that morning, working hard and fishing to two or three good trout on the fin, he'd moved precisely no fish. He was not up to it. It was my youth, he thought in a paroxysm of shame, misspent worming and spinning. I am unworthy. And there is too little time to train the eye and hand for such noble work, let alone cleanse the soul.

The three had a pleasant lunch near the river, drank some wine, ate pâté, laughed, told tales, and then headed out again. Neil Patterson, a young friend who lived on the river and would meet them later, had left a map for the American indicating that in the upper region there were some "very interesting trout." It was good, the American thought, to know young men who knew interesting trout.

The wine had been cool and pleasant and the American had perhaps drunk a glass too much of it, which made three. He did not count as one of his very few virtues the ability to drink much wine or to remember the names of the wines he had drunk. They all sounded French. The afternoon was warm and he had eaten well and he had had that extra glass of wine, and he was feeling very content and hopeful when John Goddard spotted a steadily rising fish of about two pounds at the head of a broad pool. This proved to be a most interesting trout. Despite two slap casts, three linings, and an hour of more delicate work, the fish was still rising merrily to naturals with very slow, very deliberate rises. He is lunching at Simpson's, the American thought, and he has paid a pretty ten pounds sterling for the privilege, and he will not be disturbed by the traffic on the Strand or the punk-rock crowds at the Lyceum. He is quite intent on the business at hand and knows precisely what he has ordered.

So the American was pleased when John Goddard called downstream, "When you've had enough of him, come up here. I've spotted an interesting fish." Timothy Benn, who had taken a fine two-pounder that morning, positioned himself upstream with a camera to record properly the confrontation of the American with his new interesting trout.

The fish was feeding in a one-foot eddy behind a knobby root on the opposite side of the river. The American knew that the fish would not move an inch from that spot any more than the Simpson's trout would be disturbed at his selective lunching. He knew that an exceptional cast was needed—upstream, with some particular loops of slack, in close to the bank—for the fly to catch the feeding lane and float into the trout's dining room without drag. A puddle cast.

After four short casts and another two that led to drag, the American was sure he could not manage this minor tactic. It was subtler fishing than he was used to, and he was not impressed with his ability to move Kennet trout. But he had not put it down. The occasional sip-rises in the eddy continued. The fish might be quite large.

And then the American managed an able puddle cast beyond his wildest hopes and the fly floated a foot or two and went calmly into the trout's domain, and he heard someone whisper, "He'll come this time," and miracle of miracles, the trout did.

The trout rose, was hooked, made a low jump, came clear of the stump and then streaked downstream, its back bulging the surface, its force bending the bamboo rod sharply. A very good fish. Better than two pounds.

From that point on, the American was not sure why he acted the way he did. Perhaps it was that he had just read something about getting below a fish, which proved that fishermen should read fewer books. Perhaps it was the extra glass of wine. More likely it was pure panic.

The American bolted. He began high-stepping downriver, busting, bursting the pastoral quiet of the chalkstream with his wild splashes. He heard one of his companions, in a high, incredulous, voice ask: "*Where* are you going?"

The trout, which had never witnessed a performance like this, and considered it extremely poor form, raced farther from the area in sheer embarrassment.

Then the American did something else he later could not explain. With the trout still green, he grasped for his lucky net.

The net was of the teardrop variety and had been bought in the Catskills and treasured for many years. The American carried it loose in his ArctiCreel, where it was safe from the brush. In fact, only a half-hour earlier he had advised his English friends that this was a much more suitable net than the long-handled nets they carried, and that it could be carried in the creel, safe from the brush, out of harm's way, until needed.

The American grasped the handle of the net and wrestled it from his creel. In so doing, out came his fly box. This was his prized fly box, a Wheatley, the most expensive kind of Wheatley, with compartments on both sides, and he had filled it for this trip with some of his choicest flies—flies by Flick and Troth and Whitlock and Leiser.

The fly box twisted in the meshes of the tangled net bag, teetered on the rim while the American did a jig and a hop, midstream, then popped free and landed open on the limpid water of the Kennet and began to float serenely off to the left.

The trout was headed right.

The gentleman with the camera was reloading film at the precise moment the American had to choose between the fly box and the trout, so there is no visual record of the sudden swerve to the left, the deft netting of one fat Wheatley fly box; and since the trout had turned the bend, no one except the American saw the roll on the surface and the positive smirk as one very interesting trout rejoiced that on the other end of the line there had been such a raving maniac.

Later, the men gathered near the bridge on the main river and drank a bit more wine. Neil Patterson and another pleasant member of the club were with them now, and there was good talk and the spirited camaraderie uniquely possible along trout streams. Someone suggested that the Simpson's trout was merely one of Patterson's tethered pets, and someone else suggested that it was good the American's fly had pulled loose from the interesting trout because Bernard did not like his Kennet browns festooned like Christmas trees. The American was quietly satisfied that he would never had stooped quite so low as that.

Then John Goddard mentioned the big trout beneath the bridge and the American was invited to have a go at him. Not for me, he thought. Old Oscar—the not-to-be-caught behemoth brown. Not *that* fish—and not with *this* audience.

But the fish was high in the water, on the fin, taking the odd sedge a few feet under the bridge, and in a few moments, unable to resist, the American was tying on a Colorado King with shaky hands, squinting into the angular sun. And a few moments later he had made a truly classic puddle cast, holding the rod high and stopping the line short so that the current had three feet of slack to consume before the fly dragged.

The fly came down three inches from Old Oscar's nose. The chorus of onlookers, standing in a semicircle behind him, grew ominously silent. Old Oscar turned and floated down with the fly a few inches. The chorus abruptly released breath, in a quiet whoosh.

Old Oscar took.

And the American struck, with no time to think of all the subtle minor tactics he had learned ... and neatly snapped the fly off in the fish.

In a Fishing Hut

In a fishing hut on the Bensham water of the River Kennet in Berkshire, I ate a sloppy cucumber sandwich, drank a mild white wine, and listened with the rest of the company gathered out of the storm as the stories began.

There was one about a lunatic who fished with bait and tied the line to his left big toe and got pulled in by a conger eel.

"I think someone is pulling your toe," said John Goddard, and he told a long, slow, very droll tale about a backcast that deftly hooked the ear of a Holstein cow, which then took off in high dudgeon across a muddy field, making the reel truly scream.

"They'll give you a great fight on light tackle," someone said.

It was warm in the fishing hut. The riverkeeper had started up a bright red fire in the cast-iron stove. I had caught my first Kennet brown that morning, and there was a profusion of food on the low center table and bottles of wine and thermos bottles of hot tea and coffee. From the open farmer's market in Newbury, Tim has bought fresh bright-yellow butter. rolls, cucumbers, a couple of different cheeses, a local pâté, and some sweet rolls—a feast. John had his usual pantry of delicacies. Hoagy and Kathy and Ross had their basket, and we were all sharing and drinking a little and bemoaning the fact that The Mayfly (important enough to be capitalized like that) had all but passed and the trout were surely glutted, and probably, anyway, it would be impossible to catch anything with such a sharp downstream wind in such a cold, pelting rain. Still, I had taken one—no matter that John had called: "What is it? A trout? Is that *really* a trout?"

When we came to the little wooden fishing hut, I had pointed out to Mari a few of The Mayfly spinners caught in spiderwebs at the edges of the window, *Ephemera danica*. It is a big fly, only a bit smaller than our Green Drake, and often it itches and goads every fish in the river to feed on the surface. Some of the stories, which were by now mingling like the fresh pipe and cigar smoke in the tiny room, concerned the awesome spectacle of The Mayfly. Someone said he had seen eight regularly feeding fish in fixed positions in the lower end of the huge mill pool and had taken all eight of them, just like that, carefully, in order. Someone else had taken fifty-five pounds of brown trout one day during The Mayfly last year. Merely two days ago, Neil Patterson said, he could positively have *promised* me a dozen trout.

This did not trouble me overly. I have been there before. Aren't I always a couple of days late, a week early? Times too numerous to mention. And anyway, I had taken my first Kennet brown only that morning.

Someone suggested that perhaps the heavy winds would flush all the remaining spinners out of the bushes and branches. Then there might well be some real action later in the afternoon.

For a moment the little hut was lit with quiet excitement. The Mayfly might still be on! There in the little wooden hut, crammed with John and Neil and Tim and Mari and me and Hoagy and the riverkeeper and Kathy and Ross, crammed with stories and theories and past dreams and triumphs and recollections, anything seemed possible. Hope was a thing with a big white body and gossamer wings, and I noticed one or two such things over the dark cold water outside the window.

But there was some debate about what would and what would not happen, and the consensus of those who knew suggested that even *should* there be enough spinners left to interest the trout, and even *should* the wind flush them free and they should drop on the water, the downstream wind would make upstream dry-fly casting too difficult, the flies would be whisked off the water before the low-in-the-water trout could get to them, and anyway, the fish were glutted.

The logic of this position was undeniable, and I for one was inclined to accept it. Anyway, the weather outside was truly putrid and the cucumber sandwiches with fresh butter were getting better and better. I had risen steadily to five of them.

In fact, no one was rushing outside and everyone was dipping a bit deeper into a corner or low in a chair, and it was cozily warm and the food was good and the quiet buzz-buzz of good talk was making me feel as comfortable as Winnie the Pooh. I did mention that, outside, there was a little snowstorm—or at least some flurries—of Mayfly spinners, sent fluttering in the wind. I raised myself a bit to watch the water and followed two of them down through the main pool. They floated merrily, a cucumber sandwich to any hungry trout, and then they disappeared—undisturbed—into a lower riffle. There was nothing, really, to make me get up. I liked the talk, which in one quarter had shifted to fly rods—and I was now listening intently to talk of tapers and relative performances.

Then Hoagy asked if I'd like to see a few fly rods he had with him, and I rose to that prospect very quickly. He fetched them from his car and they proved very much worth rising to. There was an odd glass Payne that felt like a hollow stalk of dried milkweed in my hand. There was one of Hoagy's own rods and though he made this a bit heavy—for his own use, as he liked them—and it was too heavy for me, the rod was clearly a superb tool and made with a master craftsman's skill. Then he took out an Everett Garrison made especially for Everett Garrison. Hoagy said the old master had given it to him on the condition that it be used, not kept in a closet. Hoagy had so treated it. I said I wished I had his guts. I have four or five pieces of fine bamboo that don't regularly see water—out of fear, pure fear. Still, I'm not a collector and fishing is what rods are made for. I made a few brave resolutions, out loud, to use my own classic bamboo a bit more often—especially on water like the Kennet.

Afraid to try Hoagy's Garrison, I tried a piece of his smoked kipper instead and then made myself another sandwich. I had had six butter-and-cucumber sandwiches, two butter-and-cheese, and three butter-and-pâté; now I tried a large butter-and-butter sandwich and found it exquisitely delicious. Mari frowned. I shrugged and told her quietly that the butter was really irresistible. She muttered something wise and glum about all food being irresistible to me. I told her this was positively my last sandwich, and anyway, could she please be wise and concerned a bit later so I could hear about the fifty—or was it eighty?— big brook trout that Hoagy and some pals were currently catching in Labrador.

Before this story was resolved, Neil was somehow in the middle of a wild, interminable trip through France, headed for the Risle with a friend who mysteriously stopped at every available bar and collected pocketfuls of sugar.

Meanwhile, John Goddard—the master of the chalkstream— was telling how, on a trip to Norway, the host had forgotten to bring the packages of food and he had to provide fish for the entire party and resorted to an old poacher's trick of sending out into the lake a dozen flies attached to a hinged instrument that ...

"And then a monstrous dog jumped out," said Neil, "and my friend plunged his hand into his pockets ..."

"You're pulling my toe!"

"The butter is really superb."

"... one hundred and thirty-seven brook trout averaging ..."

"Did the cow *really* ..."

"... and the dog lay down on the floor with all the sugar and licked his paws and smiled the most contented ..."

The flurry of spinners had stopped and so had the wind. With great effort I rose to my feet and boldly suggested we try to fish again. Wasn't that a touch of sun? No, it was lightning, someone said. Didn't *anyone* want to fish? Not particularly, it seemed. I reached for a knife to cut myself a slab of straight butter, but Mari touched my hand wisely. So I went outside and in a few moments the others followed sluggishly.

Later, as I came around the bend of a carrier into a field of cows, I looked so intently at the ear of one of them that I failed to watch where I was stepping and stepped blithely into a mud sink. A lot of cows had stomped and relieved themselves there. It was quite soft and ucky. So I sank. I sank well down to my thighs and then sank a bit more down into the muck. Neil, who was guiding me, turned and said, "What the hell are you doing?" He was standing on a hard mound of grass and seemed to be walking on top of the mud. "I didn't think such things really happened to you," he said. "I thought you made them up, that they were stories. Let me take your rod."

I gave it to him, glad it was not one of my prized bamboos, and continued to tread water in the mud for another minute or two. Something in my frantic motions made the nearby cow look intently at me and give a gigantic moo. Instantly, every other cow in the large field—there may have been a hundred of them—turned, shifted position, and eyed me intently.

Neil laughed.

The cows did not.

Later, back in the hut, I became one of the stories, and I tried to drown my embarrassment in one last cucumber-and-butter sandwich, but Mari said if I didn't eat so much, maybe I would not nearly die in the mud. There was talk that the "Wilderness" section of the Kennet had been laid fallow this year because last year I had festooned the fish with so many flies and they needed time to work them out. Neil began to recount, in some happy detail, my near demise in the mud, but I interrupted him and said that I had often heard of angling writers who walked on water but none, like him, who walked on mud.

The Fascination of What Is Difficult

"How do you cast?" I asked, eyeing the row of coarse high weed in front of me, the low-branched maple behind my right shoulder. Beyond the weeds I could still see, if barely, the vague form of the brown trout; it was two feet downstream from where the slight riffle broke, raised up into midwater, feeding. It was not small.

If my backcast was perfect—no more than four feet above the ground, with a tight loop, and if I could then just lift it slightly above the weed, and then shoot just enough line—I might possibly get a foot of clear float before the fly came over the trout. But I would have to snake the line a little. And hook it a little to the left. And I would have to turn the line over at just the right moment. And I was kneeling, on both knees, stretching high to see over the weed, then bending to get low enough to backcast under the branches. I do not cast precisely like a dream while standing and doubted if a cast from this position would be much better than a nightmare. My son Anthony was watching from behind the left side of the tree. No, I could not possibly hook *him*. Brian was safely farther left. They were watching me intently. I did not especially want to flub this cast, too.

What to do?

I had already spent ten minutes playing Toulouse-Lautrec, knee-walking, ever so slowly, to this position. The trout had not spooked yet, but I did not think I could chance another movement. I would get one cast, perhaps two. "How the blazes do you *cast*?" I asked again, in a hoarse whisper.

"With great difficulty," said Brian, a second before my backcast reached tentatively behind me, straightened, and did not come forward. It had happened like this twice before that morning; it would happen several more times before the day was done.

I was on the "Wilderness" section of the Kennet—exquisite water, perhaps the choicest in England—with Brian Clarke and John Goddard, two of Britain's finest chalkstream fishermen. It was my first day on a chalkstream, and I was being instructed— by friend and ritual and circumstance—in the fascination of what is difficult. Fascination, not frustration. Challenge, not futility.

The fish were there. Dozens of them. As we walked cautiously along the bank of the main stem and then up the smaller, clearer carriers, we could see them—fine, nearly wild brown trout in the two- to three-pound class. Brian, in the morning, and then John, always saw them first; then, following the line of a finger, peering into water as clear as that in a glass, I would catch a hint, a motion, a break in the color, and there it would be, a brightly spotted trout, facing upstream, moving on occasion to one side or the other, always wary.

I had always prided myself on my eyes. I had begun to fish on hard-pounded public rivers, and I had learned to read water because that was the only way you had a chance to take a decent fish. When I had heard, before we started out that morning, that on British chalkstreams one was expected to cast upstream with a floating line and had to fish, always, to a sighted fish, I had thought these quaint, arbitrary customs. I was willing, in England, to do as my English friends did, but I could not quite believe the code was more than an antiquated ritual, an amusingly perverse way of making a simple, lovely pastime outrageously complex. Even impossible.

"This is tough fishing, Dad," Anthony whispered to me a few times as he trudged along with us bravely, without a rod, watching, hoping I would get at least one fish.

"Too tough for me, old man," I said.

"But you're a famous fisherman," he said. "You don't want to go a whole day with these guys and not catch anything. It's humiliating."

"I've made my reputation on precisely that," I said. I said it quietly. "Anyway, it's more fun when it's hard. Isn't it?"

"I think it's fun to catch fish," he said.

After I had spooked four trout before I saw them, I realized that I was unprepared for this sort of game, out of my league. I was even tempted once, when I was alone, to shuffle out a little downstream cast—may the gods forgive me—but got a good, honorable hold on myself in time.

Yet after I had followed Brian's finger and then John's a dozen times, out over the high weed and down into some pellucid run, I realized that the laws were not merely arbitrary. I could justify them *aesthetically*—for these waters. I could also justify them as restrictions that drew forth abilities admirably suited to such demanding rivers. Brian and John had learned to *see* trout before trout saw them, just as I had once learned to read water. Shadows, hints of shadows, the slight opening of a trout's mouth, the undulating movement of its body, the minutest break in the prismic fabric of the water, the rose moles on a fish's back—these and a dozen other muted, subtle sights had of necessity become telltale hieroglyphs to these men. They saw with a finer eye, walked with gentler tread, had learned to make every cast count. No Halford purists, they had championed upstream nymph fishing, with shrimp imitations and the butt of the leader greased to announce the take; they were innovative and maverick but within the basic parameters of a difficult code that contained a built-in beauty as well as a built-in challenge. They loved this fishing especially for its difficulty.

And so, as the day wore on, did I.

Not that I managed it with even rudimentary skill; not that I managed even to move *one* of those fine, wary trout; it was *too* difficult for me that first day, a bit beyond my skill of hand or eye. Oh, Brian and John tried. They found fish for me in open water and in narrow channels. They dazzled me with what they saw and I could not see. We meandered with the river, talking quietly, becoming closer friends, watching—always watching the water. Often we would go ten or fifteen minutes before we saw a trout, ("More walking and looking than fishing," Anthony said). Then, intensely, one of us would stalk a fish, work ever so slowly into position, make one or two or perhaps three casts before the fish scooted off. They provided the proper flies, nymphs and shrimp of their own design. They even took several fish apiece before the long glorious day was over, perhaps to convince me that it could be done. ("Why don't *you* ever get one?" asked Anthony.) But I was skunked. Curiously, I was humbled but not frustrated; my imagination was piqued by it all, not turned off. I had, after all, learned immensely; my pleasure, and it was of the rarest sort, was quite independent from fish catching.

Don Zahner once advised me: "You're downgrading yourself too much, Nick. You're not nearly so bad a fisherman as you make out." I didn't mind the faint praise then, the back-handed compliment; and since that advice I have sincerely tried to catch a few fish now and then, not merely play the lunatic bumbler along the streams that touch my heart. The humbling I felt that day was a good rung or two above the embarrassment I usually feel. Without self-irony, I can report it frankly. There was no dishonor to not catching fish in the Kennet in high summer when no fish were rising. There was only an increasing fascination with what was difficult—crystalline water, wary trout, tough casts, an exacting ethic. When dark came,

I was as exhausted and shivering from the intensity of this thing as I'd have been had I taken a truly monstrous trout. And in the car heading back to London, I vowed that as I grew older, I would value, more and more, fishing that is choice and hard.

Later that week I fished Dermot Wilson's water on the Test and faired somewhat better. It was not easy fishing—at least not for me—but the fish were quite large and I was, frankly, delighted to take a few from such genial, storied water. Even then, though, I envied an English companion who quietly passed up the open water there and fished a minute nymph seventy feet across stream, across braided currents, and took some smaller but quite difficult fish against the far bank. He could not resist the greatest challenges any more than I could resist, that day, taking a few fish.

It is rumored that Dermot helped Anthony "in some small way" to catch that huge brown trout the boy kept safely for three hours for me to see. The fish was perhaps five pounds, handsomely formed, with a sharply hooked jaw and gigantic red spots. Anthony thought it even larger, and indeed it has grown in his reports of that day to eight, ten, and now even twelve pounds.

"It wasn't *that* hard," Anthony said nonchalantly, when he finally released a fly-caught brown larger than any I have ever taken. "It gave a terrific fight; it ran all over the place; but I finally got it. I could have taken ten more like that and not minded. It couldn't be too easy for me. I wouldn't have been bored. I *like* to catch big fish."

I watched the huge trout waver heavily on its side, turn back up, and at least glide off. Anthony was full of pride at his catch, regretting that he could not haul it around with him for the next six months and show it to all his New York chums. I thought of my friend who chose to fish the toughest stretch of the Test, of John and Brian and their hawk's eyes; I thought that someday I would grow young enough again to feel Anthony's delight and wise enough to take a truly difficult trout.

The Last Chalkstream Idyll

There is a story by Morley Callaghan about a pleasant chap who took a job as an itinerant hangman because his travels led him to such interesting new places to fish. Callaghan is the huge Canadian writer who once beat up Hemingway in a Paris gym; he beat him so stoutly that the timekeeper, Scott Fitzgerald—astounded perhaps—let the round go on for several extra minutes. Hemingway never forgave either of them.

One dose of the British chalkstreams some years ago and I thought I'd lost my heart to them completely—and promptly allowed myself to become an entire subsidiary in the colonies of a British firm, with the caveat that I go to England once a year, in early June, in time for the famous Mayfly hatch.

I'd hole up with the accountants and the empire builders for a week and then head off to Berkshire and the haunting Kennet River. There, hosted by Brian Clarke, John Goddard, or Neil Patterson, I'd flutter indelicately around the river, quite unlike the ghostly Mayfly spinner. It was the choicest of fishing. Neil or Brian or John would husband me along the main stem or one of the carriers, eyes peeled for a rise or a fish "on the fin." It was gorgeous water—pellucid, trouty, mined with weed. They'd spot fish I couldn't have seen with a telescope, and then I'd creep into some ghastly uncomfortable position—on my knees in high grass, perhaps—and attempt to cast to the big brown. They were good fish: better than a pound, up to three or four.

The first year I caught none; nor the second, then one year it rained and I ate cucumber sandwiches in the tiny fishing hut all day and practically did not cast. Each time the Mayfly had been on the week before and *everyone* had taken fish. I shoulda been there. The weights were all carefully remembered—"one pound eight," "two pounds four," "three pounds six," "four pounds one." Then I got one, too small to have a weight, and lost one (with all my experts watching) that, on John's sharp "eye scale," went "better than four pounds two."

All that traipsing around in hip boots, waiting for a fish to show (or someone to show one to me), was less than kind and not at all comfortable. Choice as it might be, there were times when I longed for a good old egalitarian American river, where you can spend most of the day casting, not looking. And I had more than my share of disasters: losing that big fish amid the blistering silence of my audience; wading chest-deep, in my new Harris tweed jacket, into the muck, on which I thought, perhaps, I could walk. But by my fourth year I thought I knew my way around that territory.

I had two happy days on the Kennet that year. The Mayfly was off but a friendly little brown sedge was on. They'd dredged the river to get rid of the heavy weed growth, and though it wasn't as pretty, there were more fish and fish happened to be taking all day. Never one for figures, I can't quote you the pound and ounce on them, but I must have taken seven or eight, the largest about three pounds, and I was deliciously smug about my performance.

Toward evening on my last day, I was fishing an upper reach that had just been dredged. The water was quite deep and a bit discolored from the soft soil, so I stayed on the high bank and cast comfortably to several rising fish. The two days had been immensely satisfying and without disaster; I'd taken most of the fish I hooked and felt I'd gotten to know the river better. When we walked down to the river from Neil's house, Neil had said that my success was a relief to everyone. It was surely a relief to me. I'd heard someone's wife, brought to the Kennet with some promise of seeing the American clown perform at this annual carnival, say: "I thought you said funny things happened when this bloke came here. I'm terribly disappointed." Well, you can't please everyone.

I felt quite content, standing on the rim of that mud mound, casting a little brown sedge to the circles. I looked out over the gentle Berkshire fields, at the pinkish sky along the horizon line, at the water as it slipped beneath an old wooden bridge, eddied, grew riffles, and spread out into this long flat pool, and then, suddenly, a truly large fish rose. I struck lightly, it thrashed at the surface, and then it bore upstream heavily. It was the largest fish I'd had on in the Kennet, better than four pounds, possibly five. From my height, I had the advantage on it and easily walked upstream and down, several times, to keep it above me. In ten minutes it tired and came close to the shore and I was positive it was a full five pounds. But how to net it? I was four or five feet above the surface of the water, no one was around, and I had no net with me.

I played the fish a bit more, until he turned sideways and quiet; then I lay full length on the soft dredged sod and put the rod on the ground beside me. I grasped the line, leaned as far over as I dared, and came eight or ten inches short of the fish. The 6X leader would scarcely allow me to raise it out of the water. What to do? The evening was growing late and misty and there were ten or twelve circles of rising fish in the pool. I wanted to catch another, perhaps two; I'd waited four years for a night like this. I even thought of breaking the leader off, but it would have been most ungracious to leave my fly in such a fish.

At last, not knowing how deep the water was, I decided to climb down the bank, digging my feet into the soft mud as I went. A lousy decision. I began to slip down the mud bank, couldn't stop myself, and went into the water, then went on down to the bottom of the river, which was six or seven feet deep there.

I have been dunked a couple of other times in my life, once in mud; I knew at once it could be treacherous, even fatal. So I forced myself up against the bank, got my head above water, screamed valiantly for help, and clawed at the mud wall. It didn't hold. No one came. I kept slipping back, gobs of mud in my hands, on my face, my hat off and sailing downstream, the fish gone now, mud dripping down my jacket, into my shirt, filling my hip boots. For a moment or two I was quite sure I was on my way to the Great Chalkstream in the Sky. Like Everyman, I wasn't ready.

The water and mud in my hip boots made them too heavy for me to kick, the mud kept tearing away as I clawed more and more desperately into it with my hands, and I slipped back under the water twice, gurgling and choking.

The disappointed wife would have gotten her money's worth.

I've often wondered whether the crowd of them would have been too doubled over with laughter to haul me out.

In the end, I must have levitated up that mud bank, out of fear or desperation, and when I got there, I lay full face on the ground, quietly, spitting out a bit of Kennet now and then, for a full five minutes. Then I checked my rod and headed downstream to tell Neil about all the fish that were still rising.

It's more than two years since that evening. I left England the next day, disengaged myself from that firm, and have not been back.

Recently, though, I found the photocopy of a letter Neil wrote to another friend, describing the event. He probably exaggerated when he says I looked like a water buffalo, fresh from a mud bath; and I'm sure he didn't *really* laugh for ten days—and if he did, deep down he'd have been truly sad if I'd become one with the Kennet; and I doubt if my "bum print" is worth preserving on his bathroom wall, where, still plastered with mud, I must have leaned my weary rump a moment.

I didn't please the wife during that last chalkstream idyll, but Neil seems to have gained a historic monument. He shows it to everyone. Lefty Kreh—who never falls in and has been zapping those Kennet browns and regaining the honor of the colonies—told me he had been shown that spot with great reverence. It ain't that important to me. It's just another place where I almost got hung.

Mari Lyons

Mornings

Every morning around ten, for thirty-one days, we'd stash our gear in the huge tan Suburban and head for the river. We'd head up the first hill, onto the highest bench, then rattle along the single rutted lane across the fields of wheatgrasses spotted with dark-green weed and sweet clover and pale-yellow prickly pear. There were always clusters of antelope in the fields. Often they would watch us—inert, wary, turning slightly so as always to be facing the car—until we came close enough to be a threat, though we were no threat. Often there were several spindly legged fawns with them, born several weeks earlier; Herb had seen a doe drop one in the narrow road, and he had stopped and watched and then gone around them. "Not enough meat to make a decent sandwich," he once said in his deep voice—the words always curt, final—watching a newborn antelope scamper away, already quick and lithe. Overhead, curlews with long curved beaks canted away, shrieking, and often we saw their chicks, which had no beaks yet, scuttling from us into the grasses.

Every morning, at the bluff that ended the last bench, we would stop the car and get out, and then look down into the valley, stretching off in front of us as far as we could see, with several braids of the river meandering through it like a blue ribbon stretched out casually upon a great green and tan rug. Except for the willows on the inner rim of the bench, near the headwaters of the East Branch, and the ragged line of cottonwoods in the distance, there were no trees: the river lay open and exposed and I knew at once that it would be hard to fish, with no cover, no breaks from the sun, with every movement of rod or line or person taken to be one of the trout's great predators here—pelican, osprey, kingfisher, merganser, heron, gull. An anthropologist who visited compared it to the Serengeti Plain, and it has the same broad fertile space.

We'd have the whole day, from then until dark, to fish the river. We could fish it anywhere we chose—miles and miles of it. We could fish it as hard or in as leisurely a manner as suited our fancy. We could go back to the ranch for lunch, or pack in a sandwich or some elk stick, or fish straight through, hard, intently. Sometimes Pat, Herb's wife, and Mari would bring down lunch in the other Suburban.

I soon realized that Spring Creek was the most interesting river I had ever fished or could imagine; and I learned that it was loaded with secrets that would take exceptional skill to learn. At first I felt very privileged to be fishing the river, but soon my thoughts turned chiefly to where we'd fish and what the fishing would be like and when it would come and what fishing we'd already had. Within a week, the days blurred and I had to concentrate to separate them, keep them in sequence, though I have had no trouble finding in my brain the full and vivid picture of a hundred moments, most of the fish I raised for the month I was there. Those were halcyon days and they changed my flyfishing forever.

From the top of the last bench the river looked blue, though up close it was green and blue and a dozen variants of amber, umber, coral, and beige; it was really colorless as water in a glass, pure spring water, but it took on the hues of its bottom and of the banks. Sometimes the crystalline water was slow and moody or flat; then there were the fifty or so great bends of the West Branch, some tight, some broad as avenues: there were riffles and chops and pools and tails and swampy runs and brisk runs and shallow flats a couple of hundred feet across, all in dozens of configurations, so that there were thousands of different fishing chances. Everywhere, the water was the clearest I'd ever seen, water in which the auburn, spotted forms of the trout and the wavering, hairlike masses of elodea and watercress were ghostlike. The river held trout large enough to make my eyes pop—mostly browns, all wild, with a scattering of rainbows—which would rise to flies the size of gnats. Nursed on the muddy, milky waters of the Croton watershed near New York City, where I had fished with worms and spinning lures, it all spooked me silly. The river seemed quite beyond the meager talents I thought I could bring to it.

When the wind did not ruffle the surface of the river too harshly—giving it a slate, opaque cover—the water was so translucent that you could see distinctly to the bottom of the deepest pools. What I could see in some of them, five to eight feet down, wavering like living shadows near the bottom, sent shock waves through me.

We would stop at the final bluff to look for the blue herons, which pecked holes in even very large trout and killed many smaller fish. They were astonishing hunters and several times I saw one result of their efforts: a beautiful, wild brown trout with a hole right on the top of its back, as if someone had shoved a pencil down an inch or so, very hard. Herb did not like them. "They can't even pick up some of the larger trout they stick," he said. After I'd seen three with that raw pencil hole in their backs, I felt the same, let the Audubon Society be damned. If there was a heron hunting, it would usually whirl into flight, its gigantic wings flapping heavily, merely at our appearance more than several hundred yards away. I never saw one until it was in flight, and at first mistook the six or seven pairs of sandhill cranes that nested in the valley for herons—though the sandhills traveled in pairs, the herons always alone.

We'd look for several minutes from the bluff, standing quite still and sometimes shivering from the early cold, and begin to think about the day and the weather and the flies and what had happened the day before and which section of Spring Creek we'd fish that day. Then we'd head down the last hill.

Now there was nothing to think about but the fishing. It was a truly remarkable river, but on a given day you could catch nothing; during the weeks I was there, three people—all fine fishermen— got skunked. Once I got none; Herb always got fish. Flies might hatch upriver but now down. The sun might be too bright, the wind too strong, relentless. The large pool on the East Branch might explode with feeding fish or remain perfectly placid, as if it did not contain a trout. The Two Islands Pool might go berserk. The Great Horseshoe Bend—as distinguished from many lesser Horseshoe Bends—might look barren, or might have one, three, or thirty fish rising. But once I had looked into several of the deepest pools I knew something of what the river contained, everywhere, and a shiver of expectation ran through me every time I looked at the water, anywhere, or pitched a fly into it, and still does even now, years later, whenever I think of Spring Creek.

In the deep pools, when the light was just right, you could see fifty or sixty wild browns, of all sizes—a few ten-inchers, a whole slew of fish between fifteen and nineteen inches, and a few old alligators that would go twenty-three or more. Sometimes, concentrating on some deeply undercut bank, if you were lucky, you could catch a glimpse of something dark and larger than anything your imagination could conjure. Was twenty-six or twenty-eight inches an exaggeration? I don't think so. Several times, fishing carelessly up the West Branch, I'd spook one of those old fellows and it would bolt from a dark bank—black and too slow for a trout, as if it really wasn't afraid of me or anything else in this world, though prudence dictated it move: a fish the size of a muskrat or a dog, coming right past me, black and thick, scaring me half out of my boots.

But Spring Creek was also a place where solitude and quiet camaraderie were possible. It might be a river crammed with wild trout of great average size and great wariness, a place where I had more interesting fishing chances than I could imagine having anywhere else, but it was also a place where I made some great friends and learned more than I can tell.

At the bottom of the hill there was a shallow stretch of the river that the Suburban could ford easily. But usually before we crossed we made a short trip downstream to the right and the Suburban leaned down toward the river and I leaned over Herb's shoulder to see the water. On the way back to the crossing, with the vehicle dipping low on my side now, I had an unobstructed view of the river. The water was thin here—perhaps a foot to eighteen inches deep, over a sandy bottom, spotted with waterweed. Darting across the bottom, their shadows more palpable than their bodies, were a couple dozen trout. They were long and tan—some darker than others—and from the car we never saw them at rest. They were elusive, evanescent; they seemed born paranoids, afraid of every motion, every shadow. I hadn't the faintest idea how to approach them, or how to catch such fish, but they were beautiful to watch in their wildness, and they were very large—some twenty-two inches or more—and they gave to each morning a kind of benediction. And they always roused my metabolism. I called this the Paranoid Pool and, from the beginning, I never expected to catch a fish in it, though Herb said there were times, when there was a slight chop on the water perhaps, when the fish could be caught, when you might gain entrance to the Castle. As day after day passed, I grew more and more determined to be skillful enough to catch one of these fish, fish as tough to catch as any I have ever seen. By the third week I had found half a dozen such spots on the river, many of them even more difficult to fish.

Below the Paranoid Pool there was a huge shallow flat, several hundred feet across and twice as long, and then the water narrowed, rushed against the far bank, split off into a back channel and disappeared, and the main current formed an exquisite run of several hundred yards that emptied into a broad right-angle bend as the back channel joined the main flow below the island. This was a deep pool, braided with a farrago of currents; it held a great head of trout and you could usually take a fish or two here, whatever the circumstances, but it was very hard to fish wisely and consistently well.

After we'd looked at the Farrago Pool we'd head back, then ford the river and rumble slowly up the rutted and pitted dirt track that skirted the dozens of S curves of the West Branch, looking for flies or rises, flushing more curlew and their chicks, as well as little killdeer that hugged the road and then disappeared into the grasses, spotting a white-tailed deer or a cluster of sandhill cranes beyond the fence that kept the cattle from trampling the banks of the river. In places you could see where an oxbow had silted in, grown grass, and caused the river to adjust its path. The older routes were a delicate, lighter, fresher green than the other grasses. Herb had been advised to tinker with the river, to add structures that would help prevent the silting of bends, but his principle of conservation was abrupt and final: leave it alone. He believed that the river would change, shift, adjust, suffer, flourish, and take quite good care of itself, thank you. Fencing out the cattle was an exception. And once he and I, on a scorching July afternoon, planted about a hundred willow shoots—none of which survived.

As we drove slowly down the West Branch, we'd hear the ice in the lemonade jug rattle, and we'd keep an eye peeled to the river. We'd always pass the decaying carcass of a calf struck by lightning that spring, and I'd always look to see if it was less of itself. The interior had collapsed and the skin kept getting tighter. At first there was an eager mass of insects everywhere on it, but as the season progressed the carcass kept shrinking, as if by itself, as if it was struggling to get gone from this place. The carcass always made me think of Richard Eberhart's poem "The Groundhog," where that little creature keeps decaying until, near the end, the poet sees merely the beautiful architecture of its bones and then, at the very end, when there is less than a spot, thinks of Alexander in his tent and Saint Theresa in her wild lament, and about mortality and such large matters. The calf carcass didn't vanish that summer; it was too tough. But it decreased. I tried to find some metaphor in it but decided to let it remain simply a decaying calf's carcass, several yards east of a run that led to one of the best back bends on the West Branch.

In fifteen minutes we'd be at the south end of the property, opposite a huge bend pool that pinched into a slick that you could watch comfortably from the warm car while the world warmed. We rarely saw fish move on our early trip upriver, though we often paused at several of the larger bends for a moment or two. At the south end we had an unobstructed view of a lovely run; its glassy surface and slight gradient let us see instantly the slightest bulge on the surface.

Herb usually saw signs of fish first.

He'd point and I'd have to look closely and then I'd see a dorsal slightly breaking the surface, or bending reeds near the far point, or a wake, or the delicate spreading flower of a sipping rise, or a quick black head, up then down.

Herb and I had exchanged hundreds of letters—often several a week—in the years before I first fished Spring Creek with him. Though he did not tie, his observations on fly design, the attitude of flies on the water, knots, new gadgets, leaders, fly-rod length and design and action, technological improvements of various kinds, books old and new, and dozens of other fly-fishing subjects were acute and frank. He fished only with the dry fly and his observations were directed exclusively to matters connected to a fly that floats—but the word "purist" would sound silly if I used it to describe anything about him. He had more fun fishing the dry fly; he conceded the rest of the river to the trout; he enjoyed that visual connection to his quarry—the link that occurs where our world of air meets theirs, on the surface. He could be growly on the subject, claiming that he was a "fly" fisherman, not an "artificial bait" fisherman, but the heart of the matter was less philosophy than hedonism, I think: he enjoyed the one more than the other.

He had clearly read far more than I ever will about fly fishing and he read with a shrewd and independent mind, guffawing at pretenders and second-handers and people who didn't give credit and "light-weights" (a favorite term of his), even if I had published or edited or introduced such people. An English friend—the author of half a dozen books on fly fishing—said: "he has a wonderfully grumpy, bollocking exterior which hides a man of great kindness. He is also a remarkable fly fisherman and makes me feel like a novice." I did not know when I flew out to be with him whether he was the superb fly fisher the Englishman and others said he was, but his opinions were sharp, often raw, always telling, even when they made me smart. What he did he insisted upon doing deftly. He spoke abruptly, sometimes in half sentences, often with laconic wit, in a low baritone. He scared the socks off at least one mutual friend. Thinking back, these many years later, I realize that mingled with the special expectation you feel when you sense you are about to begin the new and unknown was the nagging sense that we were from wildly different worlds, that up close the visit would prove a disaster.

I came full of expectation and some trepidation, and then, as early as that first morning, I forgot what I had expected and whatever it was I might have feared, and thought only of the water before us and the discrete possibilities of the day. The days were crammed with surprises anyway, of the kind that any great river provides, and I could not have imagined what happened any more than I have the imagination to invent a river like Spring Creek. For years it has so dominated my thoughts that I have been able to think and write of practically nothing else. Setting out to write this book has become as much an exorcism as a report, a private rage for order, for clarity. I want very much to see that period clearly, from mornings to evenings, from knowing nothing to knowing something, in all its tension, intensity, challenge, and fun, from when I met the river in late June to when I left it in the bright sun of late July.

In the mornings, when the grasses were still wet with a bright silver sheen and the antelope fled and the curlew flew ahead of us as we rattled along the rutted and pitted track across the benches down to the river, we always felt the nervous tingling of expectation.

At first I wanted to fish all of the river at once, and I felt anxious when we chose one spot. The fishing might be better upriver or down, I thought. It made me uneasy. But after a few days I settled down, took matters one at a time and carefully, and felt content as we reconnoitered downstream, past Paranoid Pool and the big flat and Farrago Pool, then looked at the first few pools on the East Branch, and then drove slowly up the length of the West Branch, noting the carcass and the old oxbows, pausing at four or five bends.

Few flies would hatch until ten fifteen or a bit later, depending upon the temperature, and we'd sit and talk quietly in the big tan Suburban, about books or fishing or the condition of the water, or not talk, and then we'd see some flies on the front window. They might be small dark caddis or the first Pale Morning Duns, a delicate and faint yellow. Herb would point and mumble and I'd give a little electric exclamation. Then the fish would show.

Was it a one-riser?

Yes, one rise, then gone.

"Not exactly a feeding frenzy," Herb might say.

But then there was another. And another. It was starting. We'd both make guttural sounds and not voice the obvious. One of us would point

"Better get your rod down," Herb would say, and I'd say that he should get his down. In a few more moments one of us, usually me, would get out of the car ever so slowly, never taking eyes from the river, unsnap the rod from the carrier on the car roof, select and tie on a fly, and prepare to fish.

In the mornings we always looked and talked first. Then the sun grew warmer and before too long we would find some fish working. The river was merely what a river ought to be—varied, fecund, wild, with large trout, skittery as hummingbirds, that pretty much liked a fly to look pretty much like the thing it was eating—and as I looked from the Suburban and then went out to meet it I always felt that the world and I were moments from being born.

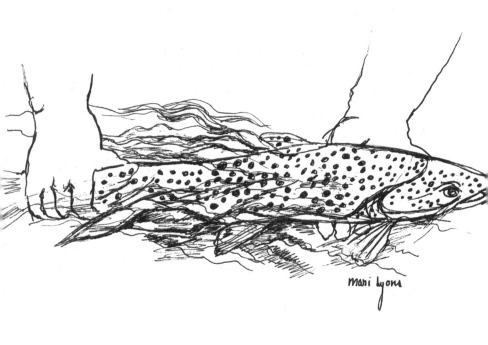

Mari Lyons

Big Fish

I had caught several large fish during the Green Drake hatch but I raised my two largest in the big pond above the Two Islands Pool on Pale Morning Duns. In both cases I'd lost the fish through stupidity. One took off in a tremendous rush of power and I simply broke it off. The other mistake was the product of letting my attention wander during some slow fishing at the pond. I had been casting and watching the tiny speck of gold on the slate water for an hour, and I had not quite believed that I could raise one of the truly large fish whose wakes we now saw streaking through the pool regularly. I turned my head for an instant, the fish rose, I turned back at the slight sound, and in haste struck late and snapped it off. I think such fish are lost because the fish has already got going in the opposite direction and you snap the line rather than pull with a steady firmness.

I had seen a lot of large fish making wakes in the neck between two of the lower pools and spent one afternoon working my way into positions on both sides of it, spoiling the pool three times, and then, finally, fixing myself on one bank, sitting down for a half hour until the fish got going good, and then fishing slightly downstream to it, on a slack line. The fish came to the Pale Morning Dun readily and took me well into the backing—

but it came back under steady pressure and at last I had it. I guess it was twenty-two inches or perhaps a bit larger, and I felt very proud of myself.

Big fish, really big fish, larger fish than you've ever seen before—except on someone else's wall or in a garish photograph—provide electric excitement, a sudden quick challenge to all you have learned in your marrowbones, and a relief from all smaller fare. And just as surely, they are a lure that hooks you to fish more. For something bigger. For a record perhaps. For a fish that has some claim to immortality. Which can be a serious business.

I know people—young and old—who live for such outsized fish. One cock of the walk is interested *only* in the biggest salmon. He is a big-fish fisherman of the first water. He's also a big fish in the art pool in which he swims and he only wants to catch big fish there, too. His talk is a litany of accomplishments; he always wants the newest, biggest, best, most; he does not "pick up a pen" for less than several hundred thousand dollars. And he generally gets the newest, biggest, best, most, which he needs, which back his advertisements for himself. He wants records and mounts; he is bored with less.

I would be too often dissatisfied if that's all I came to fly fish for—the big fish. Dreams would too often outrun reality. But there is more to those big fish, something not pathological. They nibble at my brain—albeit they're usually the fish that have gotten away. They stretch us, expand the circle that contains our sense of ourselves, the limits of some imaginative construction of what we can and cannot do. Roger Bannister spent years trying to break the barrier of the four-minute mile and then dozens did it; many fishermen catch permit regularly on the fly, though this was once rare; and more fly fishers hold larger trout than they dreamed could be held on a #20 dry fly. Big fish jolt us. They are bigger than life, or make life bigger. They swim in our brains for decades, long after lesser fare have faded—bigger, older, rarer, more difficult, unusual, commanding our hardest-won respect.

One chilly gray morning during the middle of the third week I'd been at Spring Creek, we came down the bench, headed right toward the Paranoid and Farrago pools, then drove up the East Branch to the big pond, which had shown more and more life lately.

It was a gray, trouty, drizzly, sullen day, and as I strung up my rod and put on my hip boots, I kept scanning the river, searching for a rise. The water was oddly alive. It had a mysterious energy to it. There was a slight mist on the water, turning gently, and the water was nervous here and there, with wakes and bumps on the surface that I knew were fish looking for food.

I took up a position I'd taken twice before, toward the uppermost section of the cove—sitting on a tuft of grasses just at the point, where I was able to cast upstream and allow the fly to slip down toward me and then past me at a snail's pace.

I sat quietly on my wet perch, rump wet and cold, and lay my rod across my knees, shotgun-style. There were a few golden spots on the surface, floating ever so slowly. My eyes began to flick everywhere across the surface, looking for a rise, a steady wake, a sign. I picked out individual mayflies and watched them float forty, fifty, a hundred feet. A half hour passed. The sky remained a solid mass of gray. Every fly I saw floated downriver unmolested.

Herb was fifty yards below me, in the middle of the pool, and though his fish would be farther out, he could cast twenty-five feet or more farther than I could.

We kept watching the water, not turning to the other, saying no more than a word or two to each other, a phrase, merely pointing. We both felt, in the gray silence, that something was about to burst. There was something about the way the fish were lolling, close to the surface, and the leisurely heavy nervous movement of their wakes.

And then suddenly a couple of trout started to feed.

There were three widening circles, widely separated.

We both pointed and grunted.

And then there were eight or ten or more fish up, high in the water, their dorsals out, taking the fly with an unhurried confidence. The slow rises, the slowly spreading circles on the flat surface, the slow, deliberate pinching and erupting of the water were heart-stopping. We were on one of the toughest pools on the river—a hundred and fifty feet across, perhaps three hundred feet long—and it was beginning to explode.

Here and there a dorsal fin or a tail slipped up out of the water, sharklike, and then there was a heavy wake—one hundred feet out—as a good fish moved close to the surface, less wary than ever now. And then there was another spreading circle.

My quiet patience began to give way to inner mania, which I struggled to suppress. The fish were still beyond my casting range and there was nothing to do but wait until they worked their way closer.

I heard line peel off Herb's reel as he drew out enough for a cast and then I paused from my own concerns to watch him cast toward a spreading circle.

I had a dozen versions of the PMD in my box but chose a #18 Mathews Sparkle Dun. In this especially flat, diamond-clear water the fish could examine the fly with critical care; I wanted the trout to see the body color, the silhouette, the Zelon tail or shuck.

The trick then was to cast an honest sixty or seventy feet from that sitting position—not panic and drop the back cast so it hooked the grass behind me—and to have the fly drop lightly a few feet above the feeding position of the trout, where it could pick up the minimal current and float without drag to the precise spot where the fish had taken its stand.

Miraculously, I made the impossible cast the first time. The fly fell perfectly and started its ever-so-slow float toward the spot where one of the trout was rising. I waited. The moment was charged with intensity. Someone might have kicked me in the kidneys, I'd have felt nothing. I leaned forward, waiting for the gold dot on the slate surface to disappear in the ring of that trout's rise. I muttered to the fly that it should not drag. It heard me. I waited some more. In this flat water, you could recite a couple of pages of *Paradise Lost* while a trout made up its mind, while the fly inched toward it. "He'll come to lunch," I thought. And then the fly floated merrily over the trout and on down the river.

Why? Why didn't the fish rise? There had to be a reason. Was the 6X leader too heavy? Was there imperceptible drag? Were the fish really taking the emerging mayfly and not the adult?

Herb got a good fish about noon, and then, a half hour later, I hooked something quite large and lost it, and then the water was quiet for an hour and we sat and fussed with our tackle. We'd taken no lunch along and were expected back at the ranch, but neither of us thought of eating. About two o'clock I had a delicate rise—no more than a pinching down of the water under my fly—and came up tight with a tremendous fish that race-horsed directly across the river so hard that I thought it would beach itself and go halfway up the bench. But the fish turned, jumped three time, went upstream, then down, well into my backing, and finally I urged it in. It was the largest trout I'd ever taken on a dry fly—a full twenty-two inches and perhaps six pounds, with a sharply hooked jaw.

Then, a half hour later, I took another, also a male, almost identical but a bit heavier.

That was quite enough—thank you—for a day, for the year, perhaps longer. I walked back to the big Suburban to fetch out a cup of lemonade, as an excuse for getting off the front line, as a way to try to stop the radical tremor that I had contracted in my right hand after that second huge fish. I didn't mind the tremor. It was a happy little nervous twitch, that's all, and it would stop in its own good time. One of my legs was trembling, too. I don't remember which.

I really didn't think I wanted to fish again that day. There was nothing better out there for me, and I'd taken as much as my memory could hold. I'm always astounded when I read of someone catching forty, fifty, sixty trout in an afternoon, ten of them over such-and-such size. Why? Why continue? A few good fish make a day. More make an orgy. A flurry of fish catching satisfies me completely. I don't want to catch every fish in the river. I don't want to "beat" my companion. I don't want to break records. That's the tournament mentality, and it makes the worst the best.

But I could not help but watch.

Mari and Pat came down with a wicker basket of sandwiches. Herb laid down his rod and came up to the cars. And we both chose out what we wanted and began to eat. But even as we ate, our eyes could not stay away from the water. The PMDs were still coming; there were still snouts and tails and wakes everywhere. Something else was going to happen.

Mari tried twice to talk to me but I didn't look at her. I could not haul my eyes from the water. Herb asked me about the two big fish I'd taken. Pat got excited by this but Mari merely said, in a flat tone, "That's nice, for you, dear." And then, in a whisper: "You don't talk. We don't even have a platonic relationship."

I tried to explain to her what was happening on the pond, how it happened only infrequently, how this was a Day of Days. I kept watching the water. I was mesmerized by the water. I don't even remember when Pat and Mari left, or what I said, only that Herb was soon back on his perch and I was leaning on my arms in back of the Suburban, watching him intently.

He cast sporadically, when he saw a rise or a wake heading in a particular direction. He cast a low, fast, long line, and I thought how much like wing shooting this was, watching the direction of the fish, casting quickly beyond it, into its path, then waiting with great expectation. That wait, that hesitation, was devastating.

From where I stood I did not always see the fly alight on the slate surface of the water, and now and then I'd pour myself another lemonade or fuss with my reel or line. I felt very contented. I had caught a couple of remarkable fish and that, thank you, had been quite enough. But I was facing the river and whenever I looked up I saw it and Herb and watched until whatever little drama was being played was done. I was looking up when I saw a fish rise twice, then—with a wake—drift off to the right. Then it came back and took four or five PMDs. Herb watched, tense now, waiting to cast. I wondered why he was waiting so long. Did he want the fish to get good and confident? It was clearly a very big fish, but there were a lot of big fish in this pool and it was quite impossible to tell from the delicate rise and the wake quite how large this one might be.

For a few moments the feeding stopped. Then I saw the slight bulge and dimple of the fish, about seventy-five feet out, to the right, and then I saw Herb's rapid cast.

I saw his bright yellow parachute alight four or five feet up from where the water had pinched a moment before. The cast, with only one false cast far to the left, had been exactly on target. The rumpled leader started to straighten, the fly moved ever so slightly on a current you could not see, and I felt my heart leaning out onto the water, straining after the fly—my breath slightly irregular—wanting to coax the fish into taking.

That moment was more than six years ago and memory, for me, about fishing, always mingles with fantasy and dream. But this memory is too sharply etched not to have been real.

I remember the long length of line going back and then forward, and then shooting to a distance of perhaps seventy feet. I remember the #17 Pale Morning Dun parachute dropping with a final little somersault of the leader and then picking up what there was of current and floating slowly downstream. I remember the expectation and the wait. And I remember with perfect clarity—when I run the entire scene out in my mind, in sequence—the slight pinch and bulge of the flat surface ... and then the sudden, immense, electric rush of force.

The trout took Herb's fly lightly and did not move off unperturbed by the prick, as the books say. The fish zoomed off like a bonefish—hard and fast and far, in a straight line, like any wild thing held; and then, two hundred feet up the long pool, it leaped once, erupting, exploding, splattering the air with bubbles and silver splashes of water.

"Bigger than I thought," Herb said.

He stood up now, intent, looking upstream.

"Parachute?" I asked.

Herb nodded.

I worried about the size of his leader point and asked: "Six-X?"

He nodded again.

After the jump the fish settled down to doing what a truly big fish is supposed to do. It moved off heavily, steadily, heading for the uppermost part of the pool, where the river pinched through the last narrow sections of land and broadened and slowed.

The fish was clearly larger—by a great measure—than the two fish I'd taken. Quite how large it was I could not tell. The fish was now well into the backing, perhaps three hundred feet upstream, and all you could see was the long expanse of buckskin fly line and then the smaller white backing, and at the far end a steady surge of water, as if a foul-hooked muskrat or a beaver or an otter was burrowing just beneath the surface. There was simply no way that this fish would not break off.

Herb's special Shockgum leader was decisive. He could not have held the fish without it. For with all that line out, the fish making sudden moves to the left or right, the 6X leader would surely otherwise have broken. But it did not. The fish veered off toward the far bank and the tippet held. The fish slashed at the surface and I thought that surely now it was gone; but the line was still taut when the commotion stopped. The great trout came up twice more—hugely, splattering water high, shaking, then crashing back down—with ninety feet of fly line and 280 feet of backing between it and the fly rod, and the fish was still on, and heading still farther upstream, around the bend.

You could not begin to pressure such a fish on such tackle, but you could stay with it, subtly—lean into it, drop your rod tip with it jumped, lower the rod (as Vince Marinaro advised) when the fish ran, so the line came directly off a finely tuned reel, with less friction. With abrupt, deft, athletic movements, Herb managed it all.

But then I saw him fumble with his reel and lean forward awkwardly, his rod extended as far as he could extend it in front of him. Something had happened. Was his line tangled? Surely he'd lose the fish now.

The bottom of the pool here was muddy and pocked with muskrat holes. It would be treacherous to wade toward the fish, and to get out of the pool and walk up the brushy, irregular bank could be fatal to the fight in a dozen ways. No, he had to stay in the water, where he was, in that one spot, and he had to manage the fish from that fixed position where he stood. There were no other options, no other ways to save what was becoming a desperate situation.

I did not have to stay so far from the action so I had walked to a high bank upstream where I'd have a better chance to see the great trout. I trotted back now to see if I could help Herb with whatever problem he had. The problem was this: the fish had taken the last foot of backing and for a moment—fumbling with the reel, leaning forward—Herb was trying to reach out and secure another foot or two or line before the gigantic fish broke off, which surely it would do. The fish was at the very end of the backing and sort of wallowing there, not pressing forward, finally tired perhaps, after the run, the shaking, the acrobatics. The fish could not be pressured but perhaps it could be urged, and Herb leaned his rod back a bit, then dropped it and reeled, to regain another foot or so of the line. But the line would not come back onto the spool; tied loosely, with a slip knot—the only carelessness in Herb's rig, or perhaps not—the line was circling the spool without coming back onto it. With the fish moving slightly toward him now, the line threatened to go slack.

Herb's fingers, fussing with the circling line, grew frantic for a moment.

Still leaning forward, he had to tighten the knot with his free fingers and coax line back onto the reel.

Well, that's it, I thought. A fly line with one hundred yards of backing hadn't been enough to hold this fish. If the great fish made a sudden move now, Herb would lose it for sure.

But despite the slack and the fumbling, the fish was still on.

Foot by foot Herb urged the gigantic thing back toward him, regaining half, then three-quarters of the backing as the fish turned and headed heavily, at an angle, downstream. There was no urgency in its movement now; the fish was subdued, worn, if not yet quite beaten. It could be led without being forced. The process—now done by inches—required immense patience.

Back on the high bank I kept my eyes flicking from fisherman to fish. In ten minutes the trout was back onto the reel, and I knew that it would only take a few more minutes before Herb had it at his side and would be reaching down to release it. I'd seen him handle the endgame flawlessly dozens of times.

The fish was near the surface now, canted to one side slightly, not twenty feet from me, and I could look down and see it with absolute clarity. I can see it still, all these years later. The trout looked a full foot longer than the two I'd caught, thicker by far, more than double their weight. And it was nearly beaten. I have seen larger trout come from lakes, on leaders the size of cables; steelhead are larger, even stronger; and this was fully the size of a dozen Atlantic salmon I'd seen. Why did this fish seem then—and why does it still seem—the most prodigious trout I'd ever seen? Surely the light tackle—not a affectation but a necessity for luring such a fish—and the relative size of the fish to this type of fishing played their roles. But a two-pound bluegill, even a giant of its species, is still only two pounds of bluegill, a piker. This fish was a monster.

"It's heading toward the weeds," Herb said flatly. "Can't put more pressure on."

The big head came half up out of the water and shook once, and the leader held, and Herb coaxed it slightly, firmly, away from the weeds. I felt quite sure he'd keep the great trout out of the weedbed. I felt sure he'd take it now, with only thirty or forty feet of line out.

And then the fish went a couple of feet off to the right, into the region of the weeds, and was off—and I felt then, and feel now, years later, as you must feel reading this, as all of us feel at such moments—as if I'd lost a part of myself and would forever be searching for it.

Herb reeled in quickly, checked the end of his leader, and found that the #17 golden fly had neither broken off nor bent straight, but simply pulled free. "Didn't break him off," he said. He smiled, shook his head, and said mildly, "That was a very big fish, Nick."

Now, so long afterward, I can forgive him his insouciance: a man who could fight a fish so well and lose it with so little trauma had to have caught a dozen that size.

I'd have punched myself silly.

The Intense Fly Fisherman

There was a time, some years ago, when I could fish with terrifying intensity. Give me a western lake and even the slenderest odds of hooking a ten-pound rainbow on a fly, and mules could not pull me from the water. From dark icy mornings until long after the sun bled beneath the sagebrush hills, I'd cast until my arm was numb and sun had baked the ridges of my right forefinger, wrist, and thumb a brilliant, blotched red.

I did this not once but dozens of times. I did it East and West, in Iceland and on British chalkstreams.

Sometimes I caught fish, sometimes I didn't. If I got some, I wanted more. If I got none, I had to hook a first before I left the water. If I got small fish, I wanted alligators. If I got a big one, one beyond my highest hopes, I thought there might be another, ever bigger, down there. I lived merrily, mindlessly, uncomfortably on the fringe where fishing bleeds away into madness.

Such intensity led to fierce family fights and, much worse, I thought, botched fishing. The rush of blood heavy in my head, I raged around the waters, an indifferent caster, a diffident loner. I knew little about bugs and could not be bothered to learn. At its worst, I lost my love of new and remembered waters, my wonder at the quick dart of a trout for a fly, the fun of good fellowship and a common language. Only the intensity—dumb and manic—mattered. It positively wore me out.

I had forgotten why I came to rivers in the first place. I had forgotten the meaning of the Duke's gentle words, from *As You Like It*:

> And this our life, exempt from public haunt
> Finds tongues in trees, books in the running brooks,
> Sermons in stones, and good in everything.

There was, for a time, only the hot pursuit. But then, for whatever reason, I swung to a far more leisurely frame of mind. I found I could stand passively behind a friend and chuckle as *his* fires raged out of control. Once, on a lazy little British chalkstream filled with wild browns anywhere from fingerlings to five-pounders, I spotted a fish rising just downstream of a river point topped with overhanging grasses. As the current zipped around the bend, swirled back behind the point, it brought a conveyor belt of easy food to the safe fish, which was dimpling steadily. Fingerling or five-pounder? I could not tell, though the protected lair suggested a smart, large fish.

Maples and willow on my side of the river made casts to that far bank quite impossible; there was enough current in the center to assure drag; and a cast above the point, from below, could only bring the fly whisking down past the trout's cafeteria. The rules of the river prohibited downstream fishing and that wouldn't have worked, anyway.

The one clear way to manage the classic little problem was to wade across the deep center current and cast to the fish from directly downstream. On a western river, with chest waders, I'd have done it even in my most leisurely, laid-back frame of mind. But I wore hip boots, practically the best suit of clothes I owned, and the only suit with me, and I'd caught a few fish already. So I sat down on a rock with my back against a maple and was content to watch.

After a few moments, my host came around the bend. He is a great enthusiast for fly fishing, a builder of business empires, a man not ever to retreat from a challenge.

"There's one, near the point," he whispered loudly. "Oh, he's a good one. Oh, he's a *verrrrry* good trout."

"I've been watching him," I said.

"Well have a go at him, Nick. Have a go at him. That's a *verrrrry* good trout."

"Not for me," I said. "Not today. He's all yours."

So my host got in and I leaned back against the tree to watch. He cast beautifully—a long line, hooking off to the right. But try as he might, he missed the corner by a foot, dropped his fly above and watched it sweep away from the eddy, picked up drag, got his fly caught in the willows behind him, came finally within inches of the eddy, and then stepped back and shook his head. The fish would not budge from that spot, not an inch. And my host *had* to catch it.

Sooner or later, I knew, probably sooner, he had to wade across the river in his hip boots. I felt quite smugly sure of this point.

He inched out toward the current and watched the water line rise on his boots. He cast again. Short. The angle was all wrong. He could not resist it, I thought. He *had* to have that fish. He was gut-hooked by that trout and could not possibly resist going after it.

And he couldn't.

A few minutes later the poor builder of business empires was sloshing helplessly across the river soaking his Harris tweed jacket far above the pockets. And then, just as he got to the far side and prepared to cast backhanded up toward the fish, the trout stopped feeding for the day.

I was merciless toward him, for I had been there myself, many times: I had fished late into the night when my marriage hung on the slenderest of threads; I had waded into a pool in a jacket and leather shoes; I had walked through muck as treacherous as quicksand and waded on nights so dark an owl would have gotten lost.

But I was sad and envious, too. In my new contemplative height had I lost some of that marvelous passion that is also part of the sport? Of course I had. Fly fishing was never a purely contemplative recreation. There are times when, if you don't commit your full soul, if you don't put your blood into the pursuit, you might as well be playing a quiet game of cribbage before the fire. Isn't one of the prime reasons we venture out to *use* that intensity coiled within us?

Still, I was talking to Charlie Brooks about fish passion once and we agreed that certain symptoms of it could be lethal. I mentioned the guys on the Great Lakes who had died of salmon mania when wild weather came and they would not leave the water. He told me about a guy who'd arranged to float the Madison during the salmonfly hatch. Ten minutes after the boat pushed off, the sport saw stone flies everywhere, and fish taking them. His casting grew wild, and with some help from a Montana gust of wind, he managed the unique distinction of being probably the only man to hook himself with a Sofa Pillow through the bottom lip and up into the flesh of the upper lip. Pinning his mouth shut. The guide wisely saw at once that this was a bad scene and announced that he was heading for shore and would hustle the guy to a hospital.

There was a loud, determined noise from the sport. The guide thought he must be in great pain and rowed harder toward the shore. There was a louder, raucous, this time intelligible, "*Nooooooo!*" The man adamantly refused to leave the river; he *had* to finish the float.

"That's a real fisherman!" a friend said quietly, nodding approval, when I retold the story.

A *real* fisherman?

After eight hours on the water, the man had caught a dozen good trout but his face was distended beyond recognition, infected, and he was in a state of acute shock. The guide rushed him to Bozeman and doctors were barely able to save his life.

What intensity!

What lunacy.

Winter Dreams with Sparse

He walked into my life fifteen years ago, with his pink face and slight stoop, with his three-piece charcoal suit and quarter-inch thick glasses, looking like an antique gnome or a tax collector. His first words to me were an angry growl. "You can't use it," he said. I didn't have the slightest idea who he was and told him so. "Alfred W. Miller is who, and if you think you're going to use my story 'Murder' in that blasted anthology of yours, you've got another think coming to you, buster." He liked to punctuate with "buster."

Interspersed with those growls were long, marvelous talks, perhaps in the great leather couch in his beloved Anglers' Club before a bright log fire, both our suits burning in a couple of places from hot cigar or pipe ashes. One minute he'd introduce me to a gigantic mutt named Mange, who could perform amazing feats with food and devour the refuse of his entire ambulance detachment in the mud and bivouacs of France in 1917, the next he'd be railing against salmon fishing, because when *he* caught a fish, sir, he wanted to know why the beggar took the fly. Sitting there, chuckling away, in danger of being burned to a crisp, we used to vow that someday we'd go winter camping together. He was tough enough to have done so well into his eighties; I was the cream puff.

He had a thousand tales. A dozen times I heard him tell the long, rambling, hilarious "fly in the nose" story, about a friend who got a Fan-Wing Royal Coachman caught in the tip of his nose on a Sunday morning in Pennsylvania, and though he always carried a tackle box filled with a thousand gadgets, he could not find one with which to extricate himself; the story progressed to a diner, where a waitress was terrified by his odd nose-dress, and then to the sudden discovery that his car was on fire, then a rattlesnake somehow appeared mysteriously, and finally—an hour after he'd begun the tale—his friend tumbled down a hill and knocked the senior member of the Parkside Anglers Association nearly senseless—twice. He had tales about Mr. Hewitt, whom he had known well and loved and always called "Mister," and LaBranche, Roy Steenrod, and the Brooklyn Fly Fishers; he had serious reservations about Theodore Gordon because the man had abandoned his sick mother. Sparse's other nickname was Deac, from Deacon, for his moral uprightness.

He was adamant one June when I told him I had not yet been on the water. It was a disgrace. He growled and promptly hauled Mari and me off to the DeBruce Club on the Willowemoc. We fished a little together—he was a deft left-handed caster—and he showed me where LaBranche cast what he called the first dry fly on American waters. Then he said, "You've been working too hard. You need an uninterrupted couple of hours on the water to refresh yourself, bub. I'll entertain your missus." And he sat with Mari at the kitchen table in the Krum farmhouse and told her, in great detail, for four hours—the information being somewhat more than she wanted—about ballistics and maneuvers on the Mexican Border Patrol.

He was astonishingly precise about a great variety of gadgets and contraptions, some in common use, some of his own invention—like the zipper for chest waders and the attachment that kept you from dropping your pipe into the drink. No matter that the former leaked and when the pipe slipped it only dropped hot ashes down your waders.

I'd heard the "fly in the nose" story a dozen times and I was at the lunch table five years ago when Sparse began to tell it, faltered, and his great memory failed. I did not tell him to tell that story the last time I saw him, on his ninetieth birthday. Frail, shrunken, he had lost over eighty pounds. Hoagy Carmichael had rigged him a hat with a wire brace screwed into the cloth so that he could hold a pipe in place without using his hands and not incinerate himself; the old guy loved the idea of it. I wanted to hear Sparse tell one of the old tales once more and prodded him to tell me the "prune rod" story. He did so, as well as he'd ever told it—about his father's belief (when Sparse was eight years old) in the health-giving properties of prunes, the deal struck to eat twenty-five prunes for a nickel (with a limit of fifty per week), the rod eventually bought from the proceeds of this worthwhile activity—and then he produced the huge hickory club itself.

Like the hickory "prune" rod, brilliantly waxed and protected after eighty-two years, better than it had ever been or deserved to be, whatever Sparse touched became richer, finer. A friend's prose, a lunch at which he unfolded one of his inimitable stories, a day on the Willowemoc with him, a thousand lives he touched, a memory, an Anglers' Club *Bulletin* edited with his discerning eye, an event he'd lived or carefully researched—all were brighter, more memorable for his ministrations. He could make us laugh with a fantastic story about a fifty-pound brown that devoured pieces of bread soaked in scotch and make us cry when we read "A Drink of Water." Nearly blind in one eye and with only 20 percent vision in the other, he was still the most meticulous proofreader I ever knew and always the firmest, most exacting critic. He saw more than any of us, remembered it precisely, and then crafted his words with choicest care. The trout were not taking, but a boy along on the trip "rose to chocolate bars all day long"; some of the finest fishing is in print; he always wanted to fish "not better but more." His counsel and encouragement to a hundred lesser writers, some quite famous, has yet to be chronicled properly, and his own prose remains a constant lesson.

The day after his first growl, he gave me "Murder" to use, and he kept giving for fifteen years—a score of unforgettable moments and a piece of his heart. With a roar like a werewolf, Sparse could not hide that he was really mostly a gentleman and a lamb. He practiced a code from another, nearly forgotten time, and it included strong doses of honor, steadfastness, loyalty, dignity, backbone, pride, the art of making truly careful sentences and the art of being a gentleman, and love.

He had been a reporter for the *Wall Street Journal* and then, until several years earlier, a stockholder-relations counsel; he went to work every day, well into his eighties. In his last years, old age did its best to ravage him. The doctors rummaged around inside him and did their worst; at times he had tubes attached here and there and less than a full complement of parts. But most painful must have been the loss of his beautiful and astonishing memory, which no doubt had helped him become the debating champion of New York State long before the First World War. Hoagy, who saw him a couple of weeks shy of his ninety-first birthday, reported that the only gift he wanted was "the ticket out of here." He died on Veterans Day and would have liked that.

Everyone who knew Sparse will miss him sorely—not because he was always an easy man, which he wasn't, but because there is not a chance, buster, that we shall see your likes again. He imputed to the world of fly fishing, which he loved deeply, a sense of character and tradition and wit; he saw it as a human activity, full of wonder and excitement, far beyond the mere catching of fish—an activity that enlivened the heart and sparked the imagination. It had the power to bring out the best in men—and some of the worst. He told us about the stupidity of much high-pressured "sport" and the fun we might have on our fishless days. He was far more than what he'd admit to: "Merely a good reporter, bub." He was a superb writer who will be read a hundred years from how, and a great-hearted, humorous, and perfectly remarkable man.

It is winter now and I delight to imagine us finally off someplace in the snow, sitting on a log, puffing at pipes whose ashes sizzle and sink as they hit the snow. "Why don't you just tell me that 'fly in the nose' story one more time, old friend," I say. He grunts and chuckles and screws up his face, then says, "Well, it was an early Sunday morning in Pennsylvania, buster and ..." And my face kept aching from laughter and I didn't notice the cold, and finally, like some great chord, the senior member of the Parkside Anglers Association gets knocked nearly senseless for the second time.

A Skinny Little Girl,
a Fishing Rod, a Bluegill

She was precisely the kind of little girl I would have fallen madly in love with, had I been six or seven and not her grandfather. She was skinny, with blond curly hair cut short, gangly when she ran, restless with dull adult talk, a chatterbox herself, crazy for her grandfather's stories, her two front teeth gone and paid for, not nearly so shy of seeing worms for the first time that she would not hold one.

In short, she was the perfect prospect for a fishing pal, and I had known this for a long time and had laced my letters to her with bluegill, trout, bass, hooks, bobbers. I tested a rod by asking her to pull on the line. I was lousy with indirections, determined not to force her, determined not to let the unintelligible jargon of fly fishing wreck my plot, as I had let it spoil everything with her three uncles.

I would have to wait six years for her four-month-old brother, Finn, and he might not like worms so well. So I was laying something of a groundwork in the piscatorial direction, through innuendo and cunning. I was no fool. I would not force anyone anymore. I was not at all sure why we want those we love to love what we love: but forcing never helped.

"Of course you're forcing her," my shrewd daughter said. "Don't you see yourself at all, Dad? Leave my little girl alone."

"Maybe she'll love fishing," I said quietly.

"It's a perfectly good thing to do, this fishing of yours, but some people just don't like it, Dad—and no one likes it as much as you do," she said. "That may be hard for you to imagine, but it's true."

"I have a gut feeling about your little girl," I said. "She's got ..."

"Piscatorial potential," she said. "I know. I know, Dad."

But I backed away anyway and mentioned fish not at all over the summer, until a few weeks ago. The temperature got up to 104 degrees near Woodstock, New York, the creeks were dry, the nearest lake low, and I knew I would have to make some dramatic moves or the season would be over.

At seventy, you reckon the number of seasons left.

No flies this time. No rod for me, so I could not possibly rage around rivers demonically possessed, fishing for twelve or fourteen hours at a time while my sons grew hopelessly bored, began to throw stones, and their sister, Lara's mother, had to advise them: "Be good—or Dad will put you in a story." No. The heyday of the blood, piscatorially speaking, was over. No entomology this time; no 6X leaders; no cul-de-canard winging; no big-name rivers with trout so snobby they sneered at the poorly presented fly.

We began in my backyard with a rusted can, a shovel, and the hunt for worms with each spadeful of earth turned. I remembered the ritual well. If I was going to make a hunter-fisher-gatherer of my granddaughter, the gathering was at least proving out. She had a good eye and a quick hand. We got six.

"Don't we want to get a few more, Grandpa?" Lara said.

And so we got two more, small ones, and I rigged a spinning rod without a reel, with line tied directly to the tip-top guide, to which I affixed a bright red-and-white bobber, then a length of level leader, then a smallish bait hook.

A SKINNY LITTLE GIRL, A FISHING ROD, A BLUEGILL

My friend Bill has a lovely spring-fed pond, an acre or so, filled with outsized trout, plump bullheads, and far too many bluegill. The latter were always ravenous. Perfect.

There is a photograph of us, taken recently—one old man, big as a house, on a wooden dock, and a skinny little girl, in a long pink cotton dress and sneakers and a floppy white hat. She is carrying a gigantic creel over her shoulder and holding a long rod from which dangles, unceremoniously, a pancake-sized bluegill, her first. The old man has his arms around her waist so that she will not fall in. The girl is serious about her first bluegill.

Lara's grandmother, who took the photograph, later reported that I had clearly made a convert, though I remember reflecting soberly that even our six bluegill—and all the chattering about them afterward—did not an angler make.

But the photo does give reason for hope.

Bobbers and Little Boys

On the hot and lazy evenings of high summer, I like nothing better than to sit near my little pond, toss out a simple short length of line tied to the tip of a bamboo pole, and watch the red-and-white bobber perch precariously on the surface. This is more of a big puddle than a pond, but it's filled with bluegill and fathead minnows and a couple of largemouth bass and one conspicuous orange koi.

They are always hungry. So are the mosquitoes and no-see-ums. There are far too many bugs near this almost-stagnant water, and my grandson Finn doesn't like them. Neither do I, though all septuagenarians have had lots of bugs in their lives and they matter less to us than they do to a three-year-old.

I haven't fished this way for many years. But it's the way I started, when I wasn't much older than this sturdy fellow at my side, and my head is flooded with memories.

I was born to this fishing. First in South Lake near my grandfather's hotel in the northeastern Catskills and then at a grim boarding school, where fishing may have saved my life or at least my sanity. I fished every chance I could, with bait, hook, and bobber. Standing knee deep in the murky water of Ice Pond, everything came in at the eye. I watched the water for any of its thousand messages, above and beneath the surface. My eyes were pinned to that cork float, to its slightest movement. Was that a nibble or the wind? Was that a bluegill, rock bass, or perch? The energy of the float came to me like a flash of electricity, and now it made me think, with Finn beside me, of all the high-powered fishing I had done over the many years since those first days: with surface plug for bluefish and striped bass, with deer-hair Bomber or bug for salmon or bass, with flies that drew strikes from hundred-pound tarpon, with tiny dry flies on western spring creeks.

And yet, the anticipation here at this muddy pond I've had dug out of a hillside is as great as any of that sophisticated fishing, as great as when I stood in that pond near the boarding school, watching the float and the way the refractions of the sun angled down to some mysterious point in the mysterious underwater world I probed. We used a simple cork then, from a wine bottle, threading the line through the center with a stout needle and leaving it in place for the entire season. Later I learned that the British and French had taken the float to a high level of refinement, using porcupine quills and plastic for what they called "coarse fishing" (for tench and barbell) or match fishing (a rather serious brand of competition, often with maggots for bait). For American bluegill and perch, the cheapest red-and-white bobber, with a plump foam center and a thin plastic tube running through, serves just fine. That's what I use here.

I'm not alone in my addiction to bobbers. Trigorin, the famous author in Chekhov's *The Seagull,* says that he takes no greater pleasure than to sit on the bank of a river watching a float. My friend Barbara told me of a deeper attachment. When her husband, Mark, was diagnosed with Lou Gehrig's Disease, they both quit their jobs to pursue a joint passion for fishing. They fished flies for bonefish along the Keys, and then Mark had to change from the long rod to a spinning outfit when the disease began to work its dreadful darkness. And then—near the end—

they fished in Central Park Lake, with a doughball laced with vanilla extract beneath a bobber, the way Mark had started to fish.

Finn, who is unusually full of energy, watches for a moment while I fix a worm on the hook, adjust the split shot, and slip the bobber to the proper distance from the bait.

"When it goes down, you pull," I tell him.

"Okay, Grandpa," he says. He is holding onto the bamboo pole with both hands.

"Be sure to pull hard."

"I will, Grandpa."

We lob the rig out together, and at once the bobber begins to dance. There are simply too many hungry bluegill in this pond. Then the bobber darts off at an angle, slams downward, and in an instant is so far underwater that we can't see it.

It has all happened so quickly that it's probably too late, but I announce, "You've got one," and then he yanks with all his might and the pretty little jewel of a bluegill is derricked out of the water, flies toward shore, and is soon flopping on the rocks. It has happened so abruptly that Finn is at first too puzzled to smile.

But I do.

Then I motion for him to swing the wriggling thing toward me and I grasp it, folding the sharp dorsal fin back neatly with my fingers, then holding the fish out to him.

"Want to touch it?" I ask. He doesn't. Not particularly. Not now.

Later, after his fourth bluegill on as many lobs, he heads to a little rock pile off to the side and begins to throw rocks into the pond, lefty and righty. I worry that he has found it all too easy, and that I have already failed, yet again, to hook a young relative carrying most of my genes with this sport I probably love too much.

"Well, old fellow," I ask him later, as we walk hand in hand up the hill through the high summer grasses toward the house. "Well, old man," I say, leading with my chin, "which do you like more, fishing with a bobber or throwing rocks?"

He answers without hesitation. The dichotomy that I have presented is exactly wrong, and so is his answer.

But nobody's perfect. Three-year-old grandsons, especially, are not yet perfect. Nor are their grandpas.

But there's always next year.

And there were more years, as the next section relates.

Indian Summer of a Fisherman

1

Even brains have their seasons. Mine turns lately on ponds, memories, books, and glimmers of better days to come, though they may or may not. The mix, rather too suddenly, has changed. I suppose I could call the fly box that I now use for pills a symbol. But I don't. It is just a useful way to keep in one place the dozen or so pills I take daily for heart, joints, prostate. I happen to need fewer flies these days than all those I hoarded for so many years and have taken to sharing boxfuls with neighbors who fish rivers where those flies once worked for me so well; and I ship many off to far-flung friends in France and England who might find them exotic and even useful. I still have many thousands, and a good fly pattern is not to be left for the ineluctable moth.

For several years, twenty-five years ago, I tied flies for my own use—the Hairwing Royal Coachman at a time when I thought it could do everything and when I believed in the illusion of perfect simplicity; some of Flick's Grey Fox Variants, ditto; a simple marabou leech pattern or two, for a lake that held really big busters that loved leeches but which I never fished again; a few tube flies for salmon that had once, thirty years earlier, worked in Iceland and because constructing them was an idiot's delight. That was the sad extent of it, and I confess I made some monstrously sad specimens that happily no longer exist. But I have always been a keen student of fly pattern and design. I bought, begged, and examined thousands of them, checked their attitude in a glass of water, studied the effect of water on color, insinuated myself into the trout's position, however misguided, and acquired enough to stock a rather large fly shop. I still cannot pass up an intriguing fly.

Several years ago, after we bought a summer house in Woodstock, New York, I began to fish a friend's spring-fed pond only a few miles away, and what was needed there to catch fish on a fly rod were beyond the subtlest items in my arsenal, flies that cunningly aped the naturals that hatched on some pretty moody spring creeks I had fished. I called it Bill's Pond because it belonged to my friend Bill. It was about an acre in all, with the lower end, near where it tumbled out of the cement hatchway into a little creek, warmer, filled with lilypads, favored by the bass, bluegill, and pickerel. There was a small island on which geese nested, behind which you did not want your fish to take line, and the main section, fed by a vigorous updwelling spring and numerous small springs, held trout—a lot of them and of a size to raise any fly fisher's hackles. Bill fed them delicious little round liver pellets and the biggest of the fish, the rainbows, were seven or eight pounds, and all the trout co-habitated without prejudice with a few grass carp that must have weighed more than fifteen pounds and four or five bright-orange koi—terrific moving targets to pitch to, targets that demanded you lead them like a bird hunter by just the right distance. The koi were not much smaller than the carp.

As an aging trout man, the trout—those big rainbows interspersed with a few three- or four-pound brookies and some pretty unsocial browns that kept mostly to themselves—interested me most. Bluegill and golden shiners took a fly, and the few channel cats would take a black leech fished very slowly, Bill told me, though I never tried this; but the trout were shy of what their wilder stream relatives loved. They rejected every fly I tried. They scarcely gave them a look. All of the trout smacked their lips when liver pellets came their way, found them as irresistible as the finest *escargot* or goose liver pâté or just about any item on Mario Batalli's tasting menu. So after dozens of fruitless tries with the world's subtlest Pale Morning Duns and Sulfurs and Hendricksons that I had patiently accumulated, there was nothing for it but to invent an imitation of what these picky characters preferred with their snobby palate.

It was not such hard or uninteresting work. I started with a little square cut with a single-edge razor from a wine cork, rounded it to the shape and size of the natural, dyed it the exact right shade of brown with a a permanent felt-tip marking pen, cut a slit in one side with the razor blade, put a dab of Magic Glue on the cut, and inserted a #10 Eagle Claw bait hook. It was done. With a few shrewd variations and modifications—like leaving a white patch of cork on top so I could see the miserable concoction on the water—I had my imitation, and over the next few years it became the standard on Bill's Pond, accounting (for me) for at least one memorable grass carp, one koi (by pure mistake), and three or four of the largest trout.

Sneer if you will. Kept from wading by an incrementing loss of balance that had led to three or four murderous falls—from my two new titanium hips and burgeoning waistline, all those pills in my retired fly box, or just creeping age—I gave up rivers several years ago, embraced Bill's Pond, and sucked my memories like a bear sucks its paws in winter, for sustenance.

2

There is an arc to every angler's life. It differs for each of us but we all overlap. And as the arc makes one of its last turns, we can finally see the pattern with immense clarity. Awash with memories, we see all our early bumbling and passion give way to some competence and then to preferences and choices. We see our first trout, first trout on a fly, first spring creek, first tarpon, the mastery of one or the other of the cluster of techniques we need to take a few more of the most recalcitrant trout. Each image brings a new turn of the arc and even, in some cases, leads to satiety. Some folks I know simply give it up, for golf, for spectator sports, for who knows what. One fellow I knew caught so many exquisitely difficult—and large—trout that he grew bored, just gave it over. I don't know what he did thereafter. Many, though, cannot get enough of the finest fly fishing, never grow bored, fish quite as hard at eighty, even eighty-five, as they did at forty, braving all. And a few old fly fishers, as Sparse once told me about a prominent Long Island Club, simply took to a wheelchair and suffered themselves to be hauled to the ramps near the hatchery.

For some reason, I have been blessed (or cursed) with the sharpest possible memory for just about every trout I ever caught, from the first (gigged from a late-summer Catskill creek on a bare Carlisle hook strapped to a willow branch) to dozens of the most challenging on a remarkable western spring creek. I can without the slightest effort conjure a certain Pale Morning Dun floating with the placid current on a placid pool, ever so slowly, and then the sudden leisurely lumping of the surface when a preposterously large brown that I had pitched to seven times finally took. And I can remember tough trout I saw good friends hook, which gave me much the same pleasure.

But memory is not merely such brief images. Any fly fisher's memories course through his veins and have colored all his thoughts, all that he is, like wine splashed through water.

Fishing and catching were always part of my life, from before memory, and probably began with my capturing what I could with my hands—newts, crayfish, frogs, minnows—prowling a rocky headwaters creek. At the Ice Pond near the grim boarding school I attended, I used a long cut branch and green line, a red-and-white bobber and a threaded worm, and the simple sight of the bobber on the flat pond, first still then twitching and darting beneath the surface, always stunned me ... and still does, when I watch my grandson's bobber. During my years in high school, I took long treks by subway and train, a massive full-service pack on my back, from Brooklyn to the East Branch of the Croton River and fished all night and all day with Mort and Don and Bernie. There I discovered the damage a C.P. Swing cast upstream with a spinning outfit could do, retrieved just a bit faster than the current; and there are grainy photographs of me, with a limit of faded trout atop a wicker creel. The sight, from a bridge over Michigan's Ausable, of a dry-fly man casting to a rising trout remains vivid: the electricity when the fish took the fly, the explosion in my brain when I saw fully what a fly rod could do. And when I committed myself to those feathered things, it was as if I was born again, and it all became too close to a religion, which it never should be. And then my search began and has never truly ended, not even now, to understand the architectonics of flies, the mechanics of improving my self-taught fly casting, the way in which words could become an extension of the fishing and how I wrote them and edited them, bringing all of what I had learned about words to the twin tasks, and then fishing the Beaverkill, the Willowemoc, Ten Mile River, New York's Au Sable, and the Madison, the Firehole, the Beaverhead, the Gallatin, in England and in France, salt water here and south, and finally finding the greatest challenges and sweetest rewards on a spring creek that gave up some of its secrets ever so reluctantly, some never. And when I think of that creek, I always see a fly floating serenely at dusk, a great wake easing toward it, the momentous take of the largest brown my friend had ever hooked and the twenty minutes, into the dark that he played it to a dozen feet from his rod tip until the fish simply slipped the hook. Somehow I learned a deep, slow patience on that western river, and it sloshed through me until I could feel its stillness in me when I talked to a class of students or tried to write a decent paragraph: the feelings, the spirit of the thing inside me forever. And there are the books by Haig-Brown and Plunket-Greene and Kingsmill-Moore, and John Inglis Hall's wonderful *Fishing a Highland Stream* and Romilly Fedden and Leeson, and a hundred more that all live inside me and release a sentence or two when I least expect and most need them.

And I have so many more memories—some of which I have put into my shaggy-fish tales, some that have a friend's face and words attached to them. The old maxim that youth is wasted on the young sometimes holds, but mine, my youth, redolent with the passion with which it was lived, often as potent as that in Conrad's "Youth," lives in me intact. I love it. I thrive on it, even as I press into my eighties and feel in my head and body and hips the price of that passion, of hard living.

3

A year ago I took a feeble Knox Burger, an old friend, to Bill's Pond. He had been one of the finest literary agents, outspoken, fierce in support of his authors' rights, their work, and hard on the authors, to get their best work. He had once met me on the Gallatin wearing a T-shirt that boldly proclaimed, "Honest prose and nerves of steel," his credo. He was sui generis, indelible. I knew him for more than thirty years, as a colleague in the tough-sweet world of books, a valued investor in my little publishing firm, a fishing companion, a frank and baldly honest friend.

Age that is only rarely kind had worked its worst with Knox. Though not too deep into his eighties, he was frail, feeble, ravished by cancer and radiation that had blasted his bones, hip operations that did not repair, his speech blurred, his eyes that had loved words for so long incapable of reading, his legs weak and unsure. He had lost much of his body weight. But age had not quite played its final act.

This was the last time I fished with him, the last time he fished. He had passed his Indian summer and was living a very cold and unforgiving winter.

I told him on the way to the remarkably fecund Bill's Pond that the trout were very picky about what they ate but that I had devised with immense cunning a fly that adequately imitated the liver pellets that Bill fed them.

He growled a word that I had to ask him to repeat. Loudly and slowly and with effort Knox said: "HAM ... burger."

Bill put two chairs out on his low flat deck and Knox, with deliberation, threaded his line through the guides of his old bamboo rod. It was a common-enough rod, a well-used Montague. Then he reached over toward his canvas carry-all, could not reach it, and I extracted one box of flies. One after the other he chose a dozen different patterns and I affixed them in turn, which he tried for three or four short deliberate casts each. No follows, no takes. I mentioned my pellet imitation.

"NO HAM ... burger!"

As I sat next to him, watching the water, changing his flies, I spoke of days we had spent together in Montana and the Catskills, once at a club that had recently stocked some plump fifteen-and sixteen-inch browns that were spectacularly dumb. I reminded him that he had caught a dozen of them, that a handtruck had slipped from a truck in front of us on Route 17 and nearly killed us, and how the Minetta Tavern that he loved in New York City sat directly in the spot through which the Minetta Brook, loaded with brookies, had once, hundreds of years earlier, flowed.

To each story he grimaced or smiled faintly, and grunted. He kept his eyes on the water and I did not know for sure how much of my old friend was still there.

After an hour, Knox remained fishless. I half turned from him then and surreptitiously changed his fly to one of the little dyed cork jobs in my box. He cast once, a couple of feet beyond his shoelaces, and immediately hooked one of the truly outsized rainbows that I had seen cruising close, to whom I had slipped four or five pellets, chumming.

The fish, a plump specimen of seven or eight pounds, took off at a great clip, and Knox leaned forward in his chair, dangerously close to toppling into Bill's Pond. I lurched for the back of his belt, caught it, and never let go. Then I held tight to the loose belt and played my old friend gently back into the chair. The fish was well into the backing for five minutes, and Knox could not see that it was about to go behind the island. But he kept a firm and practiced hand on the reel, and the fish gradually came back toward him, a foot at a time. Fifteen minutes later Bill brought out his gigantic saltwater net, and with one scoop the old rainbow was twisting in the meshes.

Knox passed his hand slowly along the monster's sleek flank, mumbled something I could not understand, and then Bill turned the fish back.

Then the old fellow looked at me and said in deep, clear, stentorian tones: "on ... a ... FLY."

"Yea," I said without hesitation, "on a fly."

He who loved honest prose, who had in Hemingway's phrase an infallible built-in shit detector, would have berated me loudly for it. It was the only time I lied to my late friend. And I'd have done it again.

4

The pleasure of Bill's Pond, my continuing difficulty wading, an old longing for water of my own—these led me to investigate building a pond on my hilly four acres, a bit downhill from the house. I counseled with a friend retired from the state fisheries department and he took soil samples, tested the pH, debated the strength of a few small springs; and I asked several contractors for their views on my prospects. The reports came back quickly, bleakly: the soil was far too rocky and porous to hold water unless I packed the excavation with clay or artificial clay, neither of which I wanted. I wanted it natural or not at all. The pH was marginally okay, there was no evidence that the few springs we found could supply nearly enough water to satisfy two turtles. Rainwater and road runoff, neither reliable, the latter toxic, would help a little, and perhaps the neighbor Fisher who owned land contiguous to where I wanted my pond, unwilling to sell me an acre or less of promising swamp, would allow me to sink a little pump into his wet hollow and thus gain a few drinks of cold water. He did. Being on a precipitous hillside didn't help. Even the local building inspector, though he approved my plans, insisted there was no hope for the pond and thought it merely a seasonal hole.

In the end, smarter than all these, I persuaded myself to believe none of them and went ahead with the contractor, who set up his retired father on a tractor for a week, and I watched the old guy chugging in and out of the hole, building a berm, carving out of the rocky soil an amoeba-shaped area, smoking a cigar out of the corner of his mouth, which his wife, I learned, wouldn't let him smoke at home, a quiet smile on his face, the machine indefatigable.

It was not your ideal pond though it filled for a short time from heavy rains and was actually about ninety feet across (at its longest length), and I promptly stocked it with bluegills from Bill's pond. Bill was hopeful enough to add three foot-long largemouth bass and a couple of rainbow trout, and my friend Martina deposited a single smallmouth she had caught. When all these survived not only the first late-summer drought and the frozen winter, I became emboldened and added a foot-long grass carp, three koi, a bucket of emerald shiners and sawbellies from a local bait shop, more bluegill, a few of Bill's golden shiners, even half a dozen orphs, a Russian fish. At least the bass would get a decent meal now and then.

The bluegill made their pancake beds that June and proliferated; several bass fry and then a few ten-inch largemouths appeared a year or so later, so they were reproducing; the trout lasted three years, grew fat, and then vanished en masse after an August heat wave. For the pond only had two problems: it leaked and it had no clear source of cold water.

Turtles lasted only a few months in the muddy soup and then left for more accommodating places; I got two dozen tadpoles from the bait shop and added them; I saw and heard a few frogs, then they disappeared, perhaps with the help of the blue heron that visited most mornings. I caught one bass over twenty inches long one fall, most of its body no thicker than a plump snake's, its head huge and smiling, a sure victim of near starvation: I even thought I heard it say, "Get me out of this hell hole, PLEASE," before I slipped it back.

The carp, with an appetite as great as mine, kept the pond clear of green algae; two of the koi vanished and I bought another that thrived as a younger brother or sister to the one I'd put in the first year, by then a seven or eight-pounder. There must have been six or seven dozen stunted bluegill that came toward the dock every time I approached; a couple of brookies Bill put in one fall managed to prevail, and over the years I got down for an hour or two several times a week and watched, or tossed out bread and pellets, or some wickedly expensive nightcrawlers, and now and again cast bass bugs or bright bluegill flies, or a little jig Bob Boyle had concocted, or my pellet imitation, pure hamburger.

My eldest granddaughter showed promise and fished for a time until she became a busy teenager with a smartphone, and my grandson Finn showed some interest beyond his original compulsion to pelt the pond with rocks, so we began to feed the fish together, fish now and then, knock around the odd unpromising hole a bit more frequently. We used a fly rod and something called a "noodle rod."

Finn caught bluegill by the bucketful, and one day registered some variety of Grand Slam—bluegill, golden shiner, brook trout—and then the grass carp. We had been using breadcrust, the natural not the imitation, primarily because it could be fished "dry" and because, after the great fish rose to ten similar crusts of bread, that it was to him the *plat du jour*.

The carp, caught once before, a few years earlier, then a good deal slenderer, took the dry breadcrust, swirled mightily when it realized it had been duped, sending a riot of water out in every direction, and Finn jumped as the electricity coursed through him. The noodle rod bent nearly a circle. The fish—now twelve or fifteen pounds—headed like a freight train as far from the dock as it could get and though the pond was small, the fish went everywhere it could go. After ten minutes of hauling and giving line, Finn asked whether we could get the fish onto the dock, and I told him about the net in the shed so he passed me the rod and he raced up the hill. I stopped pressuring the fish and it rested quietly, waiting for the second act. Finn came back a few minutes later with a net I hadn't used in fifteen years, which might be rotted, large enough for stripers or blues, and in the end we got the carp's head into it and I hauled it up onto the dock—the fish massive, its scales golden and tinged with brown, its little mouth gasping. Finn wanted to haul it up to the house to show parents and sister and any other potentially interested person we could hail on the road, but I reckoned the big fellow had had enough for one day. So in the end we turned it back. I decided it was best to leave the hook in its soft mouth and was sadly convinced that the long fight had done it for the great fish.

Ten minutes later, though, some bread still floating on the water, the carp was up again, wolfing down the last of this feast.

And a few years later, I'm still waiting for my grandson's next visit.

Another winter has come, my pond is frozen solid above who knows what, and my seasonable mind turns not backward but toward April. It has not been much to brag on—these past six or seven years, not really much of a true Indian summer. But I was never much of a bragger and was generally content to love my passion with unalloyed passion, grateful for every bit of it I could get. But what comes next—more meditations on my ludicrous little pond? Whatever antidotes I can find for my most maudlin moments, mostly slapstick comedy? Another trip to my beloved West? More attention to nearby rivers? The rest of this winter near some warm and gentle flats?

The pond has survived and so have I. Certainly the arc has turned. I don't need to repeat the intensity of my youth—the long days, returning tired to the bone, always reaching for the untried and most challenging, casting until my back pained, anxious to try pike in France, tarpon in the Marquesas, tough browns in a western spring creek. And I would prefer not to sit in a chair with a friend holding on to my belt, thank you, or be wheeled to a spot near a hatchery—though such a day might come.

For me a little always went a long way, even if it fell far short of all. And my brain remains that of a fisherman. All of the fishing I ever did—by whatever means—lives in me. Everything I do is colored by that fact. And if by good chance I fish in one of the best ways and places again, and I am determined to do so, I will not be more of a fisherman for it. I am all the fisherman I can be right now, and I will always be a fisherman.

mari lyons

19 July 1990